DONALD TRUMP
AND
MY EATING DISORDER

I0441571

NICOLE MARIE STORY

INDEPENDENTLY PUBLISHED

Copyright Nicole Marie Story, 2019.
ISBN 9781074423773
Created in the United States of America.
Without limiting the rights under copyright reserved above, no part of this publication may be reproduced,
stored in, or introduced into a retrieval system, or transmitted, in any form, or by any means without the prior
written permission of the copyright owner.
PUBLISHER'S NOTE
This is a work of non-fiction (reality). Some names have been changed to protect the privacy of the
individuals. The distribution of this book via the Internet or via any other means without the permission of the
author is illegal and punishable by law. Please purchase only authorised electronic editions, and refuse to
participate in, or encourage electronic piracy of, copyrighted materials. Your support of the author's rights is
appreciated.
Blog theyogaballerina.com
Twitter @yogaballerina
Instagram @theyogaballerina
facebook.com/theyogaballerina
YouTube: The Yoga Ballerina
iTunes Podcast: The Yoga Ballerina Show

TO PRESIDENT DONALD J. TRUMP

Thank you, President Trump, for your influence on my health;
and, thank you, for your influence on the health of
the United States of America.
You are a great, great man.

CONTENTS

OVERTURE

"Mittens, frozen, fingers, raw and trembling beneath, a singular, hot tear traveling along my face, I watched as he walked away. The tear warmed not my cheek. The tear warmed not my heart. And, as the cold continued to sting, the tear canceled not the pain. What the tear accomplished, however, registered as powerful. As epiphanic. As self-actualising. The tear motivated my heart to win. I earned not the love of Mr. Bikram in the manner that I wanted, so I would redevelop my plan and win the love of myself instead. As 'Trump: The Game' proclaims, the only option in life is to win! And win I shall. Always."

Appearing to author Nicole Marie Story, in the form of a dream, the words of this overture became the final piece of this book, appearing first, before everything else, before the words and sentences and stories which had been written over the course of a twenty-year period. It was a dream which delivered this book to completion. It was a dream that, with a divine kiss, sealed the content of *Donald Trump and My Eating Disorder,* sending it to the presses.

CHAPTER
I

THE FACE OF A PRESIDENT, THE FACE OF AN EATING DISORDER

THE YEAR WAS 1991. Stationed at the age of nine, I was drawn to a beautiful, sharp box resting on the floor of the closet of my parents' upstairs bedroom of our lovely, two-story, five-member family home. It was a lower, middle-class home, one bursting with love and with happiness. We had air conditioning not, designer clothing not, and fancy food not; yet we had wants not. All of our needs and desires were achieved by two honest, hard-working, dedicated parents whose passionate mission was to raise a beautiful, respectable, strong, healthy, happy family. Raising of such a family was the American dream, of that day and age, during the last two decades of the twentieth century, at least it was such in our glorious home. I wonder if they would do it, again, if they knew of how life would unfold. I hope that my parents are proud, as I am highly grateful for my foundations, and for the safe and loving environment that they fostered.

Adoring that tall, rugged house, the one in which I lived from my birth in 1982 until the age of nine in 1991, my childhood heart danced, perpetually in motion and rhythm with the pliés and grand jetés of my imagination. A four-walled cornucopia of joy, memories of that house and of the love contained inside propel my now matured heart to smile. It was before the eating disorder. Before my seventeen-year war with food. Before the realities that tore apart my place in the family home. Back then, it was as though we lived in a bubble, existing like such, for a very long time, until my eating disorder caused it to explode.

My mother managed our lives. Every birthday for three, vivacious, brunette, little girls commanded extravagant occasions, honouring our Italian, Brazilian, and Irish heritage. She cooked, cleaned, baked, and decorated for the days leading to the events. Presenting each of her children like princesses, styled in fancy party dresses, patent leather shoes, and decadent hair bows and barrettes, my mother accomplished celebrations to be remembered. She elegantly interacted with each adult, ensuring that all had food, drink, and conversation. She orchestrated the singing of happy birthday, the opening of presents, and the eating of cake, exactly in that order. And when the guests departed, my mother cleaned the aftermath, doing the work of fifteen people, all for one party. With regard to her day-to-day activities, she balanced the budget and handled the grocery and supply shopping, always buying a new children's book during our visits to Kmart, as she considered words to be important. We read together, wrote together, and coloured together. We watched *Mister Rogers*, *Fraggle Rock*, and *She-Ra* together. She chauffeured little me to and from dance school, toting my little sisters for the ride. Dinner was served nightly, hot and homemade. She performed the daily housekeeping service, too. How she made time to exercise, is beyond me, but she did. Babysitters, nannies, drivers, cooks, maids, and personal trainers were never a consideration, as they belonged to a different world. She proficiently and gracefully, with an iron fist, operated the business of our family. Conducting the symphony of our family life, leading by example, my mother taught me the art of hard work. She taught me to be on time. To be disciplined. To be organised. To be sophisticated. To do things correctly. She taught me of how to be. Applying perfection, intelligence, strength, and creativity to her charges, she was my beautiful model and teacher.

Whilst my mother managed the interior of the home, my father worked outside of the home, earning the dollars needed to support his family. And, despite his demanding hours, he attended the important things, ensuring that every birthday celebration, every visit to Disney World, every dance recital, every sled-riding adventure, included a complete video recording using a VHS camcorder. Today, video creation is second nature, but, back then, before it became as everyday reality, my father, who recorded all of our special moments, behaved as a futurist. Because of my father, I learnt to appreciate cutting-edge technology and to use it functionally. He taught me of how to install plaster to a wall, of how to lay cement foundation, and of how to drive like a man. Also, due to his influence, I learnt to salute police officers and to respect the American flag. My father taught me the art of patriotism.

And, in that old, wonderful house, in the upstairs closet of subject which contained the beautiful box of subject, I investigated with big, bright, inquisitive eyes, as though I had discovered a national treasure. Coloured in gold, printed onto the box, the word of TRUMP alluded me. I knew that "trump" formally meant to surpass one's competition by saying or doing something better, but the very bold presentation of the TRUMP lettering on this box captivated my very curious, independent, intuitive, young brain. I knew that the word of TRUMP, in this context, meant something more grand and more powerful than its formal definition as set forth by the dictionary. TRUMP, in its golden, confident, printed nature, seemed luxurious. Royal. Intoxicating. And, at the time, despite living a very comfortable life, nine-year old Nicole Marie Story knew of luxury not. I knew of royalty not. And I knew of the state of being intoxicated not. Only now, in retrospect, remembering of how I felt, back then, as a little girl, in the presence of TRUMP, might I describe the memory as such.

The box also presented the image of a heroic-looking, breathtakingly debonaire, blonde-haired gentleman dressed in a business suit, his expression instructing me, leading me, demanding me, to passionately pursue my dreams, to take on the world, to own my life, to do WHAT I WANT, and to succeed at it. To be a ballerina and an astronaut. To be a sheep herder and a writer. To do whatever and everything that MY blood running through MY veins indicated that I wanted to do and was capable of doing. He told me to do something magnificent. To ignore societal expectation and the hogwash of political correctness. To deny existence of second place trophies. To reject settlement. To do what my heart sang versus what it was told to sing. To be rational. To be relentless. To be the best. He told me to want. To think. To do. To get. TO WIN. With sophistication, pride, and ruthless honesty, the suited man's unspoken message sang with the transparency of his beautiful, blue eyes. Streaming above the handsome picture, contained inside of quotation marks, appeared one divine exclamatory sentence proclaiming that WINNING IS EVERYTHING. This declaration would become the mantra of my life. The pictured man who presented this mantra seemed oh so familiar, yet I knew of his identity not. It was as though we shared values and DNA, yet I knew of his place in this world not. I respected him. Like I did the American flag. Like I did police officers. Like I did my father. I understood this potent box featuring this handsome man's powerful image and message to be "an adult game," so I dared not to remove the lid, but I admired it, was motivated by it, in quiet. The man on the cover of the box was Donald J. Trump.

Fast forward twenty-seven years, to April of 2018 when I am stationed at the age of thirty-six years, watching the Netflix documentary of now President Donald J. Trump. The documentary, entitled, *Trump: An American Dream*, is a fantastic, unbiased piece which explores the life of President Trump, including interviews of people who love him, and of people who love him not, also featuring speaking clips from the past of our now great president. It begins with coverage of Donald Trump's 1974 business birth in Manhattan, covering significant events such as his 1976 historic restoration of the Commodore Hotel and facade of Grand Central Terminal; such as his 1983 completion of Trump Tower; such as his 1986 rehabilitation of Wollman Rink after the city failed, for nearly one decade, to do so; such as his 1988 comment to Oprah that it is easy to work with our enemies not, so he would rather "make our allies pay their fair share," leading the viewer, step by step, to the epic presidential election of 2016, and to the historic inauguration and elegant inaugural ball where his graceful, perfect, dazzling family danced, to the song of *My Way*. And, here is what took away my breath! In episode two of this excellent Netflix documentary, it is reported, of how, in the year of 1989, then civilian Donald Trump visited The Milton Bradley Company, meeting with line workers who assembled his board game. The clip shows Donald Trump interacting with the line workers of subject, supporting claims of how he has always respected the competent, manual labour involved with his grand operations. The game was called *Trump: The Game*. In addition to my breath being stolen, my heart beamed to the moon, pirouetting with surprise, joy, and relief when seeing this clip. Why breathlessness? Why surprise? Why joy? Why relief? Because, for the past twenty-seven years, I had often reminisced of THAT GAME each time that I spied something regarding the glamorous Donald Trump in the news, but I was convinced that my childhood exposure to and admiration of THAT GAME was but a figment of my wild imagination. I was convinced that my investigation of that game, in my old, wonderful, childhood home, happened not in reality. My memory was certainly from a dream, I thought, from a lovely, beautiful dream about a geometrically perfect box featuring the golden, perfect lettering of TRUMP. Featuring the image of a heroic-looking man who seemed oh so familiar to nine-year old Nicole Marie Story. Featuring the powerful words that had been the mantra of my then thirty-six year life thus far, proclaiming that winning is everything.

But it was a dream, not.

My memory, was real.

Trump: The Game, was real.

The game's beautiful tagline proclaiming that winning is everything, was real.

My childhood admiration of Donald Trump, before I knew the meaning of the Trump name, was real.

Although I was quite aware of his presence on Earth, and despite interpreting the physical image and messaging of Donald Trump as heroic during my youth, I became official Trump Fan Girl only when Donald Trump announced his candidacy for President of the United States of America. Before June 16, 2015, between my ages of nine and thirty-three, Donald Trump lived his grand life, and I lived my own. Donald Trump's life, pre-candidacy, had zero effect upon my existence. I thusly ignored his Real News. I cared not of *The Apprentice*, of Miss Universe, and of The Trump Organization. It all existed, divinely so, and, in retrospect, in recently watching his old television interviews with the likes of Phil Donahue, David Letterman, Piers Morgan, Conan O'Brien, Oprah, and the glamorous Nikki Haskell, I am highly glad that I paid zero mind to businessman and celebrity Donald Trump, because, if given just one taste, I would have listened constantly, accomplishing nothing else! His words and voice exist like poetry to my brain. So why did I ignore it all, back then, in the 1990s and early aughts? Because I was focused on one specific thing: on finding correction to my eating disorder. Nothing else mattered.

This bias on information consumption and maintaining a narrow vision with regard to the world is a lifelong personal trend. For instance, during the presidential election of 2000, stationed at the truly innocent age of eighteen, after learning of the plans and intentions of Albert Gore and of George W. Bush, I flatly decided to ignore both presidential campaigns, completely abstaining from the vote. Neither candidate aligned with what then eighteen-year old Nicole Marie Story imagined was the perfect man to lead The United States of America. Neither candidate said things that mattered to me, that excited me, that yielded rational sense to my brain. Thusly, I refused to make compromise on my strong principles, simply for the sake of voting. Why offer my vote to something that was mediocre at best? Why waste my time? Why waste my energy? My beautiful mother harvested other ideas, however, requiring that I, indeed, participate in my first "of voting age" election. Insomuch that my mother seems unaffected by "politics" and by gender equality rights, I think that her ardent desire for my participation in the vote had everything to do with human duty, and, that, in order to be a good, correct human, that I must vote.

Because I had completed my absentee ballot not, my mother fetched stubborn me from Westminster College on election day of 2000, driving for ninety minutes to my registered polling place in Moon Township, Pennsylvania. Despite at the time being registered as a Republican (in a Democrat family), I voted for the Democrat because I was obviously required to pick someone, and

Gore registered as more handsome, aesthetically speaking, than Bush. I also shook Gore's hand on March 16, 2000 during a campaign rally at the Moon Area High School gymnasium where he made a strong impression, in a J.F.K. sort of way. By this, I mean that he was cute, offered a nice smile, and firmly shook my hand. I thusly treated the presidential election of 2000 like a Miss Universe Pageant. Nowadays, Gore would never be permitted into a beauty pageant, especially the swimsuit competition! For someone who preaches so loudly about "global warming," he sure seems to be saving extra fat for a polar vortex kind of day. I hypothesise that his handshake is sweaty and weak nowadays, too. He looks and sounds like a classic antagonist of an Ayn Rand novel. But, in retrospect, despite voting for a liberal who thinks that "climate change" is more important than securing our borders, and despite the fact that Bush 41 was amazing in his service to this country, I am pleased that I rejected baby Bush, as he offered zero respect and zero support to Donald Trump in the 2016 campaign. And, although I was focused on finding a solution to my eating disorder, I was aware enough to know that Bush 43's administration was stale and slow, delivering to us eight years of Barack Obama. I ignored the Obama term entirely. Socialism threatened America, and our first lady, Michelle Obama, registered NOT as my cup of tea. Michelle Obama is like a venti chai latte with extra pumps of chai add cinnamon dolce syrup, whipped cream, and red sprinkles with Happy Holidays printed in Comic Sans font onto the huge Starbucks cup. My cup of tea is plain and elegant. A ceremonial matcha from Japan. Whisked with bamboo. With a Merry Christmas printed with sophisticated, sharp, Times New Roman lettering onto the slender cup, prepared at the fancy downtown matcha bar. A First Lady Melania Trump.

In response to this declaration about Michelle Obama, I am prepared to be insulted by radical Democrats as racist (even though I HAVE BLACK FRIENDS and would think in the same manner if Michelle Obama were white, black, or purple), as sexist (even thought I AM FEMALE), as disrespectful (even though I have simply stated MY OPINION and have the right to do so), as every bad name in the book; but before the "racist" and "sexist" and "disrespectful" jabs are offered, I challenge my dissenters to consider, "What do you think of First Lady Melania Trump?" The majority of radical liberals, including the Fake News Media, will offer a conspiracy theory with dramatic, fearful, soap opera voices to the likes of "She loves him not!," / "She travels with him not!," / "She speaks English not!," / "She lives with him not!," / "She smiles not!" / "She brushed off his hand!," / "She has an arrangement on paper!" / "She has a body double!" yada! yada! yada!. First off, how on Earth does that "information" register as opinion? It is citation of Fake News, a symptom of Trump Derangement Syndrome. Second off, I, on the other hand, see beauty, strength, glamour, intelligence, sophistication, class, heart, and the list goes on, in First Lady Melania Trump. Ironically, this is what half of you recognised and continue to adore in Michelle Obama, even after her publishing of that "autobiography." Of course the words of her book shall never cross my eyes, as I only read things that are pleasing to me. But, her commentary about the book to Oprah and to Sarah Jessica Parker, really made me cringe as it flowed through my liberal-controlled Facebook news feed. My point is, before you render judgement unto me, let it please be known that you shall be a hypocrite by doing so. Michelle Obama lovers exist, and I judge them not.

To me, Michelle Obama translates to a hybrid of Eleanor Roosevelt and Beyoncé. What does this mean? It means that the "qualities" of Eleanor Roosevelt and Beyoncé, together, equal Michelle Obama. Loud, wild clothing, non-elegant footwear, socialist, and "entitled." Eleanor Roosevelt used "female" as her entitlement card. Beyoncé uses "female" AND "black" as hers. This is disgraceful, in my eyes. But, some people like it, and that is fine. We all have personal preferences. We all have teas which impress us not. We all have humans who impress us not. And Michelle Obama impresses me not.

The girl power movement, something for which Michelle Obama seemingly stands, does nothing for me, as I am unmotivated by gender equality as a cause. International Women's Day makes me laugh. Furthermore, I am unaffected by the #MeToo movement. I think that #MeToo is an overused label by angry, liberal feminists as a way to condemn white, rich, Republican men and Bill Cosby. By the way, I think that Bill Cosby is innocent, unless one day proven as guilty. How on Earth, in 2018, did that jury create a verdict based on zero evidence? Why is Bill Cosby sentenced to prison for sexual misconduct? How is Bill Clinton's accuser of Paula Jones any different from the females who accused Bill Cosby? Zero sex crimes were proven for either of the accused. Zero evidence was provided. Thusly, based on lack of proof, neither Clinton nor Bill Cosby should be punished for sexual misconduct. Yet, Clinton is free, and Bill Cosby is unfree of these charges. Why the hypocrisy? It is because of the #MeToo craziness. Bill Cosby was charged during the time of women crying wolf and automatically being believed for it.

And, let us please explore one step further! Clinton, as a sitting president, followed to LIE UNDER OATH about his sexual relations with Monica

Lewinsky. Monica's dress featuring Clinton's DNA is standing physical proof of such lies. When found guilty of perjury and obstruction of justice, Clinton was later acquitted of these crimes during impeachment and thusly remained in office. Imagine if President Trump were to lie under oath, and to get caught, about sexual misconduct! Or to lie about stepping on, for instance, a sidewalk ant! "ANIMAL ABUSE! ANIMAL ABUSE! OBSTRUCTION! OBSTRUCTION!" shall cry the Democrats. Or, goodness forbid, the ultimate: what if President Trump tweets on what he ate for dinner, and that report is questioned by Democrats? Did he really eat McDonald's takeout, or did he actually eat a taco bowl from Trump Tower Grill because he loves Hispanics and it's el Cinco de Mayo and Trump Tower Grill makes the best? "Oh! Oh! Impeachment! Impeachment!"

Laugh out loud.

What a Democrat scam!

Also, Real News flash for Democrats: the definition of impeachment translates not to removal of office. This is a major misunderstanding about the procedure. Impeachment is simply the charging of a holder of public office with misconduct. No president who was ever impeached has ever been removed from office. As a good friend, fellow dog mother, fellow Ayn Rand lover, fellow yoga practitioner, and fellow member of my longtime underground Trump railroad recently wrote to me, "Trump will never resign. He will never quit. He won't be impeached - and if they try to impeach him, he won't leave. He will never let us down." I agree. Completely.

Yes, it is terribly awful that truth presumably exists in the recent flood of #MeToo allegations, and I want for all rapists and monsters to pay for their crimes (I, too, was wronged - by an ILLEGAL - see chapter seven; and I, too, was attacked, beaten, and mugged by an unidentified male, whom I suspect is illegal - see chapter twelve), but I believe in Due Process. And I think that the jury system is that process not, especially when it regards women and claims on sex, especially on claims dating back to thirty-six years, as was the case with our amazing now Supreme Court Justice Brett Kavanaugh. Juries nowadays seem to be overtaken by liberal wackos with zero application of rational logic. I believe in proof. I believe that one is innocent until proven guilty. And I still await proof that Bill Cosby forced drugs onto women, subsequently forcing them to engage in sexual acts with him. And, even if he did offer drugs to relax women, why are these women freed from responsibility as related to their reported decision? Why is Mr. Cosby responsible for these women and their reported acceptance of said drug? These women, if the reports are true, knew that they were in the company of a very powerful, married man who reportedly wanted extramarital sex. These women wanted the perks of being with Mr. Cosby. And then they wanted more! They turned their entitlement into a sob story of being violated. I thusly decree that these women are shameful to use their conniving brains against a man who, if the reports are true, was just being a man. Who was just being a human. Where does personal responsibility begin and end in this world anymore? As my gorgeous, eighty-seven-year old grandmother said to me recently when discussing the abuse of #MeToo: "Men have been grabbing asses since the beginning of time. These women need to get over it."

Bottom line on the feminist movement: I subscribe to it not. I am human. I believe in one race, in the human race. My favourite film, *A Woman's Face*, produced in 1941, stars the late, great Joan Fontaine and addresses the subject of humanity. Without spoiling the plot, I shall offer that in the final scene, Fontaine's character passionately exclaims that she wants to be a part of something meaningful. She wants to be human. She wants to belong to the human race. Oh, I could feel myself in her character, as throughout the film, she suffers to connect with humans because she is so very displeased with her face, one that experienced fire-related trauma during childhood. For so long, displeased with my face and my body during seventeen years of disordered eating, I found myself in a similar state of pain.

Please understand me correctly. Despite my belief that all humans are equal, I completely LOVE being a girl, especially a girly girl; and I would absolutely detest being a man, this includes both girly man and manly man, or however people identify in this age of "gender neutrality." Gender neutrality. What a joke! I respect the sanctity and existence of two conservative, formal, biological classes of sex. Man. And woman. And although I am heterosexual, I completely believe in heterosexual and homosexual relationships. To dissect this further, with regard to heterosexual relationships, I think that girls should wear sky high pumps and pantyhose, and men should open car doors. I think that girls should be sexy and therefore desired by the powerful men in their radar. Men should pay for all dates. And girls should behave like sophisticated ladies in public, as desirable play things in private. Girls should be an ornament for their powerful man. With regard to homosexual relationships, I have no experience and therefore expectation other than for the couples' achievement of joy. And, despite my belief in the heterosexual relationship power structure, I think that women should have power, outside of their sex relationship. And they do, despite Democrat claims. I believe in equal working conditions and in equal opportunities between men and women. If you are a female and want to earn more money, then work for it. Ask for it. And if you are denied, find another job. Or, create your own job. My best human friend Rebecca who is a radical Democrat challenges me on this stance, stating, "Not everyone is like you! Not everyone is born with hope! Not everyone has your drive!" Yes, this is true. But how is this my fault? Sadly, the hopeless by birth shall always exist, and solving this problem is irrational for me to consider. Although I want to help people with this book, I also recognise that my responsibility begins and ends with myself.

What makes conditions as worse in this day and age, is that the hopeless and poor are influenced by rich, liberal feminists and Bernie Sanders to flap their mouths into megaphones about unfair treatment whilst banging drums, blowing whistles, blaring loud party music, and walking in sloppy circles, mirroring a circus versus stepping up their work game and getting noticed based on merit. They prefer to scream about their gender, colour, and or poverty level, all on company time, demanding what they "deserve." Additionally, these protestors tote their young children to these strikes, influencing a brand new generation of entitled, bratty looters. Everyone wants to work a nine to five job with a lunch break and three smoke sessions and to be paid like the CEO. That is simply demented. As a side note, when the Chicago Hotel Workers struck in September of 2018, I questioned two of the striking gentlemen, who, by the way, offered pizza and soda and hugs to me daily because I treat everyone, including humans who believe in entitlement, with dignity and respect, "Are the workers at Trump Tower also on strike?" They replied with, "Hell no! Do you think that guy would hire union labour? He's a cheap mother f*****!" Obviously they missed the Real News report informing that I am President Trump's biggest fan! But, because I am kind, I laughed and nodded and accepted their hugs, declining their offer of food and drink, rather prancing onward to my destination, with my little dog Gwendolyn at my side. One day, one of these striking "workers" picked me up, twirling me around. He had alcohol on his breath.

To conclude my Michelle Obama argument, I shall state that Ellen DeGeneres recently asked a frumpy-looking radical Democrat if she would rather be stuck in an elevator with President Trump, Vice President Mike Pence, or the former Attorney General under President Trump. This is comparable to asking me, "With whom of the following would you rather be stuck in an elevator: Michelle Obama, Beyoncé, or Eleanor Roosevelt?" But, the difference is, that, unlike Ellen's interviewee, I would offer a peaceful reply. I would, like a proper, tasteful Republican, state that I shall refuse to enter the elevator with such suggested human examples and shall rather take the staircase, climbing proficiently and confidently, powered by Peloton legs, Ashtanga yoga arms, and Tae Bo abdominals, wearing sky high velvet pumps by Tamara Mellon. And sexy pantyhose. Like a girl.

When I think of a first lady, I think of a black tie date. I think of a quiet, elegant, graceful, intelligent, petite and or thin female. I think of Jacqueline Kennedy Onassis and of her infamous Valentine's Day television broadcast from the White House. I think of Nancy Reagan. I think of Melania Trump. I think not of Michelle Obama and of her loud speeches, notably the ones in support of Hillary Clinton. Could Michelle have sounded anymore rowdy with her, "When they go low, we go high" pitch? As previously suggested, Michelle Obama seems to think that black and female register as her official TRUMP cards. This black and female constitution for gain is disgraceful. When I think of FLOTUS, I think of Michelle Obama not. Nor shall I ever.

But who am I to define FLOTUS? Who is anyone to define FLOTUS? What exactly is the description of FLOTUS? To me, despite my personal preference of a reserved state of ladylike elegance for the role, FLOTUS is whomever embodies the role. It is unique. And human. And American. When Michelle Obama fulfilled the role, the hearts of my liberal friends danced. And now that Melania Trump fulfills the role, MY heart dances. The hearts of Americans are keyed with two different fittings, the matching key turning perfectly every four to eight years (in my case, every twenty eight years, or the time between President Ronald Reagan and President Trump!). Thusly, our hearts exist as either locked or as unlocked. The only difference is that when Republicans have locked, closed, sad hearts, we respect the roles of elected leadership and stay as quiet. When radical Democrats have locked, closed, sad hearts, they RESIST and DISRESPECT and OBSTRUCT, making total mockeries of their human selves and of their political party. They are disgraceful. And, at this moment, whilst Democrats cry loudly on their state of woe, my heart is unlocked, singing and celebrating joyfully! It pirouettes and smiles from sea to shining sea. FLOTUS and its ideal is open to individual interpretation. And I shall forever ignore that which appeals to me not, including Eleanor Roosevelt. Including Michelle Obama. Oh, and yes, Hillary Clinton must be added to that unappealing FLOTUS list, too. Even as a fifth grader in 1992, I knew that she was "crooked."

As previously stated, with regard to Donald Trump, from eyeing that powerful board game in 1991 until he announced his candidacy in 2015, I consumed very little. In fact, what I did consume happened by complete chance and as byproduct of another love. Of what love do I write? My liberal readers shall be very pleased to know that WE ALL passionately consumed our dashing president during one of the most amazing productions of modern entertainment. Does Carrie Bradshaw ring a bell? Or the cosmopolitan?

Yes, dear readers, we excitedly consumed Donald Trump during HBO's *Sex and the City!* As this proves, liberal Hollywood once upon a time glamourised our now great president, now abhorring him so greatly for their own evil political agenda. At this time, my eyes refuse to watch Meryl Streep filmography, even from the days of when she was thin and beautiful, even in the films of where the handsome and conservative Clint Eastwood appears, because Streep's current smug, bloated, haggard face as it relates to her vocal hatred for our dear president strums through my mind and makes me ill. And never did I think that I would silence the radio during the streaming of Madonna's *Vogue* or *True Blue* or *Take a Bow*, but, yes, such is true. Madonna has thought "an awful lot about blowing up the White House"? Well, she and her work can go to hell. And *Saturday Night Live?* I've never liked it, so no loss there! We can add *The Godfather: Part II* to that list, too. No need to announce that scoundrel's name! So, where exactly in *Sex and the City* did we celebrate our now great president? I shall hereby list the three specific occasions featuring yes, the one and only, Donald Trump.

Appearance One: *Sex and the City*, season one, episode one, entitled "Sex and the City." Aired 1998. Details: After Carrie Bradshaw is told by her longtime heartbreaker Kurt Harrington that he wants to have sex without commitment, disappointed Carrie is approached by a sexually ravenous Samantha Jones who points to the man whom we later know to be Mr. Big, boldly comparing him to Donald Trump. WHAT AN HONOUR to be referenced in the pilot episode of *Sex And The City!* And to be compared to the series hero! To Mr. Big! What other president, let alone man, on Earth, can claim this reality?

Appearance Two: *Sex and the City,* season two, episode eight, entitled, "The Man, the Myth, the Viagra." Aired 1999. Details: Enjoying a cocktail at the end of her work day, Samantha Jones notices Donald Trump who, from across the room, is conducting what seems to be a business meeting. Donald Trump makes quick, strong, sexy eye contact with Samantha then stands up, shakes hands with his meeting, and proclaims that he will be at Trump Tower if future contact is desired. And, might I please add that our then future president looked oh so handsome in this scene! I want to know two things about this cameo. What did Donald Trump think about appearing with a glass of alcohol given the fact that he has never consumed alcohol in his life and advocates against consumption of it? And, what did Ivanka, who is my age, think of her father's divine appearance? I am certain that she was very proud!

Appearance Three: *Sex and the City*, season four, episode one, entitled, "The Agony and the Ex-tacy." Aired 2001. Details: Samantha propositions a Franciscan for sex, offering to host a benefit for his church, stating, as her sales pitch, that she can confirm attendance of Donald Trump and Marlo Thomas. Enough said!

Aside from consumption of *Sex And The City*, *The Nikki Haskell Show*, *Dynasty* (Joan Collins reportedly created her gorgeous character of Alexis Colby in the likeness of Donald Trump), *Dallas* (the fine and sexy J.R. Ewing), *Beverly Hills 90210*, *The Muppets* (the Jim Henson years), and 1980s cartoons, I have rarely consumed other television entertainment. I simply am very narrow and restrictive on my consumption of things. Another example to support this fact: in school, despite receiving homework assignments to read a plethora of "distinguished" titles, I read only but a few: *The Agony and the Ecstasy* by Irving Stone, *The Once and Future King* by T.H. White, *Fahrenheit 451* by Ray Bradbury, *Animal Farm* by George Orwell, *Tuck Everlasting* by Natalie Babbitt, and *Romeo and Juliet* by Shakespeare. The story of *Romeo and Juliet* interested me because Leonardo DiCaprio as Romeo interested me. I loved the film adaptation starring Leonardo thusly I read the book to compare notes. And the film was much better! If only I had known that Leonardo would one day work to block Donald Trump from becoming president, then perhaps I would have avoided *Romeo and Juliet* entirely, as I did *Hamlet* and *Macbeth*. Why did I avoid these others Shakespearean "classics?" Well, who wants to read something depressing? Not this girl! And because I am very smart, despite having abstained from the formal reading assignments, I aced the examinations. Yes, I was almost always smarter than my teachers. Four exceptions include Mr. Rzeczkowski (Grade Four, Hyde Elementary School), Mr. Vogler (*Honours Chemistry*, Grade Eleven, Moon Area High School), Señora DeMasso (*Español II - IV*, Grades Nine to Eleven, Moon Area High School), and Ron Morris

(*Introduction to Entrepreneurial Studies,* Duquesne University). I also adored Señor Bamford (*Honours Español V,* Grade Twelve, Moon Area High School) and Mrs. Burik (Kindergarten, Cornell School District). The other teachers were a waste of my time.

This reminds me of a verbal disagreement that I once had with Mr. Bikram, about my limited scope on doing things. The September of 2014 conversation is documented at my blog (www.theyogaballerina.com/i-shall-only-do-what-i-like-to-do).

"Let's rent a cabin in the woods and go hiking for the weekend," Mr. Bikram suggested.

"No," I replied.

"Why not?"

"Because it doesn't sound like fun."

"Come on. You won't get your Lululemons dirty."

"No."

"You can bring your dog."

"I only want to do what I want to do. And I shall not do that."

"VIOLET."

"What does violet mean?"

"Watch the movie: *Willy Wonka.*"

"No, I hate *Willy Wonka.*"

"Nobody hates *Willy Wonka.*"

"I do."

"It's a classic. You cannot call yourself a film expert if you do not watch the classics."

"Then I am not an expert."

"Yes you are. I'm well versed in literature. I hate *Gone With The Wind.* But I forced myself to read the book because otherwise I'd be the less informed person in a literary discussion. Do you want to be that way about film?"

"Yes."

"You're a goon."

"Because I only watch what I like?"

"Yes."

"Then I'm a goon."

****

****

****

I am the "goon" who, on June 16, 2015, exactly nine months and twelve days after this conversation with Mr. Bikram was printed at my blog, called the presidential election of 2016.

I am the goon, who, despite receiving laughs and boos from my nearest and dearest, supported candidate Donald J. Trump from that very first day.

On June 16, 2015, an elegant, bold, sophisticated, charismatic, humorous, real man descended from the glorious, golden, confident escalator of Trump Tower to announce his candidacy for President of the United States of America. A self-funded campaign. A non politically-corrected platform. He talked about illegals and rape. About bringing jobs back to America. About wealth. About healthcare. About veterans. About making America first. About his beautiful family. About his successful business. About making America great again. And I was blown the hell away. After quickly emailing to my conservative and independent-thinking friends about my excitement for the campaign, excitement at the prospect of such a great man running the country, and also excitement about one year of pure entertainment because I knew that his campaign would be entertainment extraordinaire, I immediately thought of THAT GAME from 1991. Did I dream of it? Or was it true? Did I, as a young girl, at the age of nine, exist as so very excited about the presence of this heroic-looking man who will one day become President of The United States of America? Did I know, back then, of how to recognise greatness?

Throughout Donald Trump's presidential campaign, I experienced vivid flashbacks to those moments of little, curious Nicole Marie Story, admiring that board game. And then, watching the Netflix documentary in April of 2018 depicting Donald Trump visiting with line workers who assembled his board game in 1989, the truth became confirmed! I had, indeed, dreamt not of this great, profound experience with Donald Trump as a nine-year old in 1991. The experience, had, indeed, happened. It was, indeed, true. It was, indeed, reality. *Trump: The Game* was reality. And the game's tagline proclaiming that winning is everything, was indeed, written in stone. My childhood admiration of it, was, indeed, true. A few weeks after viewing this life-changing Netflix clip, in May of 2018, when visiting my beautiful mother for Mother's Day, I asked, "Mommy, do you remember a game that you and Daddy had? The Trump game?" And she replied, nonchalantly, "Yes. I think we still have it."

My jaw dropped.

Firstly, if you exist in my circle of confidantes, and, as previously stated, you know that on the moment that Donald Trump declared his candidacy, I called the election. Even until the very end, my "smart" and "sophisticated" and "mature" friends laughed at my confident, unwavering prediction. They, on the other hand, claimed that Donald Trump was campaigning to grow his personal brand and to build an audience to launch Trump Media. They claimed that he never wanted to be president. In fact, Mr. Bikram clings to this conspiracy theory, nearly three years into the glorious term of President Trump. I never once doubted Donald Trump's intentions.

And I was correct. Donald Trump commanded quiet America to the polls.

Secondly, if you exist in my circle of confidantes, you know that five days before Donald Trump declared his candidacy, my beautiful dog Gwendolyn posed for a picture in front of Trump International Hotel and Tower in Chicago during a one-day visit from Pittsburgh (www.theyogaballerina.com/gwendolyn-chicago). The skyscraper mesmerised me! It impressed me! Was her posing in front of it, an omen?

Thirdly, and lastly, if you exist in my circle of confidantes, you know that several months into blogging about how greatly I adored Donald Trump, into advertising on how passionately I supported his candidacy, about how I swore that I would never again vote for a president unless I loved the candidate and therefore changed my then registered political party from Independent to Republican just so that I could vote for Donald Trump in the Pennsylvania primary, THAT I WAS SILENCED.

In order to protect my work and friendships, I needed to close my trap.

I was hereby an undercover Trump supporter because, one day, out of left field, I was verbally petitioned by a client to change my politics and to therefore abandon my very strong convictions, the ones that I embodied since childhood. Mind you, work with this client enabled me, for the first time in my fiercely challenging life, to breathe. To live. To properly care for myself and for my dog Gwendolyn. To afford the proper care that Gwendolyn and I needed to be happy. To be healthy. To be peaceful. To be vibrant. Work with this client, work that I had earned by applying perfection, strength, dedication, loyalty, and skill, by jumping through hula hoops of fire, enabled me to feel like sunshine and moonshine for the very first time in my very disordered life. Losing this work would mean jeopardising my family's health. It would mean risking my peace, all because of my political and philosophical beliefs. I was unprepared to be a martyr. So, she left me with no other choice, or so I saw it, at the time. Approaching me in the mud room of her pricey Pittsburgh home with NPR strumming in the background, her beautiful, porcelain face suddenly became flushed with redness, and she spoke to me, quietly, in a tone of warning and of fear.

"I need to talk to you." She continued, "You cannot vote for that man. You do not know of what he's like. You do not know of what he's capable. He is not kind. He is not mentally well. I lived in New York in the nineties. He is not a good man. He is terrifying. My ex-husband works in real estate, and we know him. He is a very bad man. Your blog posts are scaring me."

Nicole Marie Story Trump Fan Girl could no longer publicly exist. I deleted the blog posts. I deleted the tweets. I turned it off, like a switch, as I knew, at that exact moment, that if I were to mutter one additional word about my love and respect for the heroic Donald Trump, that I would lose my work. Additionally, I treasured her friendship and felt that I needed to be loyal and supportive. Convinced that she loved me, as she treated me so kindly, I accepted invitations to her bridal shower, to her wedding, to her Christmas parties, to her dinners. None of the other "help" attended these celebrations. On many occasions, she generously sent lavish flower bouquets to my dog Gwendolyn; and she offered expensive presents, such as a Simon Pearce vase, such as a designer bag, to me. From what I know, the housekeepers' and landscapers' and caterers' dogs never received bouquets of flowers. I went above and beyond my duties, assisting with the interview of the jazz band that she employed for her wedding; fetching her "ugly" CSA collections; finding for her a landscaping team, a handyman, and the car service that she used for her wedding guests. On the day of her wedding, I drove to her house in the middle of my crazy schedule, to arm her burglar alarm system, because she had forgotten to do so before leaving, and she was insistent on having it armed. I met her driveway guy at 9pm on my thirty-fifth birthday, in the middle of a snow storm, because the driveway heating system was broken, and she wanted for it to be fixed, during her travels away from home. I joined her for a fitness class at a local boutique. I chauffeured her to a liberal political event. I attended another liberal political event with her! I dropped everything and came running across town, each time that her dog escaped from the property. Luckily, two escapes were false alarms, but on the third time, I found the sweet girl out and about, exploring the world! I did all of this, on my free time, free time that I devoted to her because she was so important to me. She private-messaged me about her feelings, about her life, about things that one, in my opinion, only divulges to a confidante or to a best friend or to a therapist. Out of character, meshing the lines between work and emotion, I felt like I needed to be there for her. I wanted to believe that she was doing this Donald Trump petition because she truly thought that it was correct and because she loved me. Putting aside my rational brain because she had been so good to me and to Gwendolyn, I wanted to believe that she needed me as much as I needed her.

But I was wrong.

And it wasn't just her. Anger and "fear" existed everywhere in this predominantly Jewish town of Squirrel Hill, a suburb of Pittsburgh, Pennsylvania, the same, little, beautiful town in which the most terrible massacre in modern U.S. history occurred at the Tree of Life synagogue on October 27, 2018. Rest in peace, my dear, never forgotten Pittsburgh neighbours who lost your lives due to the insanity of one evil monster. President Trump paid respectful homage to Pittsburgh and to the victims of this tragedy, in person at the synagogue, and during the State of The Union of 2019.

As related to the campaign, to cite examples of the anger and "fear" in Squirrel Hill, I shall state that just one week before my client approached me, I had been walking along, minding my own business, when a manly-looking, round woman driving a beautiful, black, Benz GLS-Class slowed to a stop, unrolled her window, and exclaimed, in disgust, "Come on. You're better than that! How shameful!" She was pointing to my *Make America Great Again* T-shirt. Stunned, I was perplexed at how to respond, as I had never, before this moment, been treated so hatefully, by a non-internet stranger. And, just a few days after the Benz-lady encounter, an Indian woman, probably mid-fifties in age, very plain-looking and puffy with dishevelled hair, walked in my direction. She exclaimed, with a thick, dramatic, Bollywood accent, "You can't be serious!" also pointing to my divine *Make America Great Again* T-shirt. This time I was prepared, replying to this woman, quite staunchly, "Oh, I am VERY serious." But when my client stated her position, I knew that I needed to shut my mouth to maintain my work which I needed. Which I earned. Which I loved. And I felt an obligation to this woman because I genuinely cared for her.

But there I was.

I was an undercover Trump supporter.

And it was torture.

For the next three years, I carried forward in daylight, suppressing my adoration for candidate turned President Donald Trump except for during brief interactions with a charming fellow named Jim who is amongst a handful of Republicans living in this radically liberal section of Pittsburgh. The former President and CEO of Allegheny Technologies, and, before that, CFO of Gulf

Oil, it is reported in a November 18, 2001 article in the *Pittsburgh Post Gazette* that after each of his four sons graduated from college, they visited Wall Street together, experiencing the land of where only money counts. Jim required nothing more from his sons regarding these trips - they needed not love it, nor hate it - he only required the experience. Jim, like President Trump, is a pure capitalist, pure meaning with heart.

To have earned intelligent discourse with this great Jim, now aged into his eighties, during and after the election was simply an honour. And privilege. Thank you, Jim. I miss our conversations dearly, especially during President Trump warrior moments like his summits with Kim Jong-un and being the first sitting U.S. President to step foot onto North Korean soil, like the swearing-in of Justice Brett Kavanaugh to the Supreme Court, like the previously mentioned State of the Union of 2019 of where he declared that "America will never be a socialist country," like when *The Mueller Report* confirmed that no collusion with Russia existed and that it was all a hoax created by the radical left, like when his beautiful family attended the lavish State Banquet as hosted by Her Majesty The Queen. If President Trump is extending invitations to The White House, Jim and his dear wife Mary should be at the top of that list.

Other than with Jim, on the outside, I ignored all conversation regarding our soon to be president. Nodding my head in what seemed to be agreement with my liberal client, I hid my strong beliefs. When she was horrified, I exclaimed my "wows," offering the impression that I, too, was horrified. When she hosted university students for Hillary, I smiled. I smiled to protect my work but also because of the golden rule and because I truly felt happy for her, that she was doing what she thought was right.

And, at nighttime, after completion of my hard work, behind closed doors, morphing into private Trump Fan Girl with a magical *MAGA* hat, I did what I thought was right. Celebrating Donald Trump's days and nights of speeches and rallies and tweets and debates and new book release, I voraciously consumed everything regarding this greatest man on Earth whilst passionately communicating with my underground Trump railroad. I worked so hard, all day, to come home at nighttime to watch Sean Hannity and to discuss the state of Donald Trump with my heroic friend Peter Dickerson of Australia. Peter Dickerson became my source of joy, every night, as he understood me. Peter Dickerson saw what I did, in Donald Trump. In addition to sharing words in text format, I shared my pictures with Peter Dickerson. Dressed in *MAGA* T-shirts with scissored off sleeves, revealing my perfect yoga arms and delicate edges of beautiful lacy bras by Free People, I never felt stronger or prettier. These *MAGA* selfies pleased Peter Dickerson, I think. He reciprocated by sending strong, heroic pictures of himself to me. President Trump ignited us with feelings of excitement, hope, and confidence. Peter Dickerson and I were very happy.

Every tweet, every debate, every factor of Donald Trump's campaign made my heart smile. It became my world! It all made me feel as motivated, inspired, hopeful! I ordered and read his 1987 *The Art of the Deal*, and it immediately ranked as my second favourite book of all time, second only to the grand masterpiece of *Atlas Shrugged* by Ayn Rand. In fact, *The Art of the Deal*, specifically Donald Trump's description of the Wollman Rink debacle when under city contract for many years before he swooped in to save the day, seems like a real life edition of *Atlas Shrugged*, solidifying that President Trump indeed bears the likeness of a true heroic character of an Ayn Rand novel.

The Art of The Deal begins with a very poignant statement, declaring that Donald Trump does it NOT for the money. Deals are rather his form of art. I suspected this fact about money being a benefit versus central goal of Donald Trump before reading his words. Like-minded humans are drawn to one another. Even nine-year old Nicole Marie Story was drawn to Donald Trump before I knew anything about the world. And, just as I can always sense a disordered eater, I can always sense a pure-hearted capitalist.

The Art of the Deal documents the best example on how to live. And for those who have been sitting in a hole without access to Fox News (Real News) for the past four years, the book teaches that President Trump is a very raw and transparent man. It is amazing that as he details each of his early big deals, he sounds just like the great President of today who is tweeting about Fake News and the wonderful United States of America.

In his newest book, *Crippled America*, then candidate Donald Trump begins by describing that for its cover, he posed for beautiful, professional pictures. But, despite his family's urgings to choose the resulting pretty photographs, he rejected the polished images because in those photographs, he looked as happy. And the state of America was anything but happy. America was crippled. Thusly, he wanted to match this negative temperature, looking as angry on the cover of his book.

It is incredible that *Crippled America* begins with this exact information about why Donald Trump selected an angry-looking photograph for the cover. Why incredible? Because this is the first item that Hillary's running mate Tim Kaine discussed, in a snake-oil salesman pitch, at his Pittsburgh campaign "rally" in October of 2016. You might wonder of why I know anything about a Tim Kaine "rally." The answer is that my liberal client invited me to attend. Saying no was an option not.

At this "rally" which is more accurately described as a standing slumber, everyone smiled, looking as though they had consumed magic mushrooms and smoked marijuana during a long, unproductive lunch, now holding signs decorated with rainbows, in the middle of a weekday afternoon. I estimate that approximately seventy-five people attended, approximately five of whom were Hillary protesters. I arrived to the event literally three minutes before scheduled starting time, and there existed no line, just patches of stringy-haired, middle-aged females and dirty-looking college kids with clipboards, asking for my information and for my commitment to vote for their candidate who was late for the event because he encountered cross town traffic. What a loser!

Standing very close to the stage beside my beautiful client at the quiet, sleepy campus of Carnegie Mellon University, I wanted to crawl underneath of a rock. I was hoping, mentally crossing every finger and toe and strand of DNA in my body, that the Fake News Media would capture my image not, especially given that my client had "gifted" me with an "I'm With Her" button which I displayed onto my clothing to please her. I wanted to whisper back to the protesters that I was really with them. That I belonged not amongst these Birkenstock-wearing, bohemian skirt-flowing, privileged housewives. My client, unlike the other attendees, had clean hair, perfectly manicured nails, and wore jeans, as she carries a New York privileged feminist style versus the sloppy, flower-child look of this Hillary-loving demographic of Pittsburgh. But, all in all, it was like being at my idea of Woodstock or Jamboree in the Hills.

So, what do you know, after painfully listening to liberal, whiny, disrespectful Governor of Pennsylvania Tom Wolf survey the crowd, questioning if we were planning to vote with our brains or with our hearts (proceeding to TELL us to vote with our hearts and therefore for the Hillary Kaine team, LOL), out walked this frumpy-looking male. AKA Tim Kaine. Whilst my client stood smiling with a Care Bear stare, I wanted to again crawl underneath of a rock. Kaine flaunted a pot belly and looked like everything that Ayn Rand describes as a good-for-nothing human in Atlas Shrugged. Sweating like a pig, he began his speech with a dishonest demonstration. He showed to the audience two books. The first being *Stronger Together* by he and Hillary, the second being *Crippled America* by Donald Trump. He showed to the crowd, only the covers of the books and asked (paraphrased from my memory), "Who do you want to lead the country? Someone who looks as happy on their book cover? Or someone who looks as ANGRY?!"

WOW! I wanted to exclaim, "YOU LIAR!" It was a complete misrepresentation of Donald Trump's message. "Read the first paragraph of Donald Trump's book aloud, you clown!" … "Tell to the crowd about how Donald Trump purposely selected the angry-looking picture to represent the TRUE state of America which is CRIPPLED!" I bet that Kaine never even read the book. He probably never even read his own! What a shameful weasel.

It was Fake News in the flesh. Seriously, please search for the debacle on YouTube! "Tim Kaine Rally Pittsburgh CMU 10/6/2016." And prepare to laugh! Prepare to howl! The only clip that I can find on this event sadly excludes his weasel-like opener hence my paraphrasing of it, but the speech's remainder presents the same bland, untruthful, Fake News flavour, so you shall get the gist, if you want to waste your time with watching trash. You might even spy me standing in the crowd. Toward conclusion of the "rally," my beautiful client, beaming with pride, grabbed my hand, as though to say thank you for my decision to support her candidate, and to support her.

I felt like a terrible human.

I wanted to tell her the truth, right then and there.

But I was a coward.

After the election, she "resisted," posting about impeachment on Facebook and attending the women's march on Washington. It all made no sense to me. So much money was spent by rich women to travel to D.C. and to stay at fancy hotels, all in protest of then President-elect Donald Trump. But what did this accomplish? It was whiny and unproductive which seems to be the modus operandi of radical Democrats.

But, just like the baker who refused to sell a wedding cake to a homosexual couple because of a religious objection, it was my client's right and prerogative to deny Donald Trump supporters with access to her home and to her life. She never outright said that I was required to withdrawal my support of Donald Trump. But her warning was plenty. Could she really have continued interacting with me if I had continued wearing my divine *Make America Great Again* clothing in her presence? And, even if I had reduced the Donald Trump cheer to during my personal time only, I knew that my nighttime blog posts and social media activity would continue to upset her. She followed my every move because she wanted to know and to control that which she allowed into her home. Of course she had that right. And I firmly chose to silence my heart. My freedom of speech, on my free time, was censored at my decision. And I am disappointed with my decision. I am disappointed that I continued working for her, under those conditions. Of interesting note is that despite my disappointment, I am also proud of my silenced heart because although I understood her not, I could feel her pain and torment, during and after the election. Each day that I walked into her home, she was in agony. Despite my black and white nature, because I appreciated her, because I loved her, because I wanted to believe that someone could care for me like she seemed to do, I felt sad that she felt so angry and confused. She has a REALLY GOOD HEART. I think that perhaps her heart is too big. She is a generous, beautiful, graceful angel. And I think that our daily relationship needed to end because the lines were blurred between love and work, between church and state. So I lost a client. And a friend. But I gained back myself. I did an exceptional job for her, and she paid me for that exceptional work. And because I lived as an undercover Trump supporter for nearly three years, in the eleventh hour of its twenty-year creation, this book morphed from being called, "*My Eating Disorder*" to "*Donald Trump and My Eating Disorder*," making its content so much more interesting and exciting, all because of that profound experience during and after the election of 2016.

I know that since our separation, my former client has realised the truth. She knows that I love President Trump. She knows that despite answering "Yes" to her "Did you vote for Hillary" question on November 9, 2016, that I truly voted for Donald Trump. I think that she knows of my "politics." And I think that despite her great pain, she respects who I am and that I strongly attach to my convictions, like she attaches to her own. She and I existed in each other's lives for more than our work arrangement. We truly made each other stronger. On my thirty-seventh birthday in 2019, exactly one year since our separation, she sent a very lovely, very beautiful happy birthday message to me. This was the ultimate bipartisan offering. In my heart, she is still a friend, and I shall always be loyal to her. Most importantly, I shall always be loyal to myself. To this woman, I want to say thank you for being in my life, and for loving me and my Gwendolyn.

Now let us please rewind back to the election timeline, to just a few weeks after the Tim Kaine "rally." It is now Saturday, November 5, 2016, and I dreamt, during a slumber, that I presented Donald Trump with a kiss on the cheek, like I would a King, and I said to him, "Thank you for leading our country into greatness, sir." True to form, as my dreams often materialise into reality, a few hours after awakening from this beautiful fantasy, I received a divinely exciting email from the Trump Campaign announcing that Donald Trump would be visiting my town on the next evening for a rally at 8pm on November 6, 2016. I cleared my calendar! I cleared my life! Usually, after agreeing to a social event, I regret my RSVP because I enjoy staying at home with my dog, but nothing about regret crossed my mind. The prospect of attending a Trump rally catalysed pure excitement.

Arriving to the rally at 4pm, I encountered magic. The driving line to park my Jeep Wrangler consumed one hour. The standing line to enter the event extended to easily two miles in length, coiling like a snake throughout the parking lot and beyond. IT WAS LIKE A ROCK CONCERT! Vendors! Music! Costumes! Old people! Young people! Children! From every walk of human life, people came to listen to our future president.

I waited.

And waited.

And waited, finally entering the building at around 8pm. Walking the distance of that glamorous line, following foot traffic toward the airport hangar where Donald Trump would exit from his plane directly to the podium, I knew that he would win the election by a landslide. It was like night and day, compared with the Tim Kaine "rally" at CMU, compared with the recent Hillary "talk" at the University of Pittsburgh. I attended the Hillary TALK not, thank goodness, but I chauffeured my client to the TALK and was therefore able to survey the non-traffic. I purposely identify it as a "talk" because it shows the weakness. There was no way on Earth that all of these thousands of people at the Trump Rock Concert had been polled. There was no way on Earth that such an enormous crowd would fail to dominate at the polls. Next to meeting the adorable litter of puppies to which my dog was born, the Trump Rock Concert registers as the most incredible thing that I have ever seen in my life.

Coming from a long day of passionate rallies, Donald Trump was running behind advertised schedule. He had a noon rally at Sioux City, Iowa; a 2pm rally at Minneapolis, Minnesota; and a 6pm rally at Sterling Heights, Michigan, all before flying to Moon Township, Pennsylvania. I think that Hillary was taking a long nap on that pre-election Sunday, LOL. And, as I proudly stood, shoulder to shoulder with Donald Trump lovers and fellow patriots, we chanted for hours of many, "Lock her up! Lock her up! Lock her up!" and "*MAGA! MAGA! MAGA!*" and "TRUMP! TRUMP! TRUMP!" It was exhilarating! To be surrounded by like-minded, energetic, bold human beings was powerful! Finally arriving at sometime around 10:30pm, Donald Trump spoke for about thirty minutes. Because I am small and mighty, I pushed to the front of the standing-only crowd and felt like I was seeing God. I cared not that I was hungry for dinner. I cared not that I was missing my Peloton workout. I cared not that I was potentially putting myself into harm's way with such a big crowd of people. I cared not if I appeared on the Fake News and lost my work. I got to see my future President. And that was all that mattered.

After this 10:30pm rally on November 6, 2016, just two days before the election, Donald Trump flew to Leesburg, Virginia for ANOTHER rally, arriving to that destination after midnight yet speaking with excitement, vigour, and strength to his followers. I watched the late night coverage on Fox News. Five more rallies happened on the seventh, including one in Michigan which fell into ELECTION DAY Tuesday which changed our lives forever.

The question remains, how exactly does the subject of "Donald Trump" relate to the subject of "My Eating Disorder?" The answer is that he influenced the end of it. Donald Trump influenced the end of my seventeen-year war with food. How did he do it? The short answer is that he led by example. In doing it his way, in living life according to Donald J. Trump, he influenced me to embrace the unique disciplines, rules, and rituals that yield a healthy Nicole Marie Story. He influenced me to live the healthy version of Nicole Marie Story according to myself, not the healthy version according to the world. He influenced me to be confident in my choices and differences, and to care not of societal perception. He influenced me to eat my way. To sleep my way. To exercise my way. To socialise my way. To work my way. To mother my dog Gwendolyn my way. To own my life versus being a puppet with society controlling the strings. It was amazing to, for the first time, after a long, seventeen-year war with food, live confidently and unapologetically with regard to the very simple, very basic activities of living. Before Donald Trump shined light onto my darkness, helping me to end my war with food, I was told that I would always be eating disordered. And an insomniac. And a sociopath. And a narcissist. And an isolationist. And mentally ill. The Fake News Media accuses President Trump of these same bogus "conditions!" He sleeps for minimal hours, eats fast food, and tweets at whatever hour he pleases. Is this disordered? Hell no. This is President Trump. But Fake News accuses of otherwise. When judged by my Fake News for seventeen years of disordered eating, I tried so hard to be "normal" which effectively caused me to spin out of control.

Imagine an alcoholic. I am just like an alcoholic, but my problem is FOOD. The moment that I ate one thing naughty, it turned into eating pizzas, pies, donuts, cakes, and seventeen Reese's *Peanut Butter Halloween Pumpkins*, all before midnight followed by vomiting, followed by laxatives, followed by the start of a new diet, of a new day. Nearly. Every. Single. Day. For. Seventeen. Years. The food volume and types varied, but I ate tens of thousands of calories on most days. On the random off days, I starved myself. It was a constant battle to eat and to be thin. That was my eating disorder. That was my war.

Because I cannot eliminate food like an alcoholic can eliminate her poison, I need a rigid system to exist with it. I need a rigid system to live. Otherwise I shall eat the whole house and vomit my guts afterward. I knew this from day one of the seventeen-year war. But I fought these necessary rigid systems to please the world. In trying to be "normal," I handicapped myself from living healthfully. It took President Trump's influence for me to realise that I only needed to please myself. It took embodying my self-designed rigid ways to become healthy. And I have been oh so divinely healthy for three years, ever since August 21, 2016, exactly seventeen years from the point of becoming bulimic, exactly one year, two months, and six days into the greatest campaign of the history of the world. Just as the heroic image of Donald Trump spoke to little Nicole Marie Story at the age of nine in 1991 before I knew anything about the greatness of the Trump name, Donald Trump spoke to adult Nicole Marie Story since descending from that golden escalator at Trump Tower on June 16, 2015. I relate to President Trump completely. Then and now. That is the short answer of how President Trump influenced the end of my great war with food.

What is the long answer? In 1988, Donald Trump stated to Oprah that it is easy to work with our enemies not, so he would rather "make our allies pay their fair share." This statement is analogous with my healthy lifestyle. By focusing on my allies versus on my enemies, influenced by then candidate Donald Trump, I ended my war with food. Before then, aiming to be "normal," I tried, for instance, to keep a box of cereal and jug of almond milk in the apartment. But for me, a box of cereal is the enemy. So when you end up eating all of it, the entire box plus all of the milk, by 9am, you get damn mad and continue eating liberally all day because you're all or nothing, and because you already screwed up the day so might as well keep going. Not only do you skip yoga and cycling because you feel like a big fat loser, but vomiting is off of the menu because you promised your little dog Gwendolyn in 2010 when you stopped the eleven years of bulimia that you would never again purge. So you gain weight. And lose weight. And gain weight. And lose weight. And gain weight. For another six, turbulent years. And we are talking a lot of weight, ranging between 89 and 181 pounds, for the entire length of my war with food. I continued living this ferociously disordered lifestyle, for a total count of seventeen years, until I felt empowered to completely own my virtues and strict rules during the time that Donald Trump publicly aired the owning of his.

When I finally stopped caring about what others thought, becoming honest with my friends and family in 2016, coinciding with Donald Trump's daily message as delivered through his divine *Make America Great Again* rallies, to own one's life, I confidently, regularly, announced my reality. For instance, when receiving dinner invitations, I stated, "Yes, I shall meet you for a gorgeous dinner, but I shall order food not, rather, I shall enjoy a martini or two, then order dinner for takeaway so that I may nourish with my dog Gwendolyn after returning to home. And if I, for some chance, decide to order food in your company, it shall be something elegant and tiny as I prefer to nourish afterward with Gwendolyn because nourishing in public, at "dinner," is unladylike and displeasing to me. Besides, I prefer to dine at midnight or later, like do the Europeans, and our "dinner" meeting time of nine o'clock is cocktail hour, to me. If you have a problem with this arrangement, I care not." I needed to say these things aloud because otherwise, the expectation was for me to behave like did everyone else. To eat like a hog in public. To eat early. To eat as the main focus of social activity. But doing so would only trigger me to want more food afterward, leading to a very stressful state of bingeing on food and perhaps purging of food. Dinners should be beautiful and sexy, not a stuff your face with fried chicken hillbilly hoedown.

As previously stated, I compare my reality to alcoholism. But my drug is food. Nowadays, in 2019, three years into healthy living, the outlining of my plans is required not, as my confidantes know that I will be different and that their questioning of me is simply annoying and that I shall reject it. As I heal from my war, things change everyday, and it is wonderful.

Bottom line is that I started being bold about MY unique healthy eating and living during the time that Donald Trump was being bold about Fake News, Hillary Clinton, bad trade deals, illegal immigration, and the swamp that needed to be drained. He influenced me to be confident, outspoken, and unapologetic. Similar to Ayn Rand's introduction to *Atlas Shrugged* suggests, the reality and behaviours of Donald Trump caused me to realise that others, like me, indeed, exist. People need to know that they're not alone. For a long time, I was totally alone. Until President Trump's campaign, I was alone. And if this book can reach one like-minded human who is dealing with an eating disorder, then I shall be so very happy.

In addition to ending my war with food, to yield a healthy Nicole Marie Story, I needed to end my chaotic relationship with men. I began working on this, too, in those early days of post bulimia circa 2010, but truly became bold and rigid about my manner of dating during the presidential campaign of 2016. It is quite interesting to me that I classify both food and men as things that must be sexy. And in order for me to experience an epic high, it must be controlled and beautiful. I want to eat in the cleanest of fashions. I want to conduct relationships in the cleanest fashions. This means portion control. Quality control. Presentation. And rigidity. For both food and men. My idea of clean eating is gin martinis in a fancy minimalist restaurant with midnight sashimi at my fancy minimalist apartment. My idea of clean dating is doing something adventurous in the great outdoors during early morning and daytime with a very powerful man who is my boyfriend (and my dog Gwendolyn); and, at nighttime, being in a penthouse at Trump International Hotel and Tower in Chicago with a very powerful man who is my boyfriend (and my dog Gwendolyn). Eating and conducting physical relations in an unorganised, plain environment with unclean, unproductive, unimaginative company is unacceptable. Intimacy with a radical Democrat is unacceptable. I probably need to extend that rule to all Democrats and to anyone who cares not for President Trump. And I shall be loyal to my partner, not due to rules or jealousy or control, but due to the fact that no other man shall impress me. I exist as very rigid and refuse to invest my time with anyone who misaligns with my value system. I argue not. Everything is happy. I look forward to, so much, knowing my perfect gentleman. My little dog Gwendolyn must approve of him. This is the number one requirement. She attends all social meetings. This is non negotiable.

Because of President Trump, because of his leading by example, because of his track record of winning at life, I finally found it as divinely grand to live freely by my strict rules about eating and about living that permitted me to stay as "clean." It was the first time, in seventeen years, that I found a groove that lasted for more than six months. And then, on August 21, 2016, at the age of thirty-four years, exactly seventeen years from the date of becoming bulimic, exactly fourteen months and five days after Donald Trump announced his candidacy for President of the United States of America, I found myself as existing in the longest tenure of good health of my life. August 21, 2016 was a great test, as I was managing a busy work schedule, also attending the wedding of my liberal client. Expecting to fail somewhere in the day by overeating, or by missing my workout, when I awoke on the next day in a state of divine peace with flat abdominals and hips that fit freely into size twenty-five shorts by Free People and happy memories of the day prior, it felt as though I had won at the greatest battle of my life. I had, after seventeen years, ended my dramatic war with food. I thusly found it as completely acceptable to declare myself as removed from the classification of disordered eater. Prior to this, for seventeen years, it was like Bill Murray in *Groundhog Day* crossed with *Alice in Wonderland* by Lewis Carroll, a never ending cycle of Nicole Marie Story falling into the rabbit hole, venturing into a state of anorexia, bulimia, and weight fluctuation from 89 to 181 pounds, up and down the scale, over and over again.

For me, compromise on food means poison. For me, food is nourishment or poison. To compromise and to live in the middle without rules and restrictions, only failure can result. For me, to be healthy, I must be regimented. And I am.

President Trump is black and white. Full throttle. Or sleeping. He is doing something magnificent and productive with his life, during every waking moment. The manner in which he overtook and rehabilitated Manhattan in the 1970s and 1980s - it is remarkable! The manner in which he won the love of beautiful women - I am so impressed! The manner in which he fathers and grandfathers - it is divine! The manner in which he boldly attaches his powerful name to his extravagant properties - it causes my heart to swoon! The manner in which he won the love of the country - he is the inspiration of a lifetime! President Trump lives in the middle not. In fact, he literally lives at the very top, in the penthouse of his own skyscraper! And in the WHITE HOUSE! He is divinely exciting and principled.

When I am told that President Trump looks and behaves as unpresidential, I question the naysayer with, "What is presidential?" And the Democrat replies with something such as, "It is Donald Trump not!" I answer, "Why not?" They answer with, "A president tweets not! A president bullies not! A president disrespects women not! A president runs the country like a business not! A president is friendly with dictators not!" Blah blah blah! I especially love the, "A president says what he thinks not!" My retort is, "Then what the hell does he say?"

The point that I hereby make is that there is no set definition to the face of a president. In my lifetime, I have observed many different presidential faces:

President Ronald Reagan, President George H.W. Bush, President William Clinton, President George W. Bush, President Barack Obama, and now our breathtaking President Donald J. Trump. All different. All unique. All human. All American.

The same is true for eating disorders. There is no set definition to the face of an eating disorder. As you can see, I looked as completely different during all seventeen years of disordered eating.

LITTLE GIRL WITH CURLS, 1985.

MY BEAUTIFUL FAMILY, 1987.

THE STORY SISTERS, 1988.

THE STORY SISTERS, 1989.

THE STORY COUSINS! FROM LEFT TO RIGHT, TRACY, STEPHANIE, TERRI, NICOLE, LISA, AND TAFFY THE DOG, 1990.

WITH MY BELOVED PATERNAL GRANDMOTHER, MID 1990S. AT THIS POINT, I WAS THROWING AWAY MY SCHOOL LUNCHES, TRYING TO CONTROL MY BODY.

FIVE DAYS BEFORE THE EATING DISORDER STARTED, BIRTHDAY DINNER AT DON PABLO'S, FEBRUARY 9, 1999, 135 POUNDS.

JUNIOR PROM, APRIL 1999, 117 POUNDS.

WITH MY BEAUTIFUL MATERNAL GRANDMOTHER, JULY 17, 1999, 89 POUNDS.

WITH MY BEAUTIFUL MATERNAL GRANDMOTHER, JANUARY 2001, 181 POUNDS.

SKINNY AGAIN, JANUARY 2004, 125 POUNDS.

FAT AGAIN, MAY 2005, 170 POUNDS.

SUMMER OF 2008, FACE SWOLLEN FROM VOMITING, 140 POUNDS.

JULY 2011, DRUNK AND HUNGRY, 114 POUNDS.

FAT AGAIN, JANUARY 2013, 163 POUNDS.

AND THEN DONALD TRUMP ANNOUNCED HIS CANDIDACY FOR PRESIDENT OF THE UNITED STATES, AND EVERYTHING BEGAN TO FALL INTO PLACE, JUNE 2015. 117 POUNDS.

UNDERCOVER, AT THE TRUMP MAGA RALLY, MOON TOWNSHIP, PENNSYLVANIA, OCTOBER 6, 2016.

FINALLY. EXISTING IN A VESSEL OF HAPPINESS.

Most humans assume that eating disorders can be identified by the human's exterior. Too skinny. Too fat. But what about too middle? What about the humans who look as "normal?" For most of my eating disordered life, I looked as "normal" but I assure you, I was anything but normal. I was caught in a lifestyle of restricting, bingeing, purging, manic exercising, and maintaining complete disgust for my body. At the age of twenty-five, just eight years into my bulimic tenure, caused by dramatic weight fluctuations, my breasts hung to my stomach. Thusly, I painfully duct-taped the ugly, saggy mounds around my back to achieve a flat-chested aesthetic. In addition to living with an eating disorder, I was living with welts on my breasts and back from the nighttime ripping of my skin during tape removal (See 2011 blog post, *Bulimic Breasts*, www.theyogaballerina.com/bulimic-breasts). In my late teens to late twenties, I thought that finding a rich husband would be my answer to the bulimia. If I had financial wealth and romantic love, then I would have control over food, I thought. And who can get a husband with ugly breasts, I wondered? This is why I smashed my breasts with duct tape. This is why I eventually had a breast reduction. Little did I know that I could achieve everything on my own, including peace with food, including healthy breasts, without a man.

In addition to living with an eating disorder, acting against everything for which I stand, I spent money in gross excess of my earnings, on food binges and on clothing for my fluctuating body. Struggling to pay rent and bills due to my food addiction and poor decisions, I played Russian roulette with my money and credit, writing checks before money existed in the bank and charging full tanks of gasoline when stations preauthorised for only $1. This meant that if I had $1 to my credit limit, I could drive for a few days, using another two credit cards to charge Gwendolyn's specialty dog food. Paying for her complete food requirement in one charge was impossible with my addiction, so I religiously left the dog food store, returning minutes later, acting like I had forgotten to buy everything, but I had truly returned to use a second credit card because the first had been maxed. I was too prideful to admit to the clerk that I "needed" to use two cards. Additionally, I bought Gwendolyn's monthly heart worm and flea and tick preventative in single dosages from the veterinarian because the six-month supply was outside of my allowance. It was exhausting. It was embarrassing. I worked so hard, and all of my hard-earned money went to feeding my eating disorder. My wonderful parents bailed me out, on three occasions, loaning me large sums of money, interest free, during that awful period. I repaid all loans in their entirety. And, when, in 2010, I began to confidently say no to the lifestyle of food and dating wildness, when I finally started to say yes to my black and white rainbow, I found control, stability, freedom, and health. It consumed another six years and the influence of Donald Trump to end the war completely.

I consider my eating disorder to be a condition of mental health NOT. My eating disorder happened because my personality is full throttle, and because I adore a skinny aesthetic. If anything, it is because of my eating disorder that my mental health could have been sub par. I say "could have been" because I was always positive, regardless of how much fat I carried on my bones. But I was chronically angry at myself for being so unsuccessful with food. I postponed social interactions because they could be conducted not, in the state of my imperfect, fat body, one resulting from the bingeing. As previously stated, my war was a constant battle between eating and staying thin. But in eight years of blogging about this subject, I have learnt that other reasons for disordered eating exist, reasons other than my own. Humans attribute their eating disorders to fear, to pain, to loneliness, to something other than love for food, skinniness, and perfection. They claim that they use(d) their disorder for control because they have/had control over nothing else in their life. They claim that they use(d) their disorder to inflict pain because it feels/felt so good. Likewise, they claim that they vomit(ed) because it feels/felt like a release. To stuff. And to release. They cry. They are sad. They seemed weak to me. They classify/classified their disorders as mental. As emotional. And when I started blogging, I showed to them tough love, thusly earning hate readership of my own content. I have, in eight years, learnt to simply shut up. I no longer offer unsolicited advice. In fact, I offer no advice. I simply write about my reality with hopes that my unique story can positively impact the life of another human being. As previously stated, just as no two presidents are alike, no two eating disorders are alike. Additionally, no two solutions to eating disorders are alike. I respect and offer my love to anyone who is dealing with any addiction. It is complete hell.

I think that I can reach the greatest audience by writing about President Trump because this book will appeal to humans other than those specifically interested in my first world eating disorder. It will appeal to one hundred percent of the country! To one hundred percent of the Earth! Everyone is interested in President Trump. Thusly, everyone will be interested in my book. My intended audience is therefore all humans on Earth.

This book will appeal to women and to men. During Uber rides, when questioned by male drivers on my "story," I tell the driver that I am a dog mother who is publishing a book on July 9, 2019. They reply, "What is the title of your book?" I say, *"Donald Trump and My Eating Disorder."* Erupting into laughter, they reply, slowly, "What's... it... about?" I reply, "Donald Trump and my eating disorder," Laughing, they ask, "How... exactly... do... the... two... subjects... relate?" I reply, "You must please read my book to discover the answer!" They reply with laughter, intrigue, and commitment to buy. I really hope that they do buy my work! As for the female drivers? I am usually holding on for my life because they navigate terribly and make me feel as sick, so I offer zero information to them! They will probably throw me out of their car, if they learn of my truth, anyway. I can always sense a radical female Democrat by the crazy, emotional, wimpy manner in which she drives.

Who might this book help? Maybe my book will help men to understand their daughters and or wives who do/shall experience an eating disorder. Maybe it will appeal to those humans who live with the eating disorder. Maybe it will appeal to those who have ended their own crazy war with food. It will certainly intrigue radical Democrats and the Fake News Media, because it will be appalling to them, that I am crediting President Trump with influencing the end of my war with food. Liberal perception is that President Trump's respect for women is horrendous, and they will, at first thought, think that my book will be one to blame President Trump for my former eating disorder versus the reality of my thanking him for influencing the end of it. Surprise surprise!

I think that President Trump's brutal honesty with regard to women is fabulous and refreshing. He likes beautiful women, he has a "type," and he is confident in telling a woman that she has gained weight, example being that girl WHOSE JOB WAS TO BE THIN AND BEAUTIFUL as the 1996 Miss Universe winner. Do you know that a woman was involved at the top level of construction of Trump Tower? Do you know that his first wife Ivana Trump worked at the highest levels at The Trump Organization? Donald Trump was one of the early people who employed women in the real estate and construction business. He loves and respects CORRECT and TALENTED women greatly.

It is very important to express my highest salute of gratitude to President Trump for influencing me to live according to my own value system. When my work relationship ended with my liberal client, I realised that just like during my years of disordered eating, I was living a lie by suffocating my extreme love and gratitude and respect for our great President. I began passionately resenting myself for silencing my truth about President Trump. Why could celebrities and liberal friends blast the internet with pictures of their *Pussy Grabs Back* apparel but I could not, at my blog, flaunt my beloved *Make America Great Again* gear? Why did I need to stifle praises of our great president? The conditions to which I subjected myself to restrict my speech weighed heavily on my heart. And now that I no longer mattered to my former client, or so it seemed, what was my reason? Why was I living as an undercover Trump supporter? I had no answer. Thusly, on April 6, 2018 at 11pm, walking with my dog Gwendolyn in a dark snow storm with three of her dearest of canine friends named Lana, Shae, and Miles, it hit me like lightening! I needed to tell my story! My complete story! Not just the story about my eating disorder. But also the story about how my life is forever changed because of this kind, wonderful, hard-working, intelligent, handsome man named President Donald J. Trump.

Do you know that President Trump has never consumed one sip of alcohol? In a February of 2016 interview, he talked to Anderson Cooper about his older brother Fred Trump who died from complications with alcoholism in 1981. The interview is POWERFUL. The effect that Donald Trump's brother Fred had on Donald Trump's life is breathtaking. Fred preached to never drink, and to never smoke. The interview is very emotional insomuch that the LOVE that President Trump has for his brother is worn on his sleeve. The gratefulness is, too. When I watched this interview, it occurred to me exactly why Donald Trump and his family are so successful. It is because he instilled rigid discipline in himself, and also in his children. It is the same discipline that I require in my life.

And, for the record, I find Anderson Cooper to be nauseating. In fact, Anderson Cooper is the reason that I refused to consume the "news" from 1994 until 2012. In my middle school years of "education," he corresponded as a reporter for *Channel One News*, which broadcasted to middle school and high school classrooms in the USA. And Cooper made my head spin! Back then, I thought that perhaps my young brain lacked sophistication and or that I was stupid, yielding my complete mind-boggling response to his content. But, that was the problem not. I now identify the problem accurately. It was that I disagreed with his liberal, dramatic, emotional slant on things, even as a child. He reported on the news not. He reported on facts not. He rather reported on how he felt about what he perceived to be news. It was PRE FAKE NEWS! I literally thought that I was stupid because my brain rejected his broadcasts. And then, in 2012, during an oil change at Pep Boys, in the waiting room, I spied something by Sean Hannity, and it blew my mind to have a good feeling about what I heard on a "news channel." And then Hannity appeared in the film rendition of *Atlas Shrugged*, and I was now in love with news, Hannity style! Of course that turned into a love affair with Fox News aka Real News. In true Nicole Marie Story fashion, I went from avoiding the news since 1994, to consuming it frequently in 2012, to consuming it nonstop since June 16, 2015 when Donald Trump announced his candidacy. Thank goodness for Sean Hannity! Thank goodness for Fox News! Thank goodness for President Donald Trump! Also, mind you, I have never consumed Anderson Cooper on my own free will until this Donald Trump interview of subject.

I want to tell of a second wonderful tidbit of information about President Trump, also related to his no alcohol rule. It is a lovely story, one of which I learnt by reading his first wife Ivana Trump's autobiography entitled *Raising Trump*. It is a fabulous read in which Ivana describes the night that she and Donald met. The year, 1976. The scene, a New York restaurant for dinner on the night before a modelling show that Ivana was working. She and her fellow gorgeous models from Canada awaited a fancy table. Donald, noting Ivana's divine beauty, asked if he could secure a table for her group in a quicker fashion, as he knew the manager. She agreed, Donald's contingency being that he would dine with the glamorous girls. But to Ivana's surprise, he ordered alcohol not, and rather simply ordered iced tea and a burger. And he behaved as a complete gentleman, engaging in intelligent talk, no flirting. After eating, he disappeared, quietly paying the $400 bill, mysteriously departing from the restaurant. The girls, wanting to thank Donald for his kindness, waited for minutes of ten, just in case he returned to the table; but when he returned not, they decided to leave. As they exited from the building, Donald drove to the curb-side of the restaurant, stationed behind the driver's seat of his big black Cadillac limousine, offering to chauffeur the girls to their hotel in style, all whilst exchanging a smile with Ivana. On the next morning he arranged for delivery of one hundred red roses to Ivana with a rational, affectionate note, followed by a telephone call, followed by dinner. On day three, they met for lunch before Ivana returned to Canada at which point they maintained an international telephone courtship, marrying ten months later on April 7, 1977. Such a lovely story. Like Ivana, I refer to Donald Trump's second wife as "the showgirl," and I have no curiosities into that relationship. But I do have curiosities with regard to the courtship of First Lady Melania. I assume that it was beautiful. I do hope that she will write her autobiography someday!

Does President Trump have a vice? I wonder if he considers anything that he does, to be an unhealthy habit. I am certain that he will agree, if his vice were food, that he would have an eating disorder, or, rather, because he is so glamorously successful at everything that he does, he would have a peaceful relationship, strictly managed, with food. My drug was food. I was at war with it, for a long time. I needed to end the war. I needed to make peace with food in order to live a vibrant life. I needed to learn to coexist with food. I am the leader of my body, like President Trump is the leader of our grand United States of America. I needed to win the war and to declare peace. After seventeen years of battle, I have done so. My story is unique, and my solution model can be duplicated not. Rather, my solution model can be like a shining star that healthfulness can be achieved. I am certain that most eating disorders happen like mine did, in silence, in girls and in women who appear to live very happy, very functional lives; in girls and in women who look as completely "normal." But, underneath of that beautiful, painted canvas, underneath of that smile, exists a full blown-out war. A full blown-out eating disorder. Thusly I am writing about my way because it might offer hope. It might inspire awareness. It might be the First Aid Kit for which you have searched for all of your eating disordered life. Am I speaking to you right at this very moment?

I am here to tell of my hard work. Of my discipline. Of my success. And of the chaos that preceded it. I have ended my seventeen-year war with food. I have achieved joyful living. I am existing in a vessel of happiness. It has been three amazing years and forevermore of peace. And I furthermore hereby publicly declare myself as a great supporter of President Donald J. Trump. After having lived as an undercover Trump supporter for three years, I am so divinely proud to announce my support of this great man. These two subjects considered, the president and the eating disorder, I am here to demonstrate to you that there is no set definition to the face of a president, and there is no set definition to the face of an eating disorder.

Living with an eating disorder is like living as an underground Trump supporter. You think that people will see you as a leper so you are quiet about it. You think that society will reject you. You think that you will lose your job. Your friends. Your life! I am here to tell you that it is okay to talk. It is okay to disappoint your beautiful grandmother by firmly stating, "I must decline your fancy cake, grandma, as eating cake is unhealthy for me as it will propel me into a day of gorging on food. But I shall very much enjoy a cup of ceremonial matcha!" It is okay to say, "I voted for President Donald J. Trump, and my heart beams with pride for the hard, patriotic work that he is doing." And, in doing so, in being honest, in being bold, you might end your war with food, like I did. And, you shall, one hundred percent, be doing something really good for the heart of this country by helping others to see the good that exists in our great president.

I am so very proud to touch my heart during the *Pledge of Allegiance*. I am so very humbled to stand for the *National Anthem*. I am so very grateful to salute the greatest leader that the world has ever known. Thank you, President Donald J. Trump, for your influence on my health, and for your influence on the health of the United States of America. You are a great, great man.

CHAPTER
II

LIKE A VIRGIN

THE YEAR WAS 1999. Dressed in the sexiest, tightest, stone-washed jeans by American Eagle Outfitters, size of zero and flattering to my bony Irish hips, firm Brazilian bottom, and muscular Italian thighs, I knew that I looked good. The jeans were created for a girl who existed in tip top shape. And I fitted the bill, weighing in at 89 pounds on my five-foot, three-and-a-half-inch frame, even thinner than supermodel and fellow waif Kate Moss. And I was proud of this fact. I was proud at being thinner than the poster girl of thin. The jeans were accompanied by a teeny tiny blue T-shirt featuring a yellow baby chicken cartoon with the words of "Abercrombie & Fitch" scribbling across my young, alert breasts. To complete the outfit, I adorned my feet with a pair of wooden-heeled, orange-leathered, mule-styled, three-inch pumps by Candie's. My shoe obsession, albeit formerly Candies's, began way back then, twenty years ago, during my virginity. And this outfit burns into my memory as the perfect ensemble to my first time.

I afforded these specific, divine fashion pieces with wages earned through dedicated, passionate, summertime work as drive-thru girl at Wendy's Old-Fashioned Hamburgers. My family always over-provided, especially in the clothing and shoe department, but when I began earning my own money, I took pride in my ability to buy additional nice things as a resultant of my hard work. Now, arriving to the end of a hot, sizzling summer of labour, temperatures were scalding, outside, and inside, specifically inside of my body. Everything seemed to combust on that late summer day.

It was August 21, 1999. Aged seventeen, thin and pretty, confident and poised, on the cusp of beginning my senior year of high school as a thin girl following six months of dedicated, rigorous food restriction and extreme cardiovascular exercise, I strummed my fingers impatiently along my glass of water in the back of the Hunan Chinese Restaurant of Moon Township, a suburb of Pittsburgh, a city of Pennsylvania, a commonwealth of the great United States of America.

Crossing my legs, folding my hands, posing with a smile, I sat with shoulder blades drawing together and pressing downward, with chin lifting upward in sophistication, with brain daydreaming of the passionate moment to come, all whilst waiting for the server. I knew exactly of what I wanted from this date; and the dim, intimate lighting from the flicker of a singular burning candle set the ambiance for the naughtiest time that a young, innocent, seventeen-year old girl could fathom.

Underneath of my jeans, I wore a tiny pair of panties. I dislike the word of "thong" as it seems trashy, but I must write it herein, as that is the accurate description of the style of panty that I wore. It registered as much too sexy and much too naughty for an innocent girl like me. But, for my first time, it was perfect. The owner of the restaurant visited my table, offering a warm greeting and inquiry on the state of my family, attention that made my date even riskier. Could I create the mirage of proper sophistication whilst behaving as badly as possible? Could I mask my nervousness, convincing the restaurant owner of nonchalant-ness? All whilst achieving the pleasure that I desperately needed? That I desperately wanted?

She eventually walked away, permitting space for the server to take my order. In what seemed like the longest wait of my then seventeen years, my brain occupied itself with fantasy of what would come next. I thought of one of those 1990s scrambled sex shows that I studied at nighttime from my teenage bedroom. Do you remember the scrambling of where one could slightly interpret the full breasts and erotic dances of a woman wearing lacey lingerie? Sometimes where two women could be interpreted as kissing? Or be pictured as spraying each other with hoses of water whilst dressed in string bikinis tops and high-wasted jean shorts revealing the lower firm cheeks of the bottom? Or of where sounds could be heard of a sexy woman moaning as she straddled the lap of a very powerful man? Back then, internet pornography was a thing to which I was unexposed, as the internet existed in its infancy, and the shared family computer was inappropriate for investigating such curiosities! I therefore learnt of sexuality through scrambled 1990s television. And it intrigued me. The expressive bodies did. I wanted to look like that and to be admired like that by a powerful man. And with regard to food, I got the same high. I got the same thrill that I did from watching those scrambled sex shows. The forbidden nature of both situations excited me.

As I sat there, on my big date, my mouth yearned to be stuffed. It yearned to experience. My body ached to know that I would soon have something from which I had refrained for the past six months and seven days. I would permit my firm, sexy, young, virginal body the pleasure that it had been denied.

I would permit my body to have food.

The day of my big date started with a five-mile jog at 4am. My family now lived in a quiet, middle-class neighborhood, an upgrade in value (on paper) from our first home as described in chapter one. Although my heart never moved into this house, I was fortunate to live in a safe place that permitted my jogging alone, outdoors, at such dark hours. The jog included a project whereby I mentally recited each house number in the Spanish language, as I quickly darted by each one. House number proclamation in Spanish was a ritual of mine. One of many rituals. These seemingly irrational rituals were important to me, like they were important to Jack Nicholson in the film of *As Good As It Gets*. The rituals served a role in fulfilling my constant goal of perfection. I created these little requirements, pushing hard to achieve them, all day, everyday.

Upon completion of my run, I exercised to a forty-five minute VHS plyometrics workout of *The Firm Cardio Burn* followed by ten minutes of a VHS yoga workout entitled *Karen Voight - YogaSculpt*. Followed by consumption of three-fourths of a cup of Kellogg's *Product 19* (it featured the lowest calories with the simplest of ingredients in the cereal aisle) with two-thirds of a chopped banana (I always threw away the remaining one-third), covered by half-of-a-cup of skim cow's milk. I drank skim cow's milk, without question, back then, because it was what I knew. Furthermore, Ivana Trump told me to do so. And Ivana Trump was fabulous! She advertised so perfectly for the *Got Milk?* campaign, so much that I displayed her glamorous magazine advertisement onto the wall of my then teenage bedroom.

Following my exercise and breakfast on the day that changed my life forever, I arrived to work for my duty as drive-thru girl at Wendy's Old-Fashioned Hamburgers promptly at 7am to begin lettuce prepping, salad creating, order taking, money accepting, sandwich assembling, product distributing, potato scrubbing, and dish washing. Otherwise known as: the job at which I could burn as many calories as possible for the entire day whilst earning as much money as possible on corporate clock, a clock that displeasingly limited the total number of hours that I, a then seventeen-year old, could work, also a clock that mandated a thirty-minute lunch break during which time, in the smokey break room, I consumed a fat-free yoghurt and nine mini pretzels from which I would scratch off and discard of the salt, afterward returning to my Wendy's Old-Fashioned Hamburgers duties until discharge at 3pm.

And, all day, I could think of just my date, the one to follow my work shift. The highly anticipated date at the Chinese Restaurant. I would tell not a singular human of my date, as I had zero time for regular dates in my highly organised schedule which I mapped completely and perfectly daily, rarely deviating. Each minute of my life was scheduled. And I needed to keep this date underneath of the radar because I wanted not to establish a date precedent. Setting precedent would yield future date invitations and arrangements which were undesired. Dates would yield chaos, so this date would happen just once. In secret. It would be as though it never happened.

I was a virgin. I had never been kissed. So, the plan, all day, was to stay innocent like such. I would show to the restaurant, behave like a lady, and be on my way afterward. Post date, I would drink one bottle of NyQuil to gift myself with slumber, a ritual to which I had become accustomed for the past few months as I found it quite difficult to sleep naturally at an improper, under-nourished 89 pounds. My heart raced so quickly at this weight. And when I did sleep, my dreams painted horrific stories of food. Of eating food and of becoming fat again. Of becoming regular again. I forced myself to stay in bed until 3am or later when my regular workout and Wendy's "work-out" schedule would happen like *Groundhog Day* starring Bill Murray. It was my "perfect" life.

Until August 21, 1999.

On this day, my schedule, my life, my plan, as I knew it, would be altered.

Changing from my Wendy's Old-Fashioned Hamburgers uniform in the privacy of my 1989 Dodge Caravan, a vehicle belonging to my parents but one that I drove exclusively, my body was frozen despite temperatures being hot, thusly I blasted the vehicle's heater to warm my anorexic vessel. And as I showed for my dinner date, I requested back-room seating, as I wanted for nobody to be witness to my meeting. Conducting my date in the most prim, most proper, most secretive manner, I tried so hard to be perfect, but everything got so hot, so steamy, and my young vessel needed pleasure. It deserved pleasure. I knew that no other choice existed. I would go all the way.

"Shrimp lo mein, please," I said to the waiter.

But maybe I should order two plates? Maybe one won't be enough? I thought.

Elegantly capturing the server's attention after he had walked away, another plate was ordered. And then I waited. Paint could have dried faster! *"Hurry up hurry up hurry up hurry up hurry up hurry up hurry up hurry up hurry up!"* my brain screamed, over and over.

And finally, it arrived. I can still picture the piping-hot noodles and plump, gorgeous, stir-fried shrimp covered in a beautiful white sauce. Two enormous plates. It was a perfect, hearty dinner for the big, epic date. I was ready to lose my virginity. Dinner for two had been served!

But I was just a party of one.

Twirling noodles, using fork and spoon, in the traditional, elegant manner of consuming spaghetti, I decided that I would eat just one plate, bringing the second plate to home for my little sister L whom I wanted to fatten because nobody could be skinnier than I, and L was headed in my very skinny direction. Also plummeting in weight rather quickly was my baby sister Stephanie. Thusly I would fetch a *Chocolate Frosty* by Wendy's Old-Fashioned Hamburgers for Stephanie. She would reject a shrimp lo mein gesture as she hates seafood, and permitting her to have a calorie deficit advantage on me, if even for one day, was out of the question. I was the best at being skinny. I was the best at restricting. At control. At perfection. At being an older sister. My sisters admired me, and I refused to disappoint them by gaining weight. I needed to be their perfect example.

I ate the entire first plate of shrimp lo-mein in minutes of nine.

It was a huge portion.

The second plate was finished in minutes of seven.

I was alone.

I was on a date with food.

Sitting in the back of the restaurant, pants unbuttoned because my extended stomach could no longer be contained inside of my tiny jeans after having consumed this double meal in a short period of time, I was disgusted. Mad. Hot as hell. Ashamed. Worried. Freaking out. All that I could think about was gracefully leaving so that I could get the food out.

My thong, a size extra-small, pressed so tightly onto my extended frame and newly created food baby that I wanted to rip it off. I wanted to pull so roughly on its strings, getting it to break, inviting space for my stomach to breathe. A green American Eagle hoodie now hung over my waist, hiding the cute Abercrombie T-shirt, hiding the unbuttoned state of my pants, unbuttoned because my stomach no longer fitted inside.

*What a stupid good for nothing ugly fat f*cking bitch.*

Screaming this in my head, to all 89 pounds plus two plates of shrimp lo-mein of me, I planned to immediately venture to the store to purchase and to ingest laxatives to remove this food from my system. Vomiting was yet to exist on the menu of purging options, as that would ruin my teeth and oesophagus according to what I had read on the internet about "eating disorders." Why had I searched on this subject of "eating disorders?" Why had I *Asked Jeeves*, "What is an eating disorder?" It was because I was accused by everyone of having one, and I wanted to know of their reasoning. And upon learning more, I dismissed their accusations, accusing everyone of jealousy of my control.

Assuming that passionate exercise plus laxatives was enough compensation for this singular food binge, I convinced myself that weight would be un-gained. I discovered laxatives on a family vacation of a few months prior when my then 112-pound and rapidly shrinking body refused bowel movements after a few months of severe, successful restriction. My very good, always concerned parents wanted to resolve my incontinence so offered the laxative medication to me. And of course my brilliant brain translated the resultant into "removal of food from body" into "weight loss" into "backup plan in case I eat too much" into "skinniness forever!" If I could be skinny forever, then life would be perfect, I thought. Following that vacation, I secretly used the chocolate-chewable laxatives periodically, including on the night prior to this Chinese food date when I enjoyed a piece of chocolate brownie cake and too much, or so I thought, of watermelon. This night before laxative "medication" is what made me think that it was the perfect time for a date with food, at this Chinese restaurant. I had already behaved so badly with cake, watermelon, and laxatives, thusly I would go to town! Do it up big style. There has never been a middle ground for me. And, as a side note, I absolutely hate chocolate cake! My friends call me a food racist. It still perturbs me, to this day, twenty years later, that I wasted energy on chocolate cake.

And here is what I love and remember OH SO PROUDLY.

Before departing from the restaurant, before venturing to the store for more laxatives that would afterward rid my body of the food (or so I hoped), before exercising for endless hours (or so I planned) to assist with burning of the binge calories, I proclaimed something divine. From the confines of that infamous Chinese restaurant, paying my first huge bill for binge food, angry that my hard-earned Wendy's dollars were poured into two plates of dinner plus gratuity versus just one plate plus lesser gratuity which would have happened had I behaved like a lady, I announced the most profound thing in my head.

Okay, I am bulimic now. I must stop this immediately. I must write a book about how I arrived to this place. I must appear on Oprah. I must help others to become healthy. I must figure this out. I must win. I shall win!

As the tagline of *Trump: The Game* proclaims, the only option in life is to win! My mantra since the age of nine in 1991, this statement played in my then seventeen-year old head immediately after that first binge. I knew that I had done something incorrect, and I knew that it would be a great challenge to win. I knew that I would celebrate that winning with a book about the process. It consumed two decades, but I have won. With publishing this book, I hereby set that winning into stone.

Following my first wild food binge at the Chinese restaurant, before proceeding to home, I stopped at K-Mart to buy the previously referenced laxatives. During this shopping trip, I upgraded from chocolate chewable laxatives to pink regular-strength pills. The chewable laxatives in my parents' medicine cabinet would be insufficient to cover the food bill, I thought, and I wanted a hard pill as the chewable version invited more calories and suddenly seemed weak to me. Ingesting a great overdosage of the pink pills, I felt safe from fat and wanted more food. PIZZA. I purchased a "Lunchable" containing crackers, sauce, and cheese that permitted the creation of a "pizza," feasting in a pleasure zone in the Kmart parking lot, in my parents' 1989 Dodge Caravan, the same vehicle that my mother used to transport little Nicole Marie Story to healthy dance classes, so many years before. It was like a transportation vessel of night and day. Black and white. Healthy and unhealthy.

Driving to home, I wanted more. I stopped at the convenience store, a Uni-Mart, for Hostess *Zingers*, the red and white coconut-covered ones. Three packages. The creme. The coconut. Oh my God, I needed it. I needed to stick my tongue inside of that delicious, moist cake, licking out the cream, licking off the coconut, seductively inserting the cake into my mouth as my head dived into another state of pleasure. Moaning with satisfaction, I sounded like a girl having an orgasm, yet I knew not of how an orgasm sounded or felt. In fact, I knew not that an "orgasm" was a thing. I also bought a huge bag of long-stemmed, salty pretzels to eat in the secrecy of my bedroom until just before passing out. I would suck off the salt, concurrently sucking on the stick, softening it, as permitting my family to hear the food crunch was out of the question, as they would learn of my dirty little secret and think of me as a food-restricting failure.

Choreographed like a Tchaikovsky ballet to a Rachmaninov concerto, my first food binge was passionate and tormented. I would make this my first and only ever food binge. A long binge. I had already behaved so badly, and a dash of badness afforded me permission to complete the entire day in the baddest, wildest, most chaotic of manners possible. In the most extreme of manners possible. If one is to be bad, I thought, one must be bad completely. It will be a perfect binge, I thought. And I shall write a book about it.

I shall never, ever, ever do this again, for as long as I shall live. I thought.

Steadfast on keeping my weight at 89 pounds, I planned to exercise for the entire next morning, to labour all day at Wendy's Old-Fashioned Hamburgers, to exercise all night, and to ingest twenty one laxatives on both nights to ensure that I would get everything out.

On the next day, on August 22, 1999, I had another passionate date with food.

On the next day, on August 23, 1999, it happened again.

These three, passionate dates turned into a seventeen-year war.

For eleven years, I lived as a bulimic with anorexic goals, consuming tens of thousands of calories in twenty-four hour periods, abusing laxatives (upgrading from pink regular to blue maximum strength pills), becoming a highly-skilled vomiter, spending every dollar on binge food, spending every morsel of energy to hide my secret, scrambling to pay rent, scrambling to buy my dog Gwendolyn's food, SCRAMBLING TO SURVIVE.

To follow these eleven years of bulimia would be another six years of complete chaos in the eating department, minus the vomiting and laxative abusing, but something that I like to call hell on Earth. These post-bulimic years are documented, real time, at my blog (www.theyogaballerina.com) and make a great case study / backup to the story told in this book. During the collective seventeen years of disordered eating, I weighed from 89 pounds to 181 pounds, up and down the scale so many times that I constantly stand in awe of today's healthy heart that withstood so many years of stress. I constantly thank my heart for withstanding the war.

I made catastrophes of my relationships. Of my sister-hoods. Of my best friend-hoods. I manically dated to get affirmations on my body and to find a rich man to "cure me" of bulimia, as I thought that if I could be watched by a man of prominence, if I could be under his radar, if I could be accountable to someone of quality, that I could maintain a perfect, bulimic-free, skinny-girl state. But I never had a man's love in the manner that I wanted. And I never allowed myself to be loved in the manner that I deserved. Regardless if all of the men that I dated were incorrect for me, I closed off the idea of happy love before the idea could be created. It was very sad.

Yet I looked happy.

I looked like like a nice girl with normal weight fluctuations.

A bulimic often looks not on the verge of death.

A non-anorexic albeit disordered eater usually looks as "normal."

Just as many faces exist for a president, many faces exist for an eating disorder. At this time in history, President Trump proves this reality. And, with this book, with my story, I prove it, too.

I lived functionally with a smile throughout the seventeen years of living with an eating disorder.

I worked very hard. I played very hard. I lived very hard.

But I was AT WAR.

And then, one day, a blanket of peace decorated the canvas of my life.

Exactly seventeen years to the date of becoming bulimic, on August 21, 2016, I became healthy. The eating disorder disappeared. The eating disorder suddenly mattered not, and I could live healthfully, on my terms. Ending my war with food, I entered the world as a functional human being of joy. Of gratitude. Of breath. Of space. I worked very hard to achieve this, and it was because of the influence of President Trump that I truly found divine health and wellness. I am Nicole Marie Story. And this is my story of war and peace. Namaste.

CHAPTER
III

PERFECT

MY NAME IS NICOLE MARIE STORY. I believe in human perfection and strive for that state in everything that I do. Perfection is a constant, lifelong, personal goal, one that is evolutionary. To explain this evolutionary concept, I shall state that a perfect condition for me at the age of seventeen years at the inception of my former eating disorder is different than a perfect state for me at my present age of thirty-seven years. And, both states will compare not to my perfect state of eighty years from now, when I hope to be thriving excitedly at the age of one-hundred-and-seventeen years on Mars with my perfect gentleman! Thusly, practicing flexibility in my rigid life yields ultimate, evolutionary perfection. Yoga helps with this.

If desired, perfection in life must be achieved by way of hard work and by hard work only. It is acceptable to strive for perfection. Mental health "professionals" will, however, tell of otherwise. *"Fake News" CNN, The "Failing" New York Times, The "Woe-Is-Me" HuffPost, and The "Weird" Washington Post* as hosted by the old Bob Woodward who published a trash book on President Trump plus never proved a darn thing about President Richard Nixon will certainly, in my opinion, claim that striving for perfection is unhealthy, too! I am here to flatly state, leading by example, that it is divinely wonderful to strive to be perfect. In fact, it befuddles me that a human would want to exist at imperfect form. Do people actually awaken each morning with the goal to be mediocre? Or just a little bit good? That's insane to me. Each human fosters the capability to achieve their rationally perfect version, and, just as that state is variable over time, that state is variable from human to human. For instance, perfection for my sister Stephanie, at present, might mean rising many hours before the sun so that she can exercise with Billy Blanks of Tae Bo. This early morning Tae Bo exercising permits my sister to feel good about her body, to make healthy food choices, to be a more present wife and mother, and to feel sexy and confident with gorgeous abdominals and shapely arms in the workplace amongst her fellow executive colleagues. Looking divine in a pencil skirt, blouse, and sky-high heels with everything being in a straight line versus having blubber flowing over the waistline is ideal for my sister. Add in the knocking her business requirements out of the ball park, and we have perfection. Yes, my baby sister is perfect! For instance, number two, for a human who is striving to be a zero-waste vegan like is Colleen Patrick-Goudreau, perfection might mean continuously discovering ways to reduce waste to move her life into the complete zero waste vegan format. At present, although she will only invite products with a one-hundred year life span into her home, she might use the existing disposable tissues in her bathroom before becoming entirely dependent upon handkerchiefs. Although these tissues are "wasteful," she will use them to blow her nose until they are gone. The means to the end is what yields perfection in Colleen's daily life. Just as she preaches about veganism, doing something is better than doing nothing. And, that something, in the effort to achieve something greater, can be perfect, at that exact moment in time. Have you consumed Colleen's divinely enlightening and interesting podcast called *Food For Thought*? It is incredible. I have listened since 2012 when I began experimenting with veganism for extended periods of time. Although I formally label myself as an independent eater and therefore have no formal food restrictions, Colleen's work was very instrumental in justifying my processes when I behaved/behave as a vegan. And, just to clarify: Colleen is riding on the President Trump Train not. Yet I adore her work, her mission, her gumption, her boldness, her vocabulary, and her love and voice for the animals. To me, Colleen Patrick-Goudreau is perfect. To me, President Trump is perfect. If you want to be refreshed on my reasoning, then please read an encore of chapter one. And, for me, perfection exists when MY body works itself so hard that zero energy remains at day's end, so much that my last few moments are forgotten because I am so very exhausted that I fall into a deep state of recharge, requiring every bit of accepted slumber so that I might start the clean, rationally perfect living all over, in a few hours. Personal human perfection, in these examples, is achieved by way of hard work. By my sister. By Colleen Patrick-Goudreau. By President Trump. By me. By whomever is the individual seeking their version of perfect.

There exists three instances on Earth where perfection occurs naturally, without effort, without rhyme, without reason; and, perfection in these examples thusly need not be worked toward. Underneath of the layers, of the things, of the activities, of the states, when stripped to the basics, these three things on Earth register as perfect, simply by being. These three things need not strive for perfection because they are perfect from their inception and shall be perfect from the beginning of time until the end of time. I shall hereby list, in no specific order, as they are equally perfect, the three things found in nature which, by mere factor of being, are perfect.

The first, most perfect, most beautiful, most natural thing on Earth is the skyscraper.

Standing erect, with arrogant, elegant, remarkable confidence, presiding above the intertwining, systematic veins, arteries, and organs of life as we, the sophisticated humans, know it, on Earth, the skyscraper is majestic. It is proud. Offering warmth, hope, protection, it inspires one to feel, to think, to do.

It is art.

Capturing the breath, like a formidable lover hovering its mouth centimetres from its petite, vulnerable prey, the skyscraper strongly suggests peace, purity, prosperity, safety, and sex, propelling the human mind to think to its grandest capacity whilst inclining the human heart to cherish that which has earned the right to be adored. To be tasted. To be experienced. To be unwrapped in the luxurious, raw manner as suggested by the engineering of the grand, cold figure reaching into the sky.

It is desirable.

Catalysing the human spine to extend more grandly, the core to constrict more tightly; the skyscraper triggers imagination to reach more fabulously than yesterday's daydream, more reverently than today's prayer, more powerfully than tomorrow's vibration of good will. The skyscraper, transfixing the human mind like does a hypnotist to its subject, requires one to gaze upward, outward, inward, yielding a state of physical and of spiritual consciousness, of passion, of intelligence, of innocence, of love, of morality, and, even, momentarily, causes the human body to shift and to behave like the skyscraper itself.

It triggers surrender.

And, whilst the skyscraper breathes, the spectator inhales and exhales, too, victoriously so. Inhaling at the body's base, oxygen travels the height of the solid structure, feeding it with life. Feet, rooted firmly into the Earth, legs, behaving as pillars of steel, navel, drawing inward, shoulders, pressing backward and downward, collar bone, presenting its straight, beautiful, bony line, guarding precious infrastructure of floating lungs and heart beneath. Lips, sealed. They are perfect, beautiful lips, the colour of crimson and of steel. And the nose. The nose gratefully accepts fresh oxygen, as the eyes travel upward like a moving meditation, along the body of the length of the skyscraper, holding this breath with discipline at the structure's peak, pausing with energetic force on the cusp of eruption at the crown of the head, immediately followed by exhalation, and therefore a washing of breath over the body of the skyscraper like an oceanic wave, cleansing and preparing for the next flight of inhalation grandeur. Breath is grandeur. A grandeur of gold. Breath is life. And life is gold. Breathing is the simplest of acts that must be celebrated and cherished. In Ashtanga yoga, we celebrate the breath. We cherish the breath. We celebrate the senses. Sight and quiet observation in the act of admiration is sexy. Desiring to touch something that one finds attractive but outside of one's current reach is powerful. Creating a plan and working to achieve what one wants for the purpose of self happiness, is the greatest action on Earth. This is stated with regard to the body of a skyscraper. With regard to the body of a human. With regard to both beautiful, enigmatic yet transparent bodies. When one looks at the skyscraper, when one looks at the perfect human body in a standing position, one thinks, "Samastitihi."

Firmly posing on the horizon, during any season, any year, any moment in its long history of existence, the skyscraper begs to be touched yet it can be touched not by the common man. This fact of nature reminds the world of the grandiose capacity of the human brain to perform. Yet that performance is a choice, one that is a rarity in acceptance. A rarity in fulfilment. Industrious, like a motor, the human brain is capable to create functional, fundamental beauty like that of a skyscraper, yielding an inspiration of thought. Creativity. Wealth. Production. Happiness. Love. But as for the humans who decline the moral life choice of hard work and the associated value system of pure capitalism, pure meaning with heart, pure meaning honest, passionate hard work to achieve one's happiness, then the image of the skyscraper will trigger pain. Lust. Jealousy. Want. Often disguised as selflessness. But, in actuality, is evil. The breath of those existing in pain is hot, like lava bubbling in a volcano. It is fresh not. It is glorious not. It is contrasting of an oceanic wave. It is likewise contrasting of President Donald J. Trump who is the King Of The Skyscraper. Thusly, when a hot brain accepts the information offered by a skyscraper, it drenches the human body in heat, in sweat, the resulting state being that of a looter. Of a pig. Of an excuse maker. Of a cry baby. Of a radical Democrat. Of the Fake News Media. Of one who sees the glass as half full. Of one who is a pessimist. Of one who apologises for breathing, for thinking, for acting as an individual. Of one who lives based on the value system of emotion versus practicality. Of one who subscribes to suffering and coping. Of one who complains and criticises rather than living by the golden rule. Of one who believes in entitlement. Of one who resists. Of one who obstructs. Of one who is fearful. Mind you, a looter can, indeed, touch the skyscraper without having earned it, be it by connection, inheritance, fake living, lying, crony capitalism, and other acts of badness, giving the impression that one is a pure capitalist; but that touching is like having sex with a prostitute, like socialising in a dirty house of whores, like a lazy fat guy playing in a bucket of Kentucky Fried Chicken, watching pornography in his dark apartment on a Saturday night. This lazy fat guy features gluttonous stomach, a brain of cobwebs, fingers of grease. He is wrapped into a suit by day, fraudulently entering those doors of the skyscraper, sweating like a pig, thinking that he is a a god. But he is the devil. The suit can only shield the lie for so long, as the pig will soon realise that his state of living is hell on Earth. These are the CEOs who operate based on personal bonuses versus for the good of the employees, stockholders, and customers. They have three-year plans with eventual retirement on the yacht versus having thirty-year plans to yield prosperity for all. This stale bread unfortunately frequently exists inside of the skyscraper. It is cancer. This is what creates evil in this world. Existing in the middle, in limbo, taking what one believes one should have without effort and heart is what creates evil on this planet. Believing that one should have something, anything, due to one's mere factor of existence, is wrong. Entitlement is wrong. Yet it exists. Everywhere. For so many humans, this has become a system. The accepted way of life. The learned way of living. The small percentage of those who earn the right to touch and to undress the skyscraper is why the concrete jungle exists yet it occupies a very minute percentage of the Earth. This nearly invisible percentage is why we have hope. We have hope not because of the rainforest. We have hope, rather, because of the concrete forest. We have hope because of the skyscraper. It is why we love Cary Grant in the film of *An Affair to Remember*. It is why we love *Love Affair*, the original depiction of *An Affair to Remember* because the skyscraper dazzles in black and white, and so does Irene Dunne who was so thin and bubbly and beautiful. The skyscraper is why Tom Hanks and Meg Ryan will forever be pictured happily in our brains with Jonas and the backpack as featured in *Sleepless in Seattle*. It is why, when we think of Miss Piggy, we think of the glamorous Empire State Building and of her thoughtful, passionate, productive pursuit of Kermit in *The Muppets Take Manhattan*. It is why we love Howard Roark and his sexy, firm architectural accomplishments in Ayn Rand's *The Fountainhead*. It is why we love the bareness of Dagny Taggart's apartment posing above the skyline of New York in Ayn Rand's *Atlas Shrugged*, and of the successful, powerful Hank Rearden lounging upon Dagny's sofa, representing production, sex, and power. The skyscraper is why we love Ayn Rand. It is why we love President Trump. It is why we love our President of the United States who bought air rights above Tiffany & Co. to permit extravagant building of his glamorous Trump Tower and personal penthouse made of gold! In *The Art of the Deal*, then civilian Donald Trump wrote about coming to Brooklyn as a child with his father, pleading with him to visit the Empire State Building because he loved tall buildings and it was, at the time, the tallest in the world.

Hank Rearden's character in *Atlas Shrugged* reminds me of businessman Donald Trump. Firstly, both gentlemen proudly display their names onto their properties. Secondly, Hank Rearden and President Trump harvest great power, a resultant of working hard and of subscribing to and existing under a system of pure capitalism, again, pure meaning with heart. My liberal friends exclaim that President Trump should be stripped of his money and therefore of his power. I ask, "Why? Why should President Trump be stripped of something that he has earned? Has he earned not his money? Has he earned not his power? Has he earned not his respect?" Do the words of Lil' Kim suddenly mean nothing to radical Democrats and to black people (and to white people, too) who have forever celebrated her message in the song of *Money, Power & Respect?* My radical Democrat friends, despite these great lyrics, answer that it is unfair that President Trump was reportedly given a million dollars by his father. That the rich only become richer. That the poor black man has no hope, thereby blocking him from opportunity. EXCUSE ME, BUT THIS ARGUMENT IS RIDICULOUS. IT IS A FAKE ARGUMENT. And if President Trump were black, would it make a difference in radical liberal thought? Would his money, power, and respect be seen as acceptable? The answer is yes. If President Trump were black, it would be acceptable. I hereby accuse radical Democrats as racist against white people. Should we actually strip President Trump of his earned billions and donate it to "the less fortunate" to give them a chance? Seriously, what on Earth is wrong with the radical liberal mind?! Yes, as a pure capitalist, I believe in grand charity. And I also believe that the mediator between head and hands must be the heart, but this suggests not to make everyone in the company, or even in the world, as equal. If the President and CEO of The Trump Organization earns the same dollar amount as his workers, then who runs the company?

President Trump has earned his money, power, and respect. Both in The Trump Organization and as president of the free world. Those of us who think

68

with pure, clear minds can see the amazing good and perfection in President Trump. Those who cannot see the amazing good and perfection in President Trump need to look inside and ask ourselves of why. Why are you so hot and angry? Why does President Trump's success and the world's celebration of it upset you? Why does the skyscraper upset you? The skyscraper evokes an emotion of happiness and a notion of progress in those of us who possess a pure, capitalistic, productive, positive nature. And, likewise, the skyscraper evokes emotion of regret and of greed and of jealousy and of woe-is-me in most of us who do not. (I do, indeed, love and respect a few human exceptions to this proclamation. To my friends who dislike President Trump yet work hard and adore skyscrapers and beautiful living, I think these negative things of you NOT, because I know your personal reasons for your positions, and I respect and love you. And, to my liberal friends who prefer to be surrounded by trees versus skyscrapers, the same is true with regard to you. I thank you for accepting me into your world, for considering my views, and for teaching me about the nutritional value of weeds. I respect you and love you!).

These elements of emotional response, good and bad, black and white, culminate to a divine peak in the glorious unit of the skyscraper, creating a delicious meal from a very complex, yet very simple recipe. The skyscraper is the wow of every cookbook known to man. But there exist two types of man. With regard to the first type of man, the skyscraper is the clean eating. It is the healthy meal for those of us who live and think purely. It is the machine, the catalyst, the inspiration for production. Comparatively and conversely, the skyscraper is the greasy, fast food of salt-drenched french fries, laden with chemicals, for those of us who exist as impure. The first example is strong. The second example, weak. There is a black and white to everything. And when a human mind considers the skyscraper, its reaction is either love or hate; it is something that is felt so deeply within and exists as our own personal secret and truth, and, that feeling, that response to the brain's reaction, tells the human exactly of their individual quality. They must live with that fact. They must live with that diagnosis. The skyscraper fills you with something. It fills you with joy or with resentment.

It nourishes.

From every breach of a city's borders, whether from country road, from suburban tunnel, from suspension bridge, from high atop mountain, from underwater tunnel, or from outer space, when entering the city and consuming the skyscraper, the lines of geometrical perfection, the gallery of aluminium and steel, apprehends one's breath with a temperature of cold, washed and blanketed by the heat indicative of things constantly happening, of grandiose things to come. It is comforting to observe. A relief. A presentation of happiness. A "welcome home to your beautiful city of progress" hug. It is a reminder that something will always be bigger than you, and you must therefore never stop working because you must compete to survive. Religiously catching the spectator's gaze, the skyscraper, standing nakedly in its jungle, offers not pizzazz, yet erotically seduces with simple glamour. Reduced to and existing at its highest, most natural, most purely amazing form, the skyscraper decorates the world with functional beauty. Standing to attention, it says, "samastitihi" calling us to our yoga practice, to our lives. To our bodies. To our minds. To our hearts. To our breath. To the present. To begin. Again.

The second, most perfect, most beautiful, most natural thing on Earth is the human body.

Or, rather, it should be stated: the human body has the potential to be perfect. It is perfect when at birth and when, at all other points in life, as existing under rigid discipline. It is perfect when fed with amazing things. It is perfect when expending amazing energy. It is perfect when it is pure. When it is clean. When it is stimulated. When it is calculated. It is perfect when operating under the pure practice of Ashtanga yoga. Thusly, formally stated, the second most perfect thing on Earth is the human body under the practice of Ashtanga yoga.

Like the skyscraper, the Ashtanga yoga body is clean. Lean. Long. Strong. Flexible. Calculated. Beautiful. Day in, day out, it is the same, yet different. The man practicing Ashtanga yoga in India, two thousand years ago in a cave brightened with fire, dressed in towel with holy cow by his side, starkly contrasts with the modern practitioner of Ashtanga yoga, stationed in her swanky downtown apartment tucked onto the top floor of a skyscraper, room brightened by the glimmer of neighbouring skyscrapers and by a singular lavender or vanilla scented soy candle, body dressed in something fancy by Alō Yoga moving through a led Primary Series, Full Ashtanga Method with Mr. Lino Miele on YouTube or following Secondary Series with the great late Sri K. Pattabhi Jois on YouTube using the iMac with 5K Retina display whilst soul music streams from the Amazon Alexa or whilst Sean Hannity on Fox News is broadcasting on the smart television, moving and breathing upon a beautiful, sparkly, purple, special-edition Manduka Pro mat or beautiful, red, special-edition *Year Of The Dog* yoga mat by Lifeorme which came with a price tag of

$169.95, designer mixed-breed dog snoring on the velvet chaise lounge by ZGallerie or her fluffy *Cloud* by Restoration Hardware, dog only joining the practice sometime around navasana, begging for a cookie. Demanding a cookie! She always jumps into the yoga action during navasana. Why is this? It is because the dog is systematic, too. Something about navasana triggers her to want a cookie and to passionately demand it! And, after the yoga practice is completed, after the Ashtanga closing sequence and savasana, the fancy practitioner dances like a genie, reciting the Mangala Mantra, slowly centimetre-ing her way to the little sweet dog, then slowly crawling like a dog to the resting dog, singing, "Naaa-maaa-staaay," and the little doggie remains in her comfortable position but that little curly tail wags with excitement. The little doggie senses the peace, happiness, and divine sense of accomplishment in her mommy, the Ashtanga yoga practitioner, and the tail responds in its own sweet form of celebration. Many lipstick kisses are given to the little doggie, and she returns the love with licking the sweat from her mommy's face and head. In fact, her mommy sings in her sweetest voice, "Gwendolynnnnn, I made something for youuuu! I made this goooood sweat just for youuuuu!" Pictures are then captured for Instagram where cyber space becomes the social grounds for the modern yoga practitioner. It becomes the love fest once experienced at yoga studios and in Indian caves. Both examples of yoga practitioners, the ancient and the modern, are amazing and powerful. They are disciplined. They are perfect.

Yes, conditions are completely different between the two described Ashtanga yoga environments, yet the simple caveman of India and the fancy lady of today are doing the same exact practice using the same exact vessel of a divine human body. A practice that has withstood the test of time, Ashtanga yoga takes the body onto a tour of science meets art. It is the same physical practice, day in, day out; yet the daily magic is different and new. Exercising the internal organs whilst hardening of fat, Ashtanga yoga is the most potent medicine available to the human race. When a body is existing in this heightened state of health and joy, when it is living the Ashtanga yoga life, one moves about the Earth with unwavering poise, confidence, power, energy, gratitude, and love.

And, when the Ashtanga yoga body meets the skyscraper, magic happens. They mirror each other in tradition, habit, aesthetic, and health. Consider for instance the powerful lady entering through the revolving doors of the skyscraper in the 1980s, dressed in something knee-length in pink with shoulder pads by Chanel, complimented by white stockings and curly, permed hair, lusting after a bubbly Diet Coke to be delivered to her office followed by an afternoon of fat-free yoghurt and rice cake. Compare this to the modern producer dressed in the sleekest of black Victoria Beckha flaunting a silky Brazilian blowout, huge bag by Hermès, spectacles by Chloé, four-and-a-half inch velvet pumps by Tamara Mellon, lusting after the apple carrot beet celery cold-pressed raw juice to be delivered to her office by the kind, local farmer selling his delicious juices at an exquisite downtown juice bar called *The Glam Farmer,* making personal local deliveries to the top executives within the skyscraper, followed by an afternoon raw nut bar with a quadruple tall iced espresso. Or matcha. Or matcha plus espresso! Or chaga! Followed by the most divine of cocktails: the one of cardiovascular exercise plus Ashtanga yoga. With regard to the cardiovascular component, the 1980s girl is doing something led by the leg-warmer wearing, tiny-waisted exercise goddess known as Jane Fonda on the VCR. Please search for Fonda's 1983 *Workout Challenge* on YouTube if you want to be tested physically! Although Fonda's politics are crazy, she knows of how to manage her body and has successfully done so for all of her life. She commands my respect, for this fact. Compare this 1980s girl to the modern girl who is exercising with the glamorous, fashion-forward, athletic spin instructors who stream directly to her innovative Peloton bicycle, permitting group boutique cycling classes from the comfort of one's gorgeous apartment. Followed by a few minutes of Tae Bo abdominals with the great Billy Blanks. Followed by Ashtanga yoga. Yes, both women exercise differently in their cardio, but they are doing some divine version of it; and, they are connected intimately through their Ashtanga yoga practice and through the skyscraper. They are producers. They are fashionable. And, by Ashtanga yoga, by the skyscraper, they work and live nakedly. They work and live perfectly.

The skyscraper and the human body under the practice of Ashtanga yoga are timeless. Chockfull of purpose. Resilience. Ability to adapt. To survive. To be strong. To be flexible. Even more so than a tree. The tree is what a standard mind conjures when it thinks of nature and of strength. But, in reality, the tree is weak. Emotional. It is comparable to a radical Democrat. The skyscraper and the Ashtanga yoga body are better than the tree, as they are perfect. Mind you, the skyscraper and the Ashtanga yoga body can be injured, terribly so, sometimes necessitating months, even years to recover. But they recover. They repair. They become stronger. And they never forget.

A force with which to be reckoned, the skyscraper and the human body under the practice of Ashtanga yoga are pure. Clean. Beautiful. Both, science. Both, art. Both nourish and stand with exquisite beauty, inspiring like does nothing else on Earth. They are the simplest products of sophisticated thinking. Of sophisticated doing. Of sophisticated living. Skyscrapers, and the Ashtanga yoga body, despite changing trends of fashion, stand the test of time.

They are perfect.

The third, and final, most perfect, most beautiful, most natural thing on Earth is a child resting its head on the heart of its mother.

Like the skyscraper, like the body under the practice of Ashtanga yoga, this third, most perfect thing on Earth is timeless. It is something that dances forever in heart, mind, and soul. With a simple thought of that little head resting upon my heart, memories flood of the way that we were, of the way that we are, of the way that we shall be tomorrow, and of the way that we shall be forever in my heart. In this book, I write specifically of my baby, of my dog. Of my little Gwendolyn. And of how I awaken each morning to her sleepy, sweet, little, smushie head resting upon the powerful organ in the middle of my chest cavity. Upon my heart that has continued working despite the turmoil through which I subjected my body for many years. For so long, I questioned about how my heart could rationally continue functioning without a power supply. Without a battery. Without an outside power source charging and delivering energy to that which I treated so poorly. To a heart that supported a body at 89 pounds, at 181 pounds, and at everywhere in between, several times, up and down the scale for years of seventeen. How could a standalone organ perform so religiously, powering a body to which I offered zero reckon in terms of kindness? Without a surge of artificial energy, how could a body that I treated like the dirtiest garbage in the land survive for seventeen years of disordered eating? My only conceivable answer is that it was the universe's plan to have me live in a challenging state, so hard, for so long, so that when a little, beautiful dog named Gwendolyn swooped in to save me, I would know it and love her with all of my might, changing everything.

As stated earlier in this chapter, I mediate my head and hands with my heart, but I am also focused on winning, as *Trump: The Game* proclaims is the only option in life. I am a pure capitalist with the spirit of a social worker. And, that, according to a great, dear mentor of mine, "is a very powerful combination." It seems as though, my heart, at nighttime, recharges its ability to act kindly by way of diffusion. The presence of Gwendolyn's head resting sweetly upon my heart yields a transfer of good energy, producing a heart that becomes stronger and more determined to do amazing things. My dog is my heart's metaphorical power supply. She is my daily catalyst in finding and achieving joy. She is the catalyst for my finding purpose. I hope, with all of my might, that my heart is working in reciprocation, keeping every part of Gwendolyn's little body as healthy and energised, too.

Like a Joey in her mother's basket, when we sleep, Gwendolyn seems to feel safe. Protected. Comfy. This is obvious to me insomuch that she adheres herself to my physical body, in a little cocoon formation, resembling a crescent roll, a baby shrimp, or a French horn, snoring deeply, nestling until it is time for morning exercise, moving not one centimetre whilst I consume President Trump's overnight or early morning tweets, whilst I tend to social media, whilst I write and publish a new blog post (www.theyogaballerina.com), whilst I text chat with my heroic friend and ardent President Trump supporter Peter Dickerson of Australia, whilst I snap ninety-nine pictures of Gwendolyn as she sleeps, sending resulting images to my human best friend Rebecca, breaking Rebecca's no-texting-before-6am-rule, and or whilst I snap pictures of my body to exchange with my sister Stephanie who is also conducting her early morning body assessment. I begin this work usually at 3am and generally continue until 4am or 5am when we venture outside for a five-mile walk. Well, this 5am walk ritual existed until I was attacked, beaten, and mugged in Chicago during a dark walk on December 20, 2018, but, before that point, it was an all hours walking convention. And yes, Gwendolyn is aged eleven years, eight months, and twenty nine days, and like a joyful athlete, she walks at least five miles per day. And swims on occasion! And plays with the toughest of toys until she kills the squeakers in minutes of five! And chases balls which is new! Gwendolyn is fun. And patient. And kind. She envies not. She boasts not. She is proud not. She dishonours not. She is self-seeking not. She is easily angered not. She keeps record of wrongs not. She delights in evil not, but rather rejoices in the truth. And she always, always, always protects, trusts, hopes, and perseveres.

Gwendolyn is *The First Corinthians*.

When I hold Gwendolyn in my arms as we strut through the lobby of our building, she wraps her short little hind legs about my waist, resting front paws on my shoulders, like would a baby koala. And she smiles with pearly whites, holding that cute little nose into the air, lower jaw extending forward creating the cutest of underbites on Earth. She very much enjoys being carried. It is like toting a little sack of loving potatoes. And when she walks, she prances forward like the Queen of England, recently described by a sophisticated Alexis Colby type as being "jaunty" which translates to "having or expressing a lively, cheerful, and self-confident manner." I think she gets this from me. And now I sound like the mother on *Dirty Dancing*!

Gwendolyn notoriously finds discarded pizza on city sidewalk, requiring me to wrestle it from her naughty little black mouth. The "Drop it, Gwendolyn!!!" command only works if the pizza is covered in mushroom, as she hates mushroom. Mushroom is the only of three foods which she snubs. The second is hard-boiled egg. Yes, hard-boiled egg participates not in her strict food system of raw meat, raw goat milk, dehydrated fish beams, and dehydrated chicken hearts (gross!); but, as a one off, I recently needed to trick her into consuming her Chinese medicine whilst on the go, so I stopped at the local convenience store and bought a hard-boiled egg into which I hid her pills. She chewed it with a disgusted-looking face, dropping it from her mouth, in the same fashion that she drops mushroom and the other food that I am about to describe. This third food which she snubs is banana, but, unlike mushroom and egg, she will gobble a banana if another dog is present, as Gwendolyn is very food greedy. Just as she inherited her sophistication, I think that she inherited her food obsession from me. I never share bites of my meals with other humans because that would ruin the perfection of the nourishment experience. Something tells me that perhaps I would share my food with my future perfect gentleman. Maybe. It is perfect, however, to share meals with my Gwendolyn. In fact, it is our mommy and Gwendolyn ritual. Mommy takes a bite, then Gwendolyn takes a bite. I joke that it is my secret to staying thin. She is the perfect match for me: jaunty and food passionate. If I were a dog, then I would be Gwendolyn!

My love for Gwendolyn is so grand, running deeper than any sea, higher than any skyscraper, longer than any flight from here to Pluto and back; and, as I tell her, from a formal measurement perspective, I love her from that left floppy ear, the one featuring a little point, just like mine does, all the way to infinity and beyond. "And that's a really far distance, Gwendolyn, because it never ends."

When drinking martinis and existing with an uninhibited state of la la la thinking, I often whisper to Gwendolyn that if a God exists, I ask for only one thing: that I can be her mommy forever. This verbal wish, of course, is followed by a sea of tears. But I shall be her mommy forever. Every single day for the rest of my life will be spent to honour the one little sweet thing that motivated me into a world of joy. Into a world of love. Into a world of purpose. I shall, forevermore, until my last breathing moment, honour the one little sweet thing that awakened my heart and made it smile. I shall, forevermore, honour the one little sweet thing that powered me to live vibrantly.

Yes, Gwendolyn is my heart with four legs and a curly tail, but she is also the greatest challenge of my life. She is my greatest challenge because she forced me to be a responsible human. She is certainly challenging when she is screaming at me for cookies; or when she jumps from bed at 2am and woos at me because she wants to go outside into a snow storm and or polar vortex because a food has disagreed with her digestive system; or when she activates her defiant puggle brakes and wants to go her way, not my way, on walks; or when she grabs a bag of white bread from the shelf at 7-Eleven, dragging it to the cashier without my knowledge, tearing apart the bag like a ravenous animal (I joke that my dog has an eating disorder). But, what I mean by the greatest challenge is that she would challenge this selfish human to care about herself in a one-hundred percent committed manner because without self-care, providing perfect care to my princess would be impossible and unsustainable.

My life was no longer about my eating disorder, about my challenges, about my selfishness. My life was now about my Gwendolyn. And in caring for her so deeply, I was able to simmer my personal challenges onto the back burner. It took a long time to stuff those challenges into the garbage disposal completely, but eventually I did. And she was patient with me. She was understanding with me. She was, as previously stated, *The First Corinthians*.

In those early years, on the husband hunt, I separated from her to travel with men. I left her to go on dates. And I remember coming home to her, on February 7, 2011, after a weekend trip to Florida. The doggie resort stated that she would be a bit longer before discharge because she had gone to the bathroom on herself in the waiting cage following her post-boarding bath. She was obviously so upset about being separated from her mommy that she defecated on herself. It was at that exact moment, at her age of three years, three months, and twenty-eight days, that I promised to never leave her again. It was at that moment that I realised that dating random men was a waste of my time and that Gwendolyn deserved me, all of the time. She is now aged almost twelve years, and I have kept my promise. Aside from the rare few hours apart, including during the Trump Rock Concert of 2016 when my parents babysat, including during my sister's wedding of 2011 when her Uncle Brandon took charge, including during a post-canine-dental surgery in 2015 when Uncle Brandon saved the day again, including during an evening in 2014 when I attended a baseball game with my dear friend Sheila and Gwendolyn's Uncle Jason and his greyhound girls took charge, and including during my former liberal client's wedding in 2016 when again her Uncle Brandon took charge, I have left her not. We have slept together, every single night since that awakening day in 2011. We have slept together, every single night for eight years, five months, and two days. I am the luckiest mommy on Earth to say that this is true. I love her to Pluto and back. I love her more than anything else in space. And, in fact, as I am typing this, she is resting her little sweet head upon my heart, snoring oh so deeply. I wish that we could be like this forever.

Before my perfect little girl, I was a mess.

Behaving against everything for which I stand, I lived chaotically. Food, money, men. I was out of control. And when I got my dog, she entered into the boxing ring of life with me. I was Rocky Balboa, and she was the old guy with a scratchy voice. And, despite ending my bulimia in 2010, I continued forward with the eating disorder, first living on sushi and alcohol. Then overeating again. Got fat again. Got thin again. Fat. Thin. Fat. Thin. Lost my yoga. Found my yoga. Injured my ankle. Fat again.

And then it all changed.

Donald Trump announced his candidacy, and everything fell into place.

I now have peace.

Gwendolyn and I arrived face to face with very difficult situations on several occasions, above and beyond my eating disorder, and I honestly conceive not of how I made it home to her, on many an inebriated night; or, of how she emerged through battles of her own, like the time in 2013 when she was taken into the mouth of a very large dog, on the verge of death as he shook her like a bunny. Kicking the attacking dog in the abdomen, I tried, with all of my might, to pry his mouth open with my hands. Blood, everywhere. Gwendolyn's blood. And my own. But the attacker was stronger and Gwendolyn was his prey. I was literally saying goodbye to my little girl as she stopped screaming because she lost her ability to fight. I can still, six years later, hear her blood-curdling scream arriving to a halt. Her eyes were losing life. She looked dizzy. All that I could think of was that I was a failure at the one thing at which I was good, at the one thing that I loved doing, at being her mommy. I had failed to protect her. I cried, "I love you, Gwendolyn. I love you. I am sorry. I am sorry. I love you. I love you. I love you, my baby." Even as I type this, I experience post traumatic stress, as it all comes back to me. And then, out of nowhere, I saw, CHOMP. It was another dog who existed in our pack who swooped in, biting the attacking dog, prompting the attacker to release Gwendolyn so that he could bite the heroine. The heroine was named Sophia. Sophia the greyhound. Gwendolyn ran into the bushes, and Sophia resulted with a puncture wound on HER sweet face, and, Gwendolyn, of course, survived (see blog post www.theyogaballerina.com/new-york-minute). As a side note, the dog who attacked Gwendolyn was found a new home through a listing made at my blog, and he is now a reformed canine, dressing as a fairy princess, cheering at Pittsburgh marathons, and receiving pets from little children at public events! It is an incredible story. A happy ending for all.

Gwendolyn's other big traumas include during the year of 2010 when another very big dog pawed her in the head during play, causing Gwendolyn's eye to herniate from the socket which resulted in surgery to reinsert the eyeball followed by elective surgery of canthoplasty to tighten the muscles of both eyes to prevent future eyeball herniations. Another trauma happened during the year of 2015 when she broke an incisor when playing with a toy, requiring an invasive dental surgery to remove the root where we additionally discovered that teeth existed in her gums that had never emerged during puppyhood. These, of course, were removed, too. Another trauma happened during the time that she had cancer in 2016. Another trauma happened during the time that she tore her cornea in 2017, requiring multiple surgeries and installation of a contact lens to heal the injury. And, finally, another trauma happened during the second time that she had cancer in 2018. Gwendolyn is the owner of quite the impressive medical file.

Together, we conquered. We conquered my eating disorder, and we conquered her battles, too. In learning to use my "all-or-nothing" disposition for good and healthy things, I have created a magnificent little palace of warmth and love and joy for which I am eternally grateful with every single breath that I take.

This chapter of *Donald Trump and My Eating Disorder* is written to discuss more than the perfect skyscrapers, more than the perfect Ashtanga yoga body, and more than the perfect baby's head on the heart of its mother. This novel is written to discuss the things that are imperfect, too. It is safe to declare that most humans never achieve their idea of perfection. I believe that each human has the potential to achieve their version of perfect, but that attainability level is very difficult. At this time, I am the perfect version of who I want to be. I love my life. Some call me a book definition of narcissist, something that is a diagnostic "mental disorder," and that is quite fine and dandy as labels mean nothing to me. Why is it a disorder to love yourself, I ask? To be confident? Why do many humans define President Trump as a narcissist and consider that to be a bad thing? I shall add that, like President Trump, I am a very kind human. I bother not a soul but my own. But if you try to hurt me or my beloveds, then I shall take you outside. That rarely happens anymore as I exist in such a heightened state of peace, and I am rarely challenged or agitated in a way that moves me to respond. I walk about this Earth with such happiness that my skin is tingling and my brain is buzzing with energy and zest and pride! It is fantastic beyond my grandest of dreams. I pine for each new minute of the days and nights. President Trump operates on this same energetic field.

To influence anyone who is living with a hardship, this novel is written to discuss of how, after so many years of hating on my body, of slaving to my mind, of experimenting with myself like the monster of Frankenstein, that I discovered of how to use my black and white personality to create good. To create peace. To create space. To create harmony. To create my idea of perfection. All whilst living uniquely, for me, for my happiness. This novel is written because I have a unique story to tell. One that makes me laugh, one that makes me cry, and one that makes me appreciate. One that makes my friends' eyes widen so dramatically that I've been asked, "How on Earth can a person eat so much food? How can a person do this to herself?"

I know that others exist like I do. I know that these humans have relationships with people who understand not of how to operate in the company of "conditions," or "state-of-beings" such as my former state of disordered eating. MY MOTHER was just thirty-nine years old, when I developed my eating disordered practices. That is two years older than I am today. And, of course, because my problems started under her roof, she blames herself for my former issues. Even though I am ultimately grateful for the eating disorder because I can share my story in public service, she blames herself for my years of pain. But an addict can be controlled by a doctor not, by a parent not, by a therapist not, by a friend not. An addict can control only their human self. In addition to having an addictive personality, I have an independent nature. My mother therefore had a double whammy with me! She had an independent addict! In all seriousness, if you want to help your loved one, the best approach is to talk about it. To be strict. To be rational. To be loving. To be non-judgemental. Example, don't call your child a loser. But make them understand that they will screw up their lives if they continue forward with their behaviour. Ultimately, it is the addict's responsibility to stop drinking, to stop having manic sex, to stop abusing drugs, to stop abusing food, to stop treating their bodies like a GARBAGE site. It is easy not. It is a walk in the park not. Some will require professional help such as talking with a therapist. Some will need physical restraint such as hospitalisation. Some will need to create rational plans to follow on their own. With restrictions. With guidelines. With rules. And some will never get over their issue. There is no text book or diagnostic manual that can identify and prescribe a solution to an eating disorder as all eating disorders are unique, many of which are non life-threatening, but rather exist as quality-of-life-threatening. An eating disorder is a quiet demon.

I am certain that most humans harvesting quiet demons live with their demons FOREVER. Two dear, amazing friends recently lost their beautiful, twenty-five year old son because his demons won. It was so tragic. So terribly sad. Thusly, I am, in strong part, inspired to complete this book which is twenty years in the making, and to have it published, because of this young man whose life ended too soon. His demon was an eating disorder not, but a demon just the same. And, on the night before his death, I encountered him briefly, outside of my building. He approached me and Gwendolyn, smoothly stating, "Hey, it's the pretty dog girl." I replied, in my cheerful, smiley way, "Hi! It's Kelly's son!" And, extending his hand for a shake, he replied, "Actually, I'm more than Kelly's son. I'm Alec." It was a breathtaking interaction, like from the scene of a black and white 1940s film noir. I had the wind knocked from me. It was an authentic "I want to be your friend" gesture. It was also like a cry for help. Like a request for assistance. It was as though I could read into his eyes. I could read into his soul. I could read into his pain. I existed in his place, once upon a time. Like-minded individuals are drawn to one another. Did he know of my past? Did he sense it? As I walked away with my Gwendolyn, I turned around to see a car arrive, and as Alec walked toward it, I sensed no good. The car and Alec suddenly became lost into a sea of human and vehicular traffic. That night was something that I'll never forget. On the next day, I saw the ambulance. A few days later, his mother, my friend Kelly, posted on Facebook about the tragedy. A person with an addictive personality can, in my opinion, identify another with an addictive personality. I sensed it about Alec, and it makes me so heavily sad to know that he will never tell his story. Thusly, with this book, in a way, I am telling it. Alec's smile and warmth coloured the world with gold. His was a precious, dear life that ended too soon. He is missed by his family and friends, every single minute of the day. And when I finally had the chance to hug my friend who is the mother, Kelly cried, telling me that her son's demons had won.

This confirmed my suspicion. I knew, at that moment, that it was important to finish writing this book and to have it published because maybe, just maybe, it will help someone who is experiencing pain, be it the addict, a family member, or a friend. I send a big hug to Kelly and to her family, right at this exact moment. They are so very beautiful and strong.

I have, after seventeen years of war with food, found peace. I am writing this book to reveal that light exists at the end of the eating-disordered tunnel, opening to a bright future of fluffy sheep, skyscrapers, yoga, Christian Louboutins, and puppies. It is like emerging from a dark hole. Yes, *Fraggle Rock* is a super fun place of dancing your cares away, but unfortunately, it is make-believe! Thusly, we must live in reality, in the sunshine and moonshine! Furthermore, living your cares is more amazing than dancing them away. Who wants to live for the weekend when every day can feel like a weekend? On my *OkCupid* profile, I am asked to complete the sentence of, "On a typical Friday night I am…" And my reply is, "doing the same items that I do on Monday, Tuesday, Wednesday, Thursday, Saturday, and Sunday." Why wait to do something special only on a Friday? I design every single day and night to be special. Come Friday, I want to do exactly what I did on Thursday, all over again! It was always this way not. During my war with food, I was a negative, downright chaotic ball of emptiness on the inside, always putting on a show to make others believe that I was a happy girl. But now, only after having killed the eating disorder, my life is truly a happy one. Every single day is magical. I have worked so hard for my health!

One of the questions that I am most frequently asked is, how did I stop? How did I stop the bulimia? My answer is that I just did. But when I stopped bingeing and purging on food, it took another six years of experimentation, of hard work, to achieve peace, and Donald Trump was the epic influencing factor in ending my war. For President Trump, my heart is forever grateful.

I believe that perfection is evolutionary. I have created a system of functionality throughout which to live the rest of my beautiful, precious life. This system shall evolve. My body shall evolve. My yoga practice shall evolve. My eating shall evolve. Charles Darwin, one of the greatest of minds, wrote about survival of the fittest, and, as I am quite fit in mind and in body, I shall survive.

I am so very excited, honoured, privileged, and chuffed that you are reading my book, one that I began writing twenty years ago in my head from the little Chinese restaurant, at the moment of the start of my bulimia. I knew, back then, when it happened, that I would turn my misfortune into a privilege. I knew that I would tell my story. I knew not that it would include a seventeen-year war; but, like with all wars that end, peace is the ending result. In sharing my story, I want to inspire others to achieve peace with their bodies and with food. I also want to help others to see the amazing goodness in our wonderful President Trump.

In the practice of Ashtanga yoga, at completion of each vinyasa, we stand at the front of our yoga mats, erect and strong like a skyscraper. We say "Samastitihi." This word is Sanskrit for a call to action. It is an invitation to come to the moment, to clean the slate, to stand up, to regain balance. I do this in yoga, and also in every breathing moment of my life. Each day is a new year. Each hour is a new opportunity to create. Each minute is a new chance to grow. To do. To be. To win. Each breath is another big, beautiful, new experience. A constant body in motion, I am coming to my moment, I am cleaning the slate, I am standing, I am regaining balance. Over, and over again.

Thank you, from the bottom of my heart, for reading this book. Namaste with love, and with a treasure chest of gratefulness.

Samastitihi.

CHAPTER
IV

INDEPENDENCE DAY

LIKE PRESIDENT TRUMP, I enjoy the wonderful ability to sleep minimally. Rarely have I used an alarm in my lifetime, rather awakening naturally between the 3am and 5am hours, and that included on my last day of bulimia.

My age, twenty-eight years on Earth. Time invested into bulimia, ten years, ten months, and fourteen days. The date, July 4, 2010. Independence Day. Or, as we the patriots define it, the day that America won its independence from Great Britain. Trust me, I love all things British, especially *Vogue* (until 2015); especially King Edward's scandalous descent from the crown to marry his beloved from the USA, Wallis Simpson, who later became known as The Duchess of Windsor and who coined that magical statement about richness and thinness; especially Margaret Thatcher who put an end to free school milk; especially the grammar, notably the words that classify as "The Queen's English." I love love love *Love Actually*, and, in fact, this film played a major role in my last day of bulimia. I have a forever schoolgirl crush on the old English film actor George Sanders circa the 1940s. And, many call me an "Anglophile," which, I assure you, despite my fondness of British sophistication and glamour, I am not, as I am one hundred percent chuffed to be an American. I love being a citizen of the United States of America. I love our president, President Donald J. Trump. And yes, like President Trump, I fully predicted and support Brexit.

On this 2010 morning of subject, on the two hundred thirty-fourth anniversary of my country's freedom, I prepared to attempt to free myself from my bondage, just as I had attempted every single day for the past ten years, ten months, and fourteen days. I prepared to free myself, from bulimia. Perhaps the day would exist as healthy and I would succeed after what seemed like a lifetime of failure, I thought. I hoped.

At 4:45am, I awoke and brushed my teeth because I had passed out on the prior evening before doing so. This was a common trend. I would eat so hard until just before the midnight hour, followed by pouring of my guts into the porcelain, followed by swallowing an overdosage of laxatives, followed by marching directly to the bedroom for a four-hour-ish slumber with my dog Gwendolyn until the entire process started all over again. The recommitment to starvation. The new diet. The ruination of the new diet with tasting something naughty. The bingeing on food. The purging of food. The ingestion of an overdosage of laxatives. The passing out before brushing my teeth. Over and over and over again for eleven years.

And, it turns out, my passing out, rather than mustering the energy to brush my teeth, happened to my great advantage. The second time that I met with my oral hygienist in 2010 after having been diagnosed with progressed periodontal disease a few months earlier, I confided in her that I had behaved as a bulimic for a long time. Note, I said, THE SECOND TIME. The first meeting, at diagnosis of periodontal disease, driven to the dentist because my gums bled so ferociously that my bananas were painted in red (see blog post www.theyogaballerina.com/bloody-bananas), certain that I would continue living as a bulimic, I refused suggested treatment to fix my gums, recognising that treatment would be an utter waste of time and money, as my continued bulimic behaviour would keep my bloody bananas in business. Once I had forfeited the bulimia, however, I returned to the hygienist, told her of my story, and her jaw literally dropped as she could understand not of how my actual tooth enamel could exist in such fantastic condition. First off, I am so grateful that I had a judgement-free zone. The great Spring of Aspen Dental in Cranberry Township, Pennsylvania was a mouth angel and head therapist. She listened to me, talked to me honestly, and was rational and compassionate. It was something that I needed at a time of when hardly anyone knew of my former problem despite my having lived with it for nearly eleven years. Spring was one of the first to know, outside of my biological immediate family, and even they were unaware of the extent of my problem. I explained to Spring of my process of bingeing, purging, and passing out, and the light bulb activated in her brain. She said that after vomiting, tooth enamel is most sensitive and vulnerable. Thusly, if I had brushed directly after vomiting, the brushing of vomit acid onto teeth would have worn away at the enamel. Because I was so intense, exhausting my body, leaving zero energy to brush, I actually saved my teeth. So, here is a disclaimer to bulimics: BRUSH NOT AFTER VOMITING. Wait at least four hours to brush. Spring suggests swishing with water. But, if one is repulsed by vomit odour, then swish with a gentle mouth wash. And, yes, I know that I shall receive negative review for offering such advice on how to manage with bulimia, but I must be honest and rational. I mean, come on, I continued the bulimia even after diagnosis of periodontal disease, which, in addition to meaning unhealthy gums, also perhaps indicates an unhealthy heart, as bacteria travels from gums to heart. Yes, it is my greatest suspicion that when a human's life ends due to "complications with anorexia or bulimia," it is because of heart disease. And, despite this threat of heart disease, I continued forward with my destructive bulimic behaviours. As a side note, in July of 2017, stationed at seven years clean from bulimia, my mouth accomplished the unbelievable! All of my gum pockets closed, therefore defying the chronic nature of periodontal disease. In true President Trump fashion, even my mouth is a winner! And, might I please add, I have never, in thirty-seven years, five months, and one day on Earth, produced a cavity. I am a very lucky lady.

After brushing my teeth on the Independence Day of 2010 morning of subject, I returned to the bedroom of our Sewickley apartment where my baby dog, now aged two years, eight months, and twenty-four days remained as submerged gloriously into her luxurious pillows and comforter by Vera Wang. The apartment might have been a suburban second-floor carpeted space with a slanted linoleum kitchen floor in an old Victorian home, no central air-conditioning, no washer, no dryer, no luxuries whatsoever, but the interior comfort pertaining to my Gwendolyn was fit for a princess in a grand castle. She has always had the very best, even when I could afford it not. I never allowed Gwendolyn to live like a pauper because of my eating problems.

And she loves to sleep! Most dogs awaken their human. It has always been the reverse for our family, as Gwendolyn would sleep through the apocalypse, unless, of course, she sensed breakfast. And Gwendolyn knew that 4:45am was too early for breakfast. She knew that it was time for exercise. Overweight by fourteen-and-a-half pounds, at the time, because she obviously ate extra during my bulimic food parties because we did everything together, Gwendolyn invested her everything into remaining in a luxurious slumber.

But I had other plans.

Leashing my pretty girl, I prepared to accomplish a glorious five-mile walk, intending to cleanse my mind, body, and soul of the past ten years, ten months, and fourteen days of bulimic activity. It would be an Independence Day of good health. It would be a celebration of America's independence from Great Britain. It would also be a celebration of my independence from great bulimia! Or so I thought. Or so I planned. But, living under chaotic conditions, things never happened according to plan.

What did happen proved to be more powerful than my brain's intended manuscript.

Because of my dog Gwendolyn, my manuscript required improvisation.

Because of my dog Gwendolyn, on this Independence Day of 2010, I succeeded in saying goodbye to bulimia.

I hereby present the story of what happened on that last day of bulimia, written in my raw, ugly, angry language of back then, annotated with softer thoughts of today, nine years and six days later. The italicised inner brain monologue from 2010 exists as specifically interesting and heartbreaking, as it is exactly what streamed through my head during that historic day. The reader will notice that my tone with regard to myself is now different. My spirit with regard to myself is now different. My way of existing in my skin, is now different. If I had documented this extreme language not, back then, in creation of this book, then I likely would have forgotten the harshness, as it now shocks my brain to know that I, once upon a time, could be so rough. It disgusts my brain to recognise that my entire day was about food. This story of so long ago seems like a dream to me. I know that it existed, but it is like watching a film of another girl, of a stranger, of a girl on drugs. My drug was food.

This section of *Donald Trump and My Eating Disorder* is painful for me to read. It is war. And my puppy was a soldier in the war. Reliving her participation in the war is what really breaks my heart. But in telling this past, in recounting the war, I might truly help someone. Thusly, herein, I recount the last battle, the one that ended eleven years of bulimia. This account, by no means was a goodbye to my eating disorder in its entirety, as that war with food continued for another vicious six years, but this was my goodbye to bulimia. Bulimia was a fierce battle in the seventeen-year war. And this was my bulimic independence day.

My Bulimic Independence Day
Written in 2010 * with added commentary
dated Present Day of 2019

The stage, set to healthy, we emerged from our quiet town apartment. "Yes! We beat the sun! We are winners already, Gwendolyn!" I exclaimed to my sweet, little dog.

Always concerned about winning everything, even competitions with the sun, I needed to be perfect, wanting to purge the prior night and eleven years of terrible treatment and torture that I had inflicted onto the machine of my human body. Before the star in the centre of the solar system could shine truth onto my darkness, I would mend my bulimic scabs and bruises, revealing myself in the manner that everyone expected, as the "healthy yoga girl who loves to walk her dog." Yes, I loved to walk my dog. But NOTHING about me was healthy.

"A healthy holiday it shall be!" I announced to Gwendolyn.

Gwendolyn, aged two years, eight months, and twenty four days, trotted by my side, pug nose lifted upward in sophistication, beautiful, soft beagle ears flopping in the cool morning breeze, curly piggie tail wagging at the slightest woof emanating from the grand Victorian homes of Sewickley, Pennsylvania, the old money town in which we resided. And, with her signature, underbite fashion, she pranced forward, ignoring the squirrels that passionately climbed well-manicured trees. This behaviour of paying zero reckon to squirrels was her standard except for once, during early puppyhood, when she collected a large dead squirrel into her mouth, presenting it to me like a prize, catalysing me to scream because it scared me so! She immediately dropped the dead squirrel, thank goodness! But, on this morning of subject, we encountered only live squirrels. The ones climbing trees. And their cousins, the fast moving animals of another kind: THE JOGGING HOUSEWIVES. Whom I hated. Whom I mother f*cking hated.

*F*cking anorexic.*

Stupid bitch.

*She's a f*ckig snob.*

*I hate these f*cking fake people.*

I can be one of them.

I deserve to be one of them.

Yes, I thought all of this. But, "sophisticated" and "proper," my mouth said words of another sort.

"Good morning! How are you?"

"Divine! Thank you! Do please enjoy your walk! Hello, Gwendolyn!" one runner happily replied.

I hated these runners because I was so jealous.

Of their control.

Of their talent.

Of their happiness.

Of their bodies.

Whatever. I'll start running again tomorrow. I'll get skinny again. F*ck these bitches.

Hydrating, with *"Earth's finest water"* by Fiji at very specific points during our power walk which existed for the purpose of resetting from the prior night and to burn calories, I diluted my haughty anger about these joggers and furthermore of last night's drunken escapade. I could afford this water not, but Gwendolyn deserved nothing less than perfect water and I would eventually pay for it when I married a rich man. Well, he would pay for it. That was my plan. I would, too, soon be skinny, and cared for, like the housewife joggers whom I pined to be like. It was outside of Gwendolyn's control to be mothered by someone who chronically failed at life because of her addiction to food. Thusly, Gwendolyn would want not. Gwendolyn happily sipped Fiji water from a tiny glass cup that I carried everywhere for her.

Perhaps I shall indulge in red wine after this exercise concludes. Yes, sounds perfect. Red wine shall render us into slumber so that I can stay in control, making this a healthy holiday, the first healthy holiday in eleven years. 'Love Actually' sounds like a lovely film choice. It is so romantic! Keira Knightly's thin body will inspire me to keep food away from my mouth. And we shall create a very arctic-like feeling in the apartment, setting the window air conditioner to its coldest point, yielding a perfect condition for hiding underneath of a blanket. A perfect holiday!

My mind said these things, yes, whilst also conjuring images of pizza, of spaghetti, of donuts, of extra pulpy orange juice to pair with the donuts, of peanut butter cookies, of fat free butterscotch ice cream, of salty french fries from Burger King. It was like the devil and the angel whispering to me concurrently. *"Be healthy." "Be naughty." "Be healthy." "Be naughty."* What an absolute paralysis of the brain.

I ended up carrying Gwendolyn for much of the distance because she was fat. But, so was I, thusly we were in this new day of good health determination together. After the walk, I twiddled my thumbs as my brain turned to the naughty sales pitch of the previously mentioned food sales devil. I needed to prolong the consumption of food just a bit more, so I ignored the tempting voice. I made coffee. Black. But on cup two, I added whiskey. This made me feel relaxed and therefore better.

At 9am, it was time for food. I prepared a gorgeous plate of steamed vegetables paired with pineapple salsa and ketchup for dipping. Pleased at my then interpreted conservative culinary choice, I offered broccoli to Gwendolyn using chopsticks. She is very good at eating from chopsticks. Chomp chomp chomp went her cute little black kiss-me-face.

F*ck. Did I feed her last night?

I could remember not.

At 10am, we viewed *Love Actually*, living vicariously through the cold weather as depicted in this Christmas-themed film. My bad behaviours always registered as so much worse during hot weather. August was my worst month, but July registered as a close second. My best human friend Rebecca, a radical Democrat, believes that heat causes war. This was, indeed, true with regard to my former patterns. Heat meant all out war with food.

Curtains drawn, cheap window air-conditioner filling the space with a stale coolness, we hid underneath of the blanket, closing off the world, wanting nothing to do with anyone, nothing to do with anything, except for imagining a perfect life married to a wonderful Hugh Grant or Alan Rickman, well, to their characters in *Love Actually*. Colin Firth, despite being super cute, played the character of a romantic wimp, or so I saw it, at the time. Other than imagining marriage, we wanted to freeze. To numb. To exist as alone, contained into our little suburban apartment with creaky floors, sandwiched between an old man with a cane on the first floor, a TSA agent and her cat in the attic, and our imagination.

Just one glass. Maybe I can have just one glass. To ease the tension.

I thought this, but I also knew that one glass of wine meant three, which meant one bottle followed by coffee for sobering to permit walking my Gwendolyn with dignity, maybe with another dash of whisky to sober without actually taking off the edge. But I poured that first glass anyway.

And at 2pm, we awoke.

The *Love Actually* title page on the DVD player had been streaming over and over again, the volume being much too loud for my hung-over ears.

F*ck!!!!!!!!!

Darting to the mirror, I lifted my shirt to examine my abdominals.

Fat as f*ck.

Squeezing my then size-six body into size-two blue khaki shorts by Banana Republic, shorts that had fitted loosely three years ago, we migrated to my parents' house where our presence was expected for a family BBQ. Even typing those words makes me laugh. "Family BBQ." Nowadays, things are so different, my presence never being expected for such an event. Nowadays, my family gets that I refrain from doing certain things because I only do what I like to do. But back then, in 2010, tradition was King, and one was expected to follow traditional family rules. Holidays meant biological family. And food. And lots of both.

There was no mentioning of my tardiness to the BBQ, and, more importantly, there was no mentioning of my tight shorts and stomach blubber. But, I assure you, my fluctuating weight and apparent lack of interest in formal family affairs was always the elephant in the room. As good parents do, regardless of my deteriorating state, they welcomed me and Gwendolyn into their home, peacefully. I thanked goodness for controlling the urge to arrive as intoxicated. That would have led to argument and premature departure from the party, for certain, an activity that was foreign not to my then twenty-eight-year old self; in fact, it was the standard.

Sitting outside on the deck, we chatted, pretending that life was grand. Gwendolyn was the peace maker. She was always the safe conversation subject when in the company of my parents during those eating disordered years. And of course FOOD, during those years, was involved in an overly sensitive way. In our family, it is the standard to stuff one's face with food at parties. And because I have always behaved as socially proper, refraining from eating like a hog whilst in the presence of others, I always anticipated being watched by the food police concerning my plate of raw vegetables. During those fat bulimic years, nearly everyone, at family parties, particularly my Italian grandmother, would ask, "Is that all you're going to eat?" It was so embarrassing to me because I ate like a bird publicly but my body clearly said that I was eating loads of lasagna behind closed doors. I knew that everyone was judging my imperfection. And trust me, I exaggerate not on this suspicion. My sister Stephanie will confirm that she also felt judged by the family food police on her consumption and body size.

On this particular day, thank goodness, it was just me, Gwendolyn, and the parents. My mother was so kind to buy vegan hot dogs for me that I simply needed to indulge despite having planned to abstain. Nowadays, I would never eat food from a grill or cooking device that touched meat or animal secretion and I can assure you that such was the case on this day not, as my vegan hot dogs were, indeed, cooked beside the animal hamburgers! This demonstrates of how humans can be so kind to those eating a specific diet, but little things such as animal meat plus vegan meat on the same grill are completely innocently overlooked by the meat-eating host or hostess, and it is completely okay to talk to the host or hostess about your requirements. Never be ashamed of your food rules, so long as they serve your version of wellness. Nowadays, even if someone went out of their way to present food of my liking, I would never eat food to be socially graceful. My social gracefulness lies in my polite manner of rejection.

Here is what I ate, at the family BBQ on July 4, 2010:

1. One vegan hot dog, covered in melted soy cheese, wrapped into a whole grain bun.

2. Delicious amounts of Heinz ketchup, relish, and mustard decorating aforementioned vegan hot dog.

3. Three additional vegan hot dogs, no cheese, no bun, dipped into ketchup.

4. Diet Pepsi.

With a 3,000-calorie budget for the day, I was doing good.

I need a drink right now. Why don't my parents drink!

But Gwendolyn and I stayed. And laughed. And ate some watermelon.

At 7pm, back at home, I ate a deliciously divine banana. So plump. Heavenly. Fluffy! And white. Like a cloud. It would do the trick. It would apprehend my craving for more food. *Bananas are so filling and healthy, chockfull of electrolytes, chockfull of goodness!* I thought. Knowing that I put this amazing "snack" into my body made me feel good all over, especially in the brain. Until it made me feel crazy.

I'm still hungry.

Grabbing her toy, bouncing about the room like a banana herself, baby Gwendolyn squeaked a glorious tune, as though she were leading a rag time band. She begged for me to play! That beautiful black and fawn-coloured face moved from side to side, up and down. And those black floppy ears! They flopped gorgeously in the cold apartment as she ran about the room, now graduating from banana to Tasmanian devil! Oh! She was so very happy. My puppy! Begging for me to play. Taunting for me to get down and dirty with the game of tug of war and fetch! *Squeak! Squeak! Squeak!*

And I couldn't move.

That f*cking banana. F*ck that mother f*cking banana.

"Honey bunny, mommy's tired. Let's play tomorrow, okay?"

Eyes, sad, Gwendolyn rested on her belly, chin resting on toy, ears hanging to the ground. Gwendolyn was so sad. The one little soul for which I had responsibility, was living imperfectly because I was living imperfectly. Because I was at war with food.

What the hell is wrong with me? I'm a stupid fat mother f*cking bitch. A f*cking terrible mommy. An awful f*cking human. Will this ever end?!

I looked at her. I knew what would make both of us happy.

Food.

"Honey bear, are you hungry? Let's get some good food!"

Gwendolyn, quickly lifting her head, cocked it happily, as she always became excited at the declaration of seeking food! We both darted to the kitchen, yet I ignored Gwendolyn, rather zeroing on the bullseye: on the vegan hot dogs that my mother had packaged to go. I heated these vegan babies in the microwave, covered in soy cheese, dipping the hot resultant into ketchup, shovelling the cheesy sticks of glory into my mouth whilst robotically preparing Gwendolyn's raw meat. And she was screaming! She was mad that I refused to share my delicious binge food! She does one of three barking styles, depending on her mood.

1. "Woo woo woo woo woo" - she does this when she is annoyed.
2. "Yelp! Yelp! Yelp!" - she does this when she is MAD. A sophisticated woman once asked, about this barking style, "Why does this dog bark like a seal?"
3. "Boof! Boof! Boof!" - she does this when she sees an "animal" on television..

On this occasion, it was "Yelp!" Which also sounds like a high-pitched scream. Oh she was pissed.

"Shut the f*ck up!!!!!!!!!!" I screamed.

She kept screaming.

Should I eat the buns, too? Or should I throw them away? Carbs are against my constitution, but it's Sunday. My super cheat day. What the hell. I might as well. I'll eat them, dipped into ketchup! Buns and Heinz 57 for the win!

Eating five toasted buns with melted soy cheese, ketchup, and relish, I existed in my pleasure zone. And then I freaked, realising that five more hours remained to the day, and I would likely fail at my food plan by morphing into full throttle bulimic monster mode, yet again, failing at my eleven-year and running venture on ending the bulimia for good.

Twelve vegan hotdogs. Forty calories. 40 x 12 = 480. Vegan hotdogs, buns, soy cheese, condiments, wine, banana, and breakfast. 3500. I'm over by 500. I shall be one pound heavier. ONE POUND. 3500 CALORIES. FAT. MOTHER F*CKING UGLY FAT BITCH.

"Hail Mary, Full of Grace, the Lord is with thee, blessed are thou amongst women and blessed is the fruit of they womb Jesus. Holy Mary, Mother of God, pray for us sinners, now and at the hour of our death, Amen." I prayed this aloud, praying to a God, to any higher power, for help.

Gwendolyn, watching, me, understood not. Living in the raw essence of her body, my dog cared not of what she consumed since 12:01am, of what she would expend on that day through exercise, of whether or not she would stay underneath of the established calorie ceiling. Of whether or not she would perform perfectly. She simply existed. Honestly. Purely. Kindly. Passionately. She knew better than I did. She was the teacher. I, the student. But, at the time, I was blind to all of this. I was simply trying to achieve something stupid, that something being maintenance of my "normal" weight that permitted me to squeeze into size two shorts whilst consuming as much delicious, naughty food as possible.

I hate my job. I hate being controlled. I hate the stupid people who are considered as authority. I hate leaving my dog for bullshit work meetings that matter not. For bingeing on Taco Bell in my car and purging at Target between sales meetings. Meetings for things that matter to me not! For bingeing on Dunkin' Donuts and purging at McDonald's where the five-calorie lemonade helps with my vomit spree. I spend more money on binge food than I earn! I am going to be fired. Gwendolyn's food is more expensive than I can afford. Oh well. I'll starve myself to feed her. At least I'll be skinny.

"Gwendolyn, let's take a good nap."

We laid for minutes of fifteen, rising at 8:30pm.

Being still was impossible.

Bucking wildly, my brain pined for more food.

Spaghetti Sunday it shall be! Shall overlook hotdogs. It's a holiday. Holidays are special. Hotdogs compliment Independence Day. No reason to cancel Spaghetti Sunday! Mommy always says that holidays are catastrophic for me. If she only knew.

"Yes! Bon appétit, mademoiselle Gwendolyn!" I exclaimed with delivery of our wheat pasta, in a most Italian girl of accents, wearing my cute pink cooking apron by Williams & Sonoma. I always looked beautiful, even during binges.

TWO POUNDS of spaghetti, quickly consumed, or rather, inhaled, shall exist in my memory forever. Eating my portion, and then Gwendolyn's, literally swooping her plate from the ground, taking food from my baby, and using three quarters of a container of Kraft grated parmesan cheese atop one jars' worth of

Rao's organic eggplant marinara sauce, all resting upon the beautiful mound of pasta. Like heroin to a junkie's veins, it was pure pleasure as it entered into my mouth. But when I had eaten everything, when there was nothing left to consume, the pain settled. Thinking of the future work required to remove this food from my body morphed conditions from heavenly to horrid. Horrid in my throat. In my stomach. In my heart. I felt so empty inside despite having been stuffed to the gills.

Gwendolyn looked MAD AS HELL that I had eaten her portion. Directly from her beautiful white Lenox plate. I still picture her beautiful little kiss-me face. And it said KISS ME NOT! I can still picture my fork twirling spaghetti on my spoon like a mad woman. Even in the midst of my binges, I twirled my pasta. I needed the pleasure of a mound in my mouth. A neat and tidy mound. I loved the taste of food. And I binged on it, very specifically, in very exact patterns and rituals.

New diet starts right now! Right at this moment! Screw the f*cking holiday. No more food whatsoever shall enter into this mouth. No no. I still have until midnight. I can be bad until midnight. Tomorrow I shall start the grandest of Bikini Body Diet Plans. How has it been eleven god damn years? Eleven years ago I started this. Protein will be good tonight. Portobello vegetable burgers. Yes, they're taunting me from the freezer. I need them. NOW! Mmm, fried in macadamia nut oil. Extra crispy. Dipped into ketchup. Jesus Christ I need them now!

As I prepared the vegetable burgers with impatient hands, my head quickly planned the new diet, deciding that full-blown starvation was my only option. Between planning the new diet and listening to the sizzle of frying vegetable burgers and my attempt to break-off pieces of burger to eat before the meal was cooked without burning my fingers, I thought, *Mommy is right. I'll be the old spinster with an eating disorder. I've been doing this for eleven years, and there's no end. It never ends.*

Ten minutes later, the fried portobello vegetable burgers were consumed with Heinz ketchup, tally presenting an estimated nine thousand three hundred seventy calories for the day. Unworried about gaining two-and-a-half pounds by this point, I simply planned to fully compensate before anything stuck.

At 9:30pm, I morphed into Frankenstein's monster. Gwendolyn was my bride. Travelling on foot, we stopped first at the coffee shop, purchasing three over-sized peanut butter cookies, each bigger than my head. If you're from Pittsburgh and know of the Crazy Mocha Coffee Company, then you likely know of these divinely enormous cookies. And two bottles of Diet Pepsi. I liked the taste of carbonation, and Diet Pepsi always helped the food to come up. Food contraband hidden in a brown paper bag, we rounded the corner, spying the Sewickley Confectionary.

Ah! Ice cream! Yes! But what if they are closed? Then McDonald's shall serve as backup. Drive-thru vanilla milkshake with salty french fries will be the perfect finale to this eating experience. Oh but wait! The confectionary is open! Hooray! Sorry, not sorry, McDonald's! I'll see you tomorrow for low calorie lemonade on my new starvation diet plan! Tonight it is ice cream from the confectionary!

"Gwendolyn honey, let's get some good ice cream!"

After overcoming mortifying embarrassment that my then-considered yoga "teacher's" teenage daughter was the ice cream girl on duty, I sucked in my severely extended stomach, asking, "How much do you charge for one banana?" With a smile and wink, she answered, "For you, it is free." Placing one banana into the brown paper bag atop the beautiful, mouth-watering pint of fat-free butterscotch ice cream, she seemed so proud to gift her mother's pet yoga princess with something special. I was, indeed, her mother's pet student, as she toted me to yoga workshops and used my brain to remember choreography for doing "the other side" during her boutique vinyasa flow classes. Thusly, swan diving into a mud cave, I tightened my ponytail, followed by placing two dollars into my yoga "teacher's" daughter's tip jar. I had never tipped for a To-Go binge in eleven years. I had never tipped for delivery binges either, but deliveries were very far and few between as I preferred the high of seeking my own food. Call me a former bulimic hunter and gatherer? It was a part of the thrill for me, often times driving at very dangerous speeds whilst under the influence of alcohol. I am so ashamed of this driving under the influence fact. And, with regard to my infrequent food deliveries, we're talking before the time of GrubHub. We're talking about when calling and placing an order was very tedious and stressful because I had no control. Thusly, delivery binges were rare. As a side note, I think that if delivery apps had existed in my bulimic days, my spending and weight fluctuating would have been so much worse. I imagine myself ordering pizza, Chinese, peanut butter, and donuts all in one night. Thusly, I feel extra bad for bulimics of this day and age. And, for the record, the only other binge, besides this ice cream binge, for which I tipped happened on that first day, during the first binge of eleven years ago, during my first time as a bulimic, at the Chinese restaurant. See chapter two for recount of that episode.

Independence Day food secured, we ran like lightening to our home. Upon reaching the door, I realised that I had misplaced my keys, exclaiming, "Ahhhh! Where are my mother f*cking keys?" Looking at little, overweight Gwendolyn, she cocked her head.

There is no way in hell that I will call the creepy landlord at this late hour. He will insist on chatting. And I need to eat before midnight arrives! I need to get this done!

So I decided to retrace our steps. The keys would either be at the confectionary or at the coffee shop. Or perhaps I had dropped them in the walking path of our great food hunt. Thusly it was me, my then overweight two years, nine-month old Gwendolyn, the pint of melting fat-free butterscotch ice cream, three over-sized peanut butter cookies, two Diet Pepsis, and one banana storming like heck back to the confectionary in eighty-degree nighttime temperatures. Luckily, we quickly found the keys sitting upon the counter of the confectionary. Gracefully curtseying to my yoga "teacher's" daughter, I smiled and exclaimed, "Happy Independence Day!" Once outside, we trekked back to home.

Shovelling everything into my mouth over the next hour, I ignored Gwendolyn, I ignored the film, and I ignored me. Only the food mattered. The cookies. The ice cream. The pro bono banana (which I pretended was cake and ate with a fork). The Diet Pepsi. Offering the impression that I was well into my third trimester with a food baby, developed from a beautiful morning starting at a pudgy 135 pounds on a five-foot, three-and-a-half-inch, non-pregnant frame, I wanted to pop my fat extended stomach like a balloon. It was now or never. Absorb the calories that I had ingested, or get them the f*ck out.

Must ingest laxatives now. Twenty-one pills. Ingesting laxatives beyond finish line of midnight will contaminate the new, clean, fresh diet of tomorrow. Laxatives activate in eight hours, so they'll handle tomorrow's breakfast if I slip with two yoghurts before yoga. Laxatives are my safety net. My buffer. But I shall slip at breakfast not. I shall eat nothing. I shall successfully starve all day. Yoga's at 9:30am. But vomit must come up before laxatives go down. Let's get this party started.

And with that thought, the vomit rushed whilst I sat upon the sofa. It came without force. Racing to the toilet, removing my Gwendolyn necklace, I regurgitated the ice cream. Cold and smooth along my oesophagus, surging along my throat, past my lips, into the porcelain which I had reached just in time, ice cream always burrowed the tunnel for an effective commencement of vomit session. It reminded me of winter.

Fingers had yet to touch my throat, but the food continued flowing on its own. Activating the bathroom fan to block the upstairs and downstairs tenants from listening to the purge, from learning my secret, I vomited in as ladylike of a fashion as I could.

Next traveled the peanut butter. Its texture, rough and clumpy, ruptured my throat, forcing tears to my big, brown eyes. It was like forcing very thick globs of mud against gravity. Globs from stomach to oesophagus to mouth to toilet. As it reached its final destination, toilet water splashed onto my face.

Dear God, please get everything out!

Elated to greet vegetable burgers, I was convinced that with my warrior perseverance to vomit, zero chance existed for food to remain in my fat body, therefore eliminating the potential of gaining even a single pound. In fact, I was hopeful to lose one.

I'll come out weighing less in the morning.

Peanut butter and vegetable burgers, sayo-f*ckin-ara!

At this point, consuming grand amounts of water to assist the vomit, my process was entirely mechanical. Drink. Fingers. Vomit. Drink. Fingers. Vomit. Religiously storing a gallon of H20 underneath of my sink for emergencies, I had all of the tools that I needed. Fingers and water were my tools.

Every time was an emergency.

Jamming fingers into my throat, vomit spilt everywhere, onto floor, onto breasts, onto hair. But my Gwendolyn locket remained untouched, uncontaminated. It was customary to remove my locket containing Gwendolyn's photograph before each and every vomit session.

Needing a break, I sat onto the ground, faucets running wildly, fans pounding at their highest of speeds, knees bent upward, elbows on knees, hands on head, mouth exclaiming, "What the f*ck!!! How did this happen?! Never ever again!!!!!!!!!"

Then flowed the second round of hotdogs, buns, soy cheese, ketchup, and relish. It surprised me that these items were still recognisable, many hours later. Relish was pleasant to vomit, helping to slide the soy cheese, otherwise a difficult food to recall, along my throat.

Spaghetti.

Red snakes filled the toilet.

Hotdogs, buns, ketchup, relish, and mustard from my earlier indulgences of the day surged forward. Topped with a banana. I kept pushing. Like an athlete. My breakfast of vegetables, pineapple salsa, and ketchup danced in the grand finale. And when the vegetables and salsa completed their performance, the ketchup continued flowing. Like lava. It was like a race for the finish line, for midnight.

I knew that it was over, that I had won, that I had achieved my goal, when red continued pouring into the toilet but it no longer tasted of Heinz 57. It tasted of blood. I was vomiting blood. Thusly I had accomplished my mission of removing everything from my big, fat, ugly bulimic body that I had consumed during the day.

Now I can take laxatives and pass out. Twenty-one pills. Extra strength. Blue. They'll activate by morning. I'll walk Gwendolyn. I'll attend yoga with a skinny stomach. And then Gwendolyn and I shall walk all afternoon. It's a company holiday so I'll have all day to get skinny for my sales meetings of Tuesday. I'll never do this again. Unless I slip. I must continue to get drunk on Sundays, and maybe I can avoid this sh*t entirely.

As I collected myself from the bathroom floor, restoring my Gwendolyn necklace to its proper position about my neck, I was ready to overdose on laxatives and to pass out with my dog, but I first cleaned the toilet from top to bottom. Leaving evidence and starting the next day imperfectly was unacceptable. So I cleaned. And upon finishing, as I opened the bathroom door, intending to venture to the kitchen where I hid my laxatives (from myself) and then venture to the bedroom, to Gwendolyn's safe place on the bed, where she hid smushed into a cloud of fluffy pillows during my purging activities, I took not one step.

Gwendolyn sat in front of me, just outside of the bathroom door.

Perched onto her little bottom.

Ears darting backward as though she were hearing alarms.

She was hearing the alarms of my body.

The alarms that said, "You have done this for the last time, and if you do this again, you will hurt yourself and in the process, you will hurt me, your beloved Gwendolyn."

She whimpered.

"Mm Mm Mm Mm Mmmmmmmmmm"

Three years before this Independence Day, Gwendolyn's "purchase" meant that someone would now participate in this crazy life of eating disordered hell with me. And although I tried to establish new rules, new behaviours, and new schedules to stop my bulimic activity to permit a healthy life with Gwendolyn, nothing changed. I only continued with getting more manic. Just a few months before this Independence Day, Gwendolyn became injured, requiring intensive surgery. My good mother babysat for me, one day, when I needed to be at work, and I shall never forget the shame of stopping for binge food before coming to home after that stupid sales meeting. The audacity of me to be so triggered, even during my baby's state of distress, was wretched! Yet Gwendolyn judged me not. And, always, despite her knowledge of what I did behind closed doors, she was the one thing that would judge me not. She would simply love me, in my best, in my worst. It never occurred to me, until this particular day, that my selfish behaviour could truly hurt someone other than myself, that it could truly hurt my beloved Gwendolyn.

Gwendolyn relied on me, loving me without obligation, yet I was staging our lives for failure. Because of my addiction. To food. I spent all of our money. Wasted all of our time. Instead of giving belly rubs, I was focused on either starving or stuffing or emptying my mouth. I did everything wrong. And, on this day, Gwendolyn was hurt. On this day, I hurt my Gwendolyn.

Collecting her into my arms, we moved to the sofa. She hooked her little hind legs onto my waist, resting front paws onto my shoulders. Yet she turned away that sweet little face. She snubbed me.

"Gwendolyn, give mommy a kiss."

She refused.

"Gwendolyn, give mommy a good kiss."

Refusing to look at me, Gwendolyn knew that something was wrong with her one thing. With her mommy.

This is it.

I am done.

No more.

"Gwendolyn, give mommy your little paw," I whispered.

"Please, my honey."

Again, turning her sweet little kiss-me-face away, she ignored my request.

I repeated, "Gwendolyn, please give mommy your little paw."

Collecting her little paw into my pinky, I clutched her tightly. Gazing at my tear-filled eyes with her sweet, little, big eyes, she offered warmth. Compassion. Forgiveness. Hope. Love. All things that I had not, until that point, completely received in my life by anyone affected by my eating disorder.

"Gwendolyn?"

"Gwendolyn, do you hear your mommy?"

She cocked her little head.

"I pinky swear to end my bulimia on this day."

She cocked her little head.

"I shall never, ever, do this again."

She cocked her little head.

"My Gwendolyn, I promise that it's over."

She cocked her little head.

"Mommy loves you more than anything else on Earth."

She licked my eyes, cleaning my tears.

And then she gave me a gnome kiss.

With that loving gnome kiss, I ended eleven years of bulimia.

On July 4, 2010, with my promise to my dog Gwendolyn, with a pinky swear, with a gnome kiss, I turned off the bulimia, like a switch.

It would consume another six years and the ultimate influence of President Donald J. Trump to annihilate my eating disorder in its entirety and to end my seventeen year war with food.

CHAPTER

V

PLUTO

I QUITE FANCY MUSING that my formative years were lived on Pluto. Despite the fact that I physically resemble my little sisters, that I mirror my graceful, late, great-grandmother's perfect skin and luscious, thick head of hair, and that I have inherited my parents' divine Peter Pan-like youthfulness as I am carded for lottery and liquor at the fine age of thirty-seven, I often joke that I am likely an alien from outer space. In fact, as a child, I passionately hoped that such was, indeed, true, as it helped little Nicole Marie Story to justify my "weirdness" and ever-present feeling of being an outcast.

To play further on this alien theory, when I am questioned about how on Earth can I do complicated, pretzel-like Ashtanga yoga poses such as Leg Behind The Head (Eka Pada Sirsasana), such as headstand with fingers pressing into shoulder blades (Baddha Hasta Sirsasana D), such as frog (Bhekasana), I reply that such yoga poses are taught not on Earth, but rather on Pluto, and that my yoga education happened when I lived there as a baby.

In addition to Pluto, I consider two other fantasy locations for my "hometown" that seem all too real and perfect and matching for my human character. The first is Shangri-La, a land which serves as setting in *Lost Horizon*, a 1937 film by Frank Capra based on James Hilton's 1933 novel of the same title. Shangri-La is a hidden utopia in the mountains of Tibet, home to a society of good people characterised by peace, quiet, hard work, sustainability, trade, good health, cleanliness, purity, harmony, and love. I identify with the group of protagonists who, by way of abduction, come to and fall in love with this perfect land where there is no war, poverty, or sickness. The oldest member of the Shangri-La society is aged to two-hundred and twenty years because he lives correctly. All members of this society age more slowly than do humans elsewhere on Earth. The architecture is clean. The air is fresh. The food is real. The wine is divine. And there is a dog!

The third land that would be fitting for me, during adulthood, such as in the late thirties as I am now, at the point in my life where I have dealt enough with bad people and have developed a lifelong trend of refusing to cooperate with them, would be Galt's Gulch, a hidden land in the Rocky Mountains as presented in Ayn Rand's *Atlas Shrugged*. On Galt's Gulch, I shall exist with the pure capitalists of society, pure meaning with heart. Refusing to lend our brains to corruption, we shall work together in our secret land, creating a self-sufficient frontier of innovation, prosperity, and joy. When the outside world extinguishes due to failure at living on socialism principles, we shall return to takeover the United States of America once again. Members of the Gulch shall include President Trump and family, Elon Musk, Sean Hannity, Gary Vaynerchuk, Ryan Seacrest, my sister Stephanie, my heroic confidante Peter Dickerson of Australia, my yoga girlfriend @rebeccahleigh of Instagram (inspiring stroke survivor), and a few very good friends who shall remain as anonymous because I want not to give away their "politics." My baby Gwendolyn shall be the first dog living on the Gulch. Of course!

As a baby, my mother reports that I never wanted to be held or snuggled. In response to my rejection of her physical affection, she thought that she was parenting me incorrectly, that was, until my sisters were born. They, in contrast, accepted snuggles galore. My mother therefore deemed me as "different." I was formula fed versus breast fed. And, I think that my mother made an excellent choice in feeding me in this manner. Ivana Trump fed her children with formula, and, just like the Story girls, the Trump children turned out marvelously. In fact, the Story family and the Trump family make a good case as to why children should be formula fed. Dollars and Versace dresses aside, my mother reminds me much of Ivana, based on what I read in Ivana's *Raising Trump*. Both are nononsense. Both are strong like bulls. In fact, if my mother writes a book, it should be titled, *The Iron Fist*.

In my early years, gravitating toward rational, quiet activities, I competed with myself. Everything required perfection: colouring, printing, dancing, memorising things, you name it! Each time that I did something, it needed to be done as better than on my prior attempt. As I entered into the formal schooling system, I became competitive with classmates but quietly insomuch that nobody probably remembers me as being competitive but rather remembers me as being the quiet girl. As being the socially graceful girl. I was proper in all public places, including in school where I was attracted by the things that men conventionally enjoy: mechanical drawing, metal shop, health science, the solar system, chemistry, and calculus. And yet, I could articulate my male-like pleasures in words, with a pen, like a lady. I could make rough and gruff and manly sound as pretty and delightful. I do the same thing today. When friends want to say "F you" when a big mistake is made by a business, they first give the underdog a chance to fix it. And when it is fixed not, they ask for me to morph their message of dissatisfaction into something pretty, and we dash off an eloquent email to the CEO. My sister Stephanie and I have labeled our mutual ability to write beautifully and to get things accomplished as *The Story Escalation Clause*. We give you one chance to fix a problem, and if resolution is unachieved in a timeframe that we deem as acceptable, then we go straight to the top dog.

Yes, as a child, I loved the rational subjects and embraced them madly. What failed to capture my interest? The romantic things. My mother tells the story of how I lost interest with decorating the Christmas tree after installation of one ornament, of how I lost interest with decorating Easter eggs after dyeing one egg, of how I lost interest with decorating sugar cookies after creating just one, of how I lost interest with colouring more than one page in a colouring book but ensured that that one page was coloured as perfect, etcetera. You get the point. And as I grew older, in middle school and high school, I cared not of Henry the Eighth and of his six marriages, or that Martin Luther King fought the laws of segregation, or that FDR created something that sounded as terrible to me, that terrible thing being The New Deal. That all happened, sure, but I was certain that it would serve me not. To know about it and to talk about it was a waste of my time. I cared only about the now, about progress, about the future. I might be the only kid to say that Disney World unimpressed, except for a few attractions. I enjoyed riding *Dumbo the Flying Elephant* with my father in 1985 at the age of three. My sailor girl outfit and curly pigtails were divine! I remember the outfit and hairstyle as though it were worn yesterday! The experience was all about looking beautiful and flaunting my divine fashion sense, even at the age of three! And, in 1990, rather than standing in queue to see *Mickey Mouse*, I wanted to analyse the *Carousel of Progress*, comparing it to my viewing from 1985 to determine if the world was on track with becoming *The Jetsons* age! I wanted to ride *Space Mountain*, as it made me feel like an astronaut. And, I enjoyed *The Muppets* attraction. Although I cared not for *Mickey Mouse*, I madly adored *The Muppets* because they were funny and interacted with humans. Also in line with this discussion on "make-believe," I enjoyed *Mister Rogers Neighborhood* as Fred Rogers was a kind, rational, creative man from my hometown of Pittsburgh. He made little Nicole Marie Story know that I was loved, just the way that I was. I would often think of Mister Rogers's message when nobody talked to me in elementary school, when called a "hairy dog" in middle school, and when bullied throughout my life by "authority." Ironically, in my early thirties, Tod Browning's film entitled *Freaks* from 1932 made me feel the same way as Mister Rogers did during childhood. It made me feel like I was a part of something.

I was a robotic, independent-thinking child, similar to how I am now a robotic, independent-thinking adult. When I reminisce, I am certain that my childhood mannerisms would nowadays be classified as autistic. My ways now, as an adult, can be classified as such, too. For instance, I read that a characteristic of autism is memorising train schedules. I shall take that one step further! In addition to knowing the schedules, I can look up and see a train, and without reading its label, know to where it's destined and to where it connects and everything else about it such as whether or not it will be filled with Cubs jerseys, homeless people, suited people, nannies, construction workers, party animals, or old school Chicago gentlemen from the South Side headed to a poker game. It is humorous to me that knowing about train schedules can mean autism in this day and age.

In order for someone like me to own who she is, then she must be confident. And I am. But for a child to be so "different," it was hard because I lived in a house of where offering my "different" opinion was translated to "talking back" (according to my mother) which was considered as disrespectful and therefore as incorrect. Being disrespectful and deviating from the rules was grounds for punishment. This sounds very normal, yes, as children need rules and discipline. But just as President Trump does things his way, I have always done the same. Thusly, my childhood, although it was very wonderful, was also painted with punishment.

I distinctly remember during one afternoon in 1986 whilst my sisters napped that we enjoyed our regular, special, beloved Mommy and Nicole reading time. Laying on our stomachs, propped onto our elbows, in front of the big box television in the living room of our old dear house, she read to then four-year old me from the book of *Sleeping Beauty*. In my little, soft voice, I repeated her every sentence. And she commanded me to stop, as it was annoying to her. But I continued. *"Once upon a time,"* she read. And my little voice repeated, *"Once upon a time..."* *"Long ago there lived a King and Queen."* *"Long ago there lived a King and Queen."* Rather than continuing our story time, my mother closed the book. Also at age four, I remember admiring her ironing work and staring at the beautiful metal tool that made clothing look as perfect. My mother warned, "Nicole, don't you dare touch this hot iron!" Of course I touched it. In fact, I distinctly recall reaching up to touch the iron and of the resulting hot burn. We were standing in her bedroom at the old house, directly beside the door behind which *Trump: The Game* would later be housed. See chapter one for details on *Trump: The Game*, and of my childhood admiration of it. A third episode of badness, also at age four, happened when I created my own rules at *Candy Land* which, of course, was interpreted as cheating. I disliked that I was losing at a game of chance. It made no sense that a spinning wheel could determine if I were a winner or loser. So what did I do? Out of turn, I moved my board piece ahead of the others. Why should I accept losing something that was outside of my control? This is what my four-year old brain rationalised. In response to my perceived cheating, my mother ended the game, hiding it in the china closet for many months. She said that I was a cheater and therefore playing privileges were suspended. Well, it belonged in the china closet as *Candy Land* is garbage. It teaches no skill and that life is based on luck versus hard work. My mother and I have since discussed these episodes, and she does feel badly for silencing my repetition of her words at story time. She now admits that I was only doing so because I enjoyed memorising things, and I wanted to read beautifully as she did. And, regarding *Candy Land*, back then, at age four, I told not a sole of my reasoning. I simply moved my board piece ahead of the others. If I had explained my move, then perhaps we might have continued with playing. In all fairness, my mother deserves a gold medal for having mothered me! And, ironically, all of these "bad Nicole" examples that I remember happened only under my mother's watch. I recall not ever being punished for something as related to behaviour around my father. Was this because I respected him more because he is a man? I know, as a young girl, that I interpreted men to be the leaders. So is this why I behaved appropriately for him and acted poorly with my mother? Or perhaps it is because my mother spent the most time with me compared to my father, so more chances existed to be "naughty" under my mother's watch? But why were my sisters never seen as bad? Or were they? I do remember that my father hit me using the paddle with three holes, and sometimes with his belt, and sometimes with his hand, but I think that these whoopings happened to carry out my mother's orders for something "bad" that I had done under her care. In the later years of my living at home, in my late teens, then just freshly eating disordered, I do remember pulling fists with my father, and he threatened to punch me (and maybe I deserved it), but I can think not of an example of where I actually misbehaved for my dad. In recently talking to my mother about my "bad behaviours," she told me that I talked back (as previously mentioned), that I picked up glass when I was told to leave it (as a young child), and then in my late teenage years, after the eating disorder began, my mother tells of how I was disruptive, making loud noises as I entered the house after my work shifts ended at 11pm, making loud noises as I fixed my breakfast in the early morning, and again making loud noises as I exercised whilst everyone else slumbered. I followed the rules not, she tells me. Thusly I was considered as a bad child. But, in creation of this book, she and I have discussed these items, and, in retrospect, she considers me to have been a very good child. "You just did things your way," she said. "You mean like President Trump?" I asked. And we both laughed.

Honestly, I can recall of only five scenarios for which I deserved punishment. The first time happened in 1986 when visiting Moraine State Park. Again, I was stationed at the age of four. Fresh tar, appearing on the road after a hot day of installation by road workers, taunted me. I wanted to run across it. I wanted to experience this interesting terrain! My parents, of course, instructed for me to walk around it. Doing what I wanted, I took off, running across the black mess. And I became stuck! Abandoning my flip flops (gougounes), running through the tar to freedom, I became stuck in the tar again, this time in my bare feet, screaming for my father! Screaming for help! He accordingly found a clean patch of asphalt on which to stand and saved me, carrying me to the red station wagon where baby wipes for my sister Stephanie's diaper-changing morphed into tar-covered feet cleaners!

The second time that I deserved a beating happened in 1987 when I instructed my sister L to insert the metal prongs from Operation (the game) into a wall socket. She got zapped, and I got beat. Ha ha.

The third time that I deserved a beating was when I instructed L to insert the letter of "F" into her late 1980s (might have been 1990 or 1991) computer smart speller. The game involved the computer offering all but one letter to a word. The human player was to think and to insert the missing letter. For this particular scenario, the computer offered _ u c k. I informed L to insert "F" and to say the resulting formed word aloud. When she said the word aloud, I ran and told my mother about L's "naughty" mouth. My sister, motioning into wailing tears when she realised that she had done something "bad" in response to my direction, became hysterical. But I was punished, rightfully so, because my mother figured it out. My mother washed my mouth with soap. She was so kind about it, though, as rather than sticking the soap directly into my mouth, she rubbed soap onto a wash cloth, sticking the wash cloth into my mouth. Dressed in my favourite purple silk nightgown featuring white lace on the V-neckline, I remember the moment like it was yesterday.

The fourth time that I deserved punishment was sometime in the middle of the 1990s when I significantly delayed returning to home, after being dropped by the school bus, about one-quarter-of-a-mile away in distance. Engaging in a snowball fight with the neighbourhood boys, I played whilst my mother worried and waited for her birthday daughter who otherwise was normally unsocial and therefore on time. The social snowball fight registered as completely different than my usual character, thusly my mother worried versus thinking that I could actually be doing something interesting. She had prepared, for my birthday, a special, homemade macaroni and cheese dinner, with edges burnt per my request. Yet I was nowhere to be found. This was during a time before cellular phones, so she waited, worrying, with the lonely macaroni and cheese and the Heinz 57 ketchup that I wanted as accompaniment. I deserved to be punished on this day, but my mother let me off of the hook. It was my birthday, she rationalised.

The fifth time that I deserved punishment happened in ninth grade in 1997. A dancer in the school's musical, *The Sound of Music*, I felt repulsed by the costume that I was assigned to wear on stage. I mean, come on, I was a starlet, or so I thought, (ha ha!)! So I told my parents that if we wanted, we could seek our own costumes. They drove me to downtown Pittsburgh to the exquisite costume shop where we rented a gorgeous purple ballgown which I wore, without permission, changing into it just before running onto the stage. I was seriously such a determined brat! Years later, and we are talking just last year in 2018, my long time friend James Randall Harper who starred as Rolf Gruber, told me that his late father commented, way back then, that he couldn't take his eyes off of me, as I danced on that stage. When Randy told this to me, it made me feel like someone was out there, seeing the correctness in who I was, in who I am. It was like getting a "143" from Mister Rogers. I'll always be grateful to Randy for telling me about his father's commentary. I am so sorry that Randy lost his father, much too soon. Just as I wish that Fred Trump were alive today, to see the greatness in President Trump, I wish that Randy's father could be alive, to see the greatness in Randy.

In all four of these scenarios when I actually deserved punishment, I received one not. The most prominent times in which I was whooped happened on family vacations where I caused a ruckus from the backseat of whatever automobile we traveled. I complained, moaned, groaned, picked on my sisters, etcetera. And, it turns out, my discomfort existed because I had car sickness. When I think of the Appalachian Mountains, I think of getting beat. To this day, my parents feel bad about punishing me for being "bad" during our travels. I know not if it is related to control or to motion or to both, but sitting in the back seat made me feel ill, and still does, to this day unless I am riding in a shiny fancy LincolnMKZ or Cadillac with Uber Premium in which case I pretend to be Alexis Colby of *Dynasty*.

Trust me, I was abused not, and I think that human kids deserve a beating when they are jerks, but when I did things that seemed as defiant, things that my adult brain now interprets to have simply been independent and different from what my parents considered to be correct, I was whooped. But the whoopings never stopped me from expressing my independent spirit and for doing things according to Nicole Marie Story.

Barbie disinterested me. I always thought that her breasts were repulsive and that her bottom was too big. She was curvy, unintelligent, and boring. I kept my Barbie dolls neatly organised, mostly in their original boxes or in the box organisers that my parents provided. I remember coming home from kindergarten on early dismissal in 1987, finding my sisters, on the floor of my bedroom, in a sea of my Barbie and Jem dolls, with the dolls' clothing swapped and mismatched and everything being a sea of chaos! I literally wanted to pass out because the sight of this made me sick to my stomach! I have yet to forgive my sisters for the mental distress which they caused by turning my neat dolls into party town. Unlike Barbie, I very much loved Jem, and it had nothing to do with her body; it rather had everything to do with her multiple personality and zest for richness, glamour, and business! Prim and proper by day, with the touch of an earring, she turned into a rad, fabulous, dazzling rock star by night! Jem taught me that one needed not to be just ONE thing. It was the same message that I gleaned from Donald Trump during my investigation of his board game in 1991. I had no idea of WHAT I wanted to be, when I grew up. How could I choose between astronaut, ballerina, sheep herder, and writer? And why, in my later years, did high school guidance counselors and universities press me to be things that seemed so boring? Thusly, I was THAT GIRL who changed her major every semester until I stopped attending formal university entirely. I was THAT GIRL who refused to settle on just one thing. One of my favourite lessons by Gary Vaynerchuk is when he told a podcast listener to be a wuzzle. He went on to describe that a wuzzle is a 1980s cartoon character comprised of two different animals. I knew this, of course, as I viewed *The Wuzzles* during childhood. Gary used this analogy to address a problem posed by this listener who was unable to decide on what she wanted "to be." This listener enjoyed doing several activities that could all work as businesses. Gary basically said in counsel, to do it all.

When did I first become aware of my body? The year was 1990. My age, eight. Traveling to Florida during a family vacation, I overheard a conversation between truckers on the CB Radio that my father used for communication about traffic and emergencies.

"Got your ears on?"

"Copy that!"

"Yahoo! Look at that sh*t! Cottage Cheese Legs! Sooey! Sooey!"

My father immediately scrambled with the radio equipment, switching off the power.

There were some F words that transmitted over the airwaves before he deactivated the sound. The vulgar truckers also identified the particular car in which the woman they described sat. I knew not of what any of it meant except for the cottage cheese part. I was focusing on my homework, as my parents had removed us from school for one week to take this grand adventure, but now my attention was directed elsewhere: to my legs which were resting on the back of the middle seat of the 1989 Dodge Caravan SE.

Cottage cheese is lumpy, I thought.

The truckers were therefore defining the woman's legs as lumpy.

Looking to my legs, I thought, *Hm, they're lumpy.*

I harvested a childhood love of cottage cheese complimented with mandarin oranges. I still remember eating bowls of this concoction in the downstairs living room of my parents' first house, the house that I loved. Thusly I knew cottage cheese very well. And it was lumpy. Imperfect. Fat.

Like my legs.

Therefore, I began my first diet.

I am not one of those crybaby humans who reference childhood realities as reasoning for adulthood problems. I think that good can come from whatever circumstance you are dealt. Example: I think that poor children living in the projects have a competitive advantage in life. Why? Because they know of hard times and therefore have hard work built into their circuitry. They must hustle, to survive. To thrive! A perfect example is Pitbull the music artist and business man. His rags to riches story is phenomenal. Pitbull is such a divine sensation that he queries BEFORE THE DOG BREED when searched for on the internet!

The same hustle advantage is true, in my opinion, of black children. *Black Man Privilege* is a book published by a black man. I learnt of this book by way of a Gary Vaynerchuk podcast episode where Gary interviews the book's author. The author describes the book as one that discusses that black people certainly do, for the most part, get born into less fortunate circumstances. But that exists. That shall never change. So instead of moping about it, attack it. Find the privilege that you have to be a human being on this Earth, and drive like hell at whatever you want to achieve. See yourself as privileged, which you are, to exist, and this will be your guiding strength and light in the pursuit of success and therefore happiness. Capitalise on your perceived handicap. In my case, it is the old eating disorder. In other cases, it might be having the skin colour of black.

Because I find zero value in identifying "the root cause" of any addiction or unwanted behaviour, therapists hated me because I never offered the information which I am offering now to my readers. Learning of my childhood was their goal. Pulling this information from me, was there failure. I interpreted discussion of such items as a waste of time, energy, and money, even when my parents footed the bill. Yes, my good parents were quick to find head doctor care for me when they discovered my bulimia at my young age of seventeen. They tried really hard to make things as correct for me, by doing what they thought was right, by finding me a psychologist. At the time, to my parents, and to most of the world, "bulimia" meant "mental illness" because bulimia did, indeed, carry that official mental illness label, one likely created by a radical Democrat. But, I was different than conventional labels. Nothing about me could ever be labeled. I was tough. I shall talk more on "therapy" and "mental illness" in chapter ten entitled *Trump Derangement Syndrome*.

For the next nine years, from the age of eight to seventeen, I was always on some sort of diet. At school, in the late elementary years, I sold the "sweets" from the gourmet lunches that my mother had lovingly prepared. And, on Fridays, when given money from my parents to buy pizza, I upgraded to the salad bar, using the money that I had earned from the selling of sweets to cover the extra cost of the salad. As the years progressed, I would throw away my lunches or eat only a very small portion of them. Food was my drug. I was trying to control it, even as a child.

I envied the bodies of the girls whose legs went straight up and down. At dance school, I was jealous of the girls without kangaroo pouches in their leotards. I really thought that my body was gross and that I had missed the thin gene. My father called my thighs, "DiGiandomenico Legs" because my Brazilian great grandfather DiGiandomenico reportedly had massive Herculean thighs. It turns out that I am just one of those people who needs to work really hard to be thin!

In childhood, I was given everything that I wanted, within reason. My father worked outside of the home for a corporation. My mother worked inside of the home, raising three beautiful children and caring for her husband. They did an amazing job at parenting someone like me. They likewise did an amazing job with parenting my sisters. My father made the money and told the jokes. My mother managed the home like a business. She was the one who said no. My father was the softy. They balanced each other. Although it was their dream to raise a perfect family, at least that is how I interpret their goal based on the manner in which they parented, I regret nothing about being a difficult child. I am proud of the little girl who embraced her brain and heart. But I do think it is sad that my eating disorder seems to be the element that tarnished the family dream. The eating disorder was something that my family wanted to hide. I, on the other hand, wanted to wear it on my sweater like Hester Prynne's "A." But we were hush hush about it. Nobody outside of our home could know, aside from the therapist. And when we discussed it, I was made to feel like an incorrect person. I was told that I knew better. I was told that I represented the family name and needed to therefore stop these behaviours. Perhaps my family can offer a more compassionate account of this moment in time, but this is my interpretation of what I experienced. It was something that we should have worked on together versus letting it tear us apart. I honestly know not if we could have rationally cooperated to have made things different. But I do think that sharing our failure as a family with regard to the eating disorder will help others to fix their issues before it turns into a lifetime of their own discomfort.

The four greatest things that my parents did for me, were as follows.

1. Dance classes. These taught to me confidence, poise, and discipline later translating to yoga. And, of course, I was a defiant little dancer. I remember, in third grade, meeting with the owner of the dance studio because I believed that I belonged in a more advanced class. The studio owner argued that because of my age, the class that I desired was inappropriate. Being promoted to this class meant mixing with girls who were much older than I, who were reportedly more talented than I. But it mattered not. I wanted to be challenged. The class upgrade was approved, and I earned my first trophy during that year. It was the 1990-91 trophy for "Best Jazz Class" at

The Ronald Matty Dance Arts Centre in Coraopolis, Pennsylvania. Nobody talked to me in the class. But I got my way. I won across the board, now having a first place trophy to prove it. And, in my opinion, I was, indeed, the best dancer in class.

2. They taught me to be non-judgmental. It was Christmas Eve in the late 1980s. My father and I shopped for last minute gifts for my mother at Super K-Mart. I remember looking at a pile of purple sweat suits, exclaiming, "Ew! Who would buy these ugly things," in the process seemingly hurting the feelings of a woman who was looking at the merchandise, perhaps as for a gift for someone that she loved. My father explained that not everyone was fortunate to have money to buy nice things. I felt very bad on that night and shall never forget that woman's face. It was at this moment that I decided that all humans are equal regardless of income, so long as they work hard and passionately. The janitor and CEO hold equal importance in my brain. Therefore, it hurts me, nowadays, when my dad considers wealthier people to be better than himself. He was the teacher who instilled the value system in my brain that physical assets make not the person. He taught me that what is inside is what matters. I wish that he could remember this lesson that he taught to me. It was one of the greatest lessons of my life. Like President Trump, my father is a very good man, and I am proud to be his daughter.

3. To be charitable. And to be taken advantage of not.

4. To work. It was the first thing that we did on the summer of my sixteenth year: my mother took me to apply for a work permit. But even before that, I was taught to work for what I wanted. For instance, in 1992, I sold the most girl scout cookies of my troop. But, unlike most of the troop members' parents, my father refused to sell my cookies at his workplace. I was SO ANGRY at the time, that he refused to solicit my cookies to coworkers, so I literally walked DOOR TO DOOR as a fourth grader, EARNING my cookie sales. Boy, my mother and I had so many cookies to deliver afterward! I am so grateful that she helped me to fulfil my orders. I would do the same, in years to come, for every school fund raiser, be it magazines, Christmas wreaths, Christmas garland, gourmet pies, etcetera. School assignments unmotivated me, but school sales contests set my world on fire! And I always sold the most. In fact, in the sixth grade, I won the limousine ride to McDonald's for selling of the most magazines in my grade. Nobody talked to me in the limousine or at McDonald's but I can still remember

dipping my chicken nuggets into BBQ sauce at that wonderful Moon Township branch of the fast food giant. I felt like I was dipping nuggets of gold! I was so pleased to have won the sixth grade sales contest. Nothing else mattered.

My parents were very wonderful. I wish that my brain could flow with memories that I could mention here. They drank alcohol not. They did drugs not. They had a social life not, outside of the family. We were their hobby. We were their lives. And, in a sense, I am that way with my life. Despite my excitement for life, I am boring and straight laced. President Trump, despite his exciting personality, seems to be very much the same, disliking parties and small talk as discussed in *The Art of the Deal*.

We all have something in our lives which is imperfect at one point or another. My imperfection was the eating disorder. My family's imperfection existed, because of my eating disorder. It consumed nineteen years for me to discover a painful fact about my interpretation of their reaction to my eating disorder that stunted my adulthood experiences. I am proud of my discovery, because in working hard on myself to end my war with food, I found my true problem, something more than the food. See chapter nine entitled *Worthy of Trust* for restricted details on this subject.

My childhood was very good. I had few friends, always a best friend, but never a big group. My sisters were my besties. My core. The eating disorder tore apart my place in our relationships, and it consumed a long time to mend our wounds. Stephanie and I worked very hard on our friendship, and we now in 2019, exist as best friends. She is incredibly special to me. In fact, I named her. About one year before Stephanie's birth, I created an imaginary playmate named Stephanie. When my parents asked on what I'd like to name the new baby, I answered with Stephanie. On the day that Stephanie was born, my imaginary playmate disappeared. I saw Stephanie as a present that my parents created for me. Stephanie is the baby. I am the eldest. L exists in the middle. I think, even as a two-year old, that I saw her as competition. I was jealous of her existence. I was mad that I was required to share the attention of my parents with L. As an eight-year old, I saw her legs as straight and beautiful. Mine, on the other hand, were lumpy and ugly. From that point forward, seeing her as prettier than I saw myself, I pushed her away. Thusly, despite playing within the walls of our childhood home and despite having her in my childhood core, our relationship lived, but it aged without nourishment. I took her for granted. And I know that my resentment of her made her feel very bad. I was mean to her. And then things just completely fell apart with the eating disorder. She was better at restriction, and I really resented her for it. What a sad reason for breaking up with your sister. I was the fat bulimic and she looked like a model. And our relationship died. On December 29, 2017, I contacted her. On April 2, 2019, she responded. And it changed my life. We will be okay. For the first time in twenty years, I have two sisters again.

In this next section, I mention important items with regard to individual characters involved with my childhood. Firstly, my mother. As previously stated, my mother's job, in the 1980s and 1990s, was to manage the family, including my dad, two little sisters, and myself. She was the best mother. In elementary school, she chaperoned all of my field trips, I think, because she distrusted other humans to be in charge of my care. I was so glad that she attended. None of the other kids talked to me, so I loved spending the day with my beautiful mommy. In later years, specifically in seventh grade, she wanted to chaperone a field trip for my symphonic band performance at Sea World. I cried and resisted, telling her that it would be embarrassing to have my mother on the trip. I was such a bitch. And she cried. I'll never forget making her cry. At the last minute, I changed my mind, begging her to attend, but it was too late. I spent that entire rainy day at Sea World in a state of lonesome misery. Not only did I hate playing the clarinet because I thought it was a manly instrument, but nobody talked to me at Sea World. I just wanted for my mother to be there! My favourite childhood memories with her include visiting the Coraopolis Memorial Library to check-out books, retreating to my grandparents' pool one Saturday in the 1980s when she had had a fight with my father, and her denying me the *BookIt* personal pan pizza from Pizza Hut in 1988 because I rebelled against the nurses taking my blood and closed down the medical centre which required a trip to the hospital because I was having surgery soon and blood needed to be drawn. I really put up a fight, and it took several huge people to restrain me to collect the blood. I actually deserved to be punished with no pizza! I am the way that I am, I am a warrior, because my mother taught me to be so. When she had her hysterectomy in 1998, I was so upset because I had never been without her, for all of my sixteen years, to that point. She had never been sick, to that point. Remembering her, laying in that hospital bed, vomiting into the little tray, still delivers sadness to my heart. And I shall never forget of how devalued she felt, when it came time to complete my college applications. When requesting information on her profession and income, the reply was, "housewife" and "zero." She was so embarrassed about how she looked on paper. She told me to never find myself in such a place. She me told to never rely on a man for money. It upset me badly because my rational brain knew the truth. My mother NEVER rested. Not one single time during my childhood. She worked so very hard, from before sunrise to after sunset, to in the middle of the night, that it is completely maddening that one stupid little elitist application for "higher education" could make her feel so badly. She was the reason that my dad could work outside of the home. She was fifty percent of the reason of our family. Sure, things were imperfect, as I was clearly nuts and developed an eating disorder, but things were as perfect as I could ever want them to be. My mother was incredible. I think of her natural beauty, especially in the 1980s. The black, soft, hair. The clear, white skin. The firm, Italian face. She was a beauty but a brute at the same time. She had brains. And she was the boss. I remember, in the late 1980s and early 1990s, at Christmastime, she operated a cookie business from the confines of our home! People traveled to our home to buy the BEAUTIFUL cookies that she baked during the day between our activities or during our schooling and during the nighttime after my sisters and I retired to our slumbers. I was so intrigued by her operation, by the beautiful, elegantly boxed cookies, by the cash, by the referrals, by the buzz amongst my school teachers that MY MOTHER was the creator of the gorgeous Italian delicacies at their Christmas soirées. And, in retrospect, I realise that my mother was a natural, divine entrepreneur! She was doing entrepreneurial things in Pennsylvania whilst Donald Trump was doing entrepreneurial things in New York. The only difference is that instead of building designer cookies, President Trump was building designer buildings. Dare I say that my mother is Trumpian? Yes, I say it! I am so proud of her work. In fact, if President Trump is seeking a chief pastry chef for the White House, or if The Trump Organization is hiring for the same, then I recommend, passionately, my mother. Her style is unique, original, elegant, and beautiful. I am very proud to be her daughter.

My Aunt Linda. My godmother. She is one of the hardest workers, one of the kindest souls, and one of the most beautiful humans on this Earth. She has loved me so fiercely since my birth, and I love her back. I am so grateful for her. I would do anything for my Aunt Linda and for her family.

My paternal Grandmother. Writing about her makes me smile and cry because we have that kind of grandmother granddaughter bond that is so very special that you know when you're one hundred and seventeen years old, you will still cherish it passionately. I have admired her, always. Her stories. Her fashion. Her strength. We made snow angels together in the snow in the 1980s.

We sewed pillows together in the 1990s. We drank martinis together in the early 2000s. And then I got my Gwendolyn and because my grandmother is a dog lover not, and because I bring Gwendolyn everywhere, we stopped spending time together, but the way that we feel about each other remains as unchanged. In fact, in recent years, she will always ask first about Gwendolyn on our telephone conversations, dubbing Gwendolyn as "Little Miss Prissy." And when Gwendolyn had surgery in late 2017, my grandmother texted me on that same night to ensure that everything went smoothly. She is eighty-seven years young, and daily, she embroiders using a machine that receives patterns from her computer. In fact, she surprised me with an embroidered towel featuring a Victorian pug! I shall forever treasure that towel. Also, at age eighty-seven, having never used an Apple product, she bought and taught herself how to use an *iPhoneXR*. We follow each other on the Friend Finder app. Seeing her location and knowing that she is out there, in this world, connected to me, makes me so happy. And, trust me, she is always doing something and going somewhere! She is my inspiration. Also, it is necessary to mention that I have a special love for her mother, my great-grandmother. I remember every detail about my interaction with her mother until her death in 1988. My grandmother is my special grandmother who has always loved her little Nicole even during those turbulent eating disordered years, and I have reciprocated that love and respect and shall always do so. I hope that she will be proud of this book. President Trump is my hero. My paternal grandmother is my heroine!

My Polish grandfather. He is an incredible man who treats my aforementioned grandmother like a QUEEN. When I was a little girl, he took me fishing and watched Little Red Riding Hood with me. One time, whilst I misbehaved in the car, he told me that the road construction cones were used to punish bad children and unbuckled my seatbelt, pretending as though he was going to put me underneath of one, ha ha! He honourably served as a Pennsylvania State Trooper for many years, retiring only when the African American quota required filling and he was overlooked for the promotion that he deserved and earned. And because I respect him so fiercely, I always thank police officers for their brave service by smiling and curtseying. I never understood of why my father waved to every police officer during my childhood. Now I do, especially during this present time in history of where radical Democrats so fiercely oppose law enforcement. Yes, dear readers, #BlueLivesMatter. And I must mention his amazing mother - she worked for Heinz 57 before it was acceptable for women to work outside of the home. My grandfather and grandmother have never argued in their fifty years of marriage, and I hope to one day meet a wonderful, peaceful, brilliant, creative, kind man, just like my grandfather.

My maternal grandparents. They are wonderful. I spent summers of many, watching soap operas and *The Oprah Winfrey Show* with this grandmother who, by the way, resembles the dazzling Joan Collins of *Dynasty*, then and now! And, during each visit, my grandfather always gave to me a dollar. Little capitalist Nicole Marie Story loved these dollars very much! He tells a wonderful story about his hometown of Pacentro, Italy, stating that it is located "three days from Rome by donkey, two weeks by horse." Why does the donkey arrive sooner than the horse? The horse will travel too quickly, spraining its leg, requiring rest, of course! His analogy to patience is epitome. It translates to my relationship with yoga and to everything that I have ever loved. My grandfather is a very smart man. I must say that I felt very judged and therefore hurt by these grandparents during my twenties and early thirties, with regard to whom I dated and with regard to my body, but they are from "the old school," as my mother defends, and I thusly try to think only of the good times, when reminiscing. I try to forget the moment of when they spied me at Walmart with the illegal whom I discuss in chapter seven. They tried to ignore me. But I insisted on greeting my grandparents because I was raised to respect them. And when I started my blog, my grandfather refused to attend my sister's wedding, because I had asked not for his "permission" to write about my life publicly. My mother smoothed things over, and he ended up attending. What an awful time in our lives. I can only imagine the pain that they felt, and I am glad to have moved onward from it. They both love my Gwendolyn, which, at the end of the day, is the only thing that matters.

Amethyst and Tracy. My cousins! My divinely beautiful sun-kissed cousins from Florida. I have so much love for these girls and look forward to celebrating with them after my book is published. #CousinCruise.

And my father. We recently had one amazing day together in 2017 when I packed my Pittsburgh apartment and moved to Chicago. I grossly underestimated the labor needed to load my U-Haul truck, and he saved the day. We finished this day by celebrating his birthday with Chinese food. I happily cherish memories of eating "dippy eggs" and watching Saturday morning cartoons with him in the 1980s. I remember that when he returned home from work in the evenings, my sisters and I raced to the door, because we each wanted to be the first to greet him. Of course I always won. Dogs love my dad, and that says everything about a human's character. He literally has the biggest heart and strongest work ethic. He will drop everything to help anyone. This includes pulling people from cars at accident scenes, helping a little old lady to cross the street, and fixing someone's garage door. He can fix anything! His brain is intelligent and creative. I definitely get my brain style from him. And he is hysterical! On July 4, 2019, he asked, "So, what is the title of your second book? *Kim Jong-un and My Life*?" He had me in stitches of laughter, the kind of pure laughter that rendered me to tears as a child. I am very proud to be his daughter.

In childhood, I was popular NOT (I lost the sixth grade election for secretary). I was the pretty girl NOT (I never kissed a boy until college). I was the girl who could dance gorgeously and classically, but I danced for the school NOT, rather for a private dance company, so this put me into that black swan bucket where the dance team and cheerleaders ignored me. I was the smartest NOT, but I was the most competitive, so I always got myself included into the honours and advanced placement classes. Nobody talked to me at lunch during elementary school, so I got myself a job answering telephones for the school secretary to avoid sitting alone or at the "dorks' table." I was rebellious, but only insomuch that I wanted to be the owner of my brain and ideas and life. For instance, when my academic advisor for the high school newspaper denied me the permission to use grammar, my way, I dropped out of journalism class during my junior year, and I thusly stopped writing for the school newspaper. That was a big blow because I really wanted to be a "writer" and thought that a formal studying of it and participating in the subject was my only avenue for achieving that goal. This dropping out of activities became a consistent trend until I realised that I needed to create the activity, my way, in order to do it peacefully and successfully. Thusly, we have my blog. We have this book. We have my yoga practice. Everything that I do, is done because I create the environment. I am an entrepreneur of my human self and always have been such.

I was very strong and determined in everything that I did.

And this included the diet which I started on February 14, 1999 at the age of seventeen. The one that shuttled me into half of a year of anorexia, eleven years of bulimia, and six more years of very chaotic, very ugly, downright turbulent, disordered eating.

CHAPTER

VI

ANOREXIA

WHEN THE SONGS OF KAREN CARPENTER stream on the radio, especially at Christmastime, I experience chills of mystification as related to my self-identified sixth sense. This sixth sense is characterised by a history of premonitory dreams, and by connections that seem almost unbelievable.

One of such connections involves Ayn Rand. In her grand masterpiece of *Atlas Shrugged*, the date of September 2 is recurring and important. In fact, lovers of Ayn Rand have deemed September 2 as official "*Atlas Shrugged* Day." Written numerically, *Atlas Shrugged* Day is 9/2. My birthday is February 9. Or, 2/9. Which is *Atlas Shrugged* Day reversed. And, Ayn Rand, according to conservapedia.com, wrote the character of Dagny Taggart in 1946 to be born in 1982. I was born in 1982. Of all fictional characters ever written, Dagny Taggart of *Atlas Shrugged* is the one to whom I relate. *Atlas Shrugged*, moreover, is my favourite book. Additionally, Ayn Rand was born on February 2, seven days before my date of birth, albeit seventy-seven years apart. And, lastly, Ayn Rand died on March 6, 1982, less than one month after my birth, at the age of seventy-seven. The number of seven hereby seems foretelling of something! I think that I am Ayn Rand's true intellectual heir. Another great example is my connection to President Trump which is discussed in great detail in chapter one of this book. Also, interestingly, *The Fountainhead* by Ayn Rand is reported to be President Trump's favourite book, thusly our favourite books, although different, are written by the same author.

Another great example of connection is, as previously stated, Karen Carpenter. My parents, at their wedding of forty years ago on June 16, 1979, danced to *We've Only Just Begun* by The Carpenters as their first dance. Did this forecast that all of their daughters would, one day, develop an eating disorder? Also as a side note and additional "connection," on my parents' thirty-sixth wedding anniversary on June 16, 2015, handsome Donald Trump and his beautiful wife Melania descended from the golden, glamorous escalators of Trump Tower to announce Donald Trump's candidacy for President of the United States of America. Everything is just so connected!

With regard to my sixth sense, I see more into the story of Karen Carpenter than does the rest of the world. It is like a cosmic connection exists between myself and this late, oh so beautiful of a human being who sang like an angel. When a person hears the name of Karen Carpenter, they think of anorexia. They think of an eating disorder. They think of a skin and bones girl who seemingly refused to eat proper amounts of food to sustain a healthy life. They think of someone with a brain disease. I think none of this. I rather think of a girl, of a grand performer, of an outstanding human who sought perfection, the perfect body included in that seeking. The goal hurt her not. It was rather the method that did the hurting. And, I say this, again, based on pure intuition of my sixth sense. In viewing filmography of her story, in reading articles of her story, in seeing her passionate pursuit of excellence, I also see myself. The moment that I tasted ultra thin at the age of seventeen in 1999 was the moment that I became ultra obsessed with keeping it. But my full throttle personality with regard to bad food behaviours won for years of seventeen. Every single day for seventeen years, taking me from the age of seventeen to thirty-four, I tried passionately to return to that state of ultra thin. And even though I no longer live with an eating disorder, that disordered call to action, that call to stuff my face with food and to rid myself of it, oh it still exists. I simply know of how to control myself and of how to pick and choose my battles. I know of how to avoid starting my World War II. And, on some days, such as recently when I clipped into the Peloton bike but knew that a plate of succulent sashimi sat in my refrigerator, I wanted oh so badly to unclip, to make a martini, and to relax with the pleasure of film and food with my little dog Gwendolyn. But the willpower in my brain, the discipline in my soul, the rigidness in my schedule, and the amazing Peloton high fives from my "virtual" friends kept me as riding strong. It kept me from eating my dinner ahead of schedule and wanting more food later. It kept me committed to my workout. It kept me as healthy. Trust me, a lot has changed from the early days of Peloton. Nowadays it seems to be geared toward Beverly Hills housewives versus toward athletes, but the early days, and especially the amazing classes by former Peloton instructor Jennifer Jacobs, were instrumental to my health. Riding with girlfriends @cece.carson, @helenehopyoga, and @ericapetralia of Instagram was instrumental to my health. Karen Carpenter seemingly had no support from like-minded exercise-obsessed people, like I did with my Peloton crew. Karen Carpenter had only opposing viewpoint and fear mongers who convinced her that she was "sick," propelling her deeper into her doom. She was in the spotlight at such an early age that she had no chance to be a loner for a few years, to find herself. To discover the healthy systems that worked for her unique human being. According to what I have watched and read, Karen Carpenter's life ended not from complications with anorexia. Karen Carpenter's life ended from complications associated with her pursuit of unrealistic perfection.

And this is where it gets complicated because I do, indeed, believe in human perfection. I believe that each human has the capability to achieve a perfect, healthy state for their individual character. Who wants for a single quality of their life to be imperfect? Each time that my parents argue, I exclaim to my mother, "You should get a divorce!" And she tells me that I am unrealistic as no relationship is perfect, that no relationship is without battle. But I disagree. If one day I fall into romantic love, then the relationship must be perfect and therefore peaceful. No arguments. No angst. No discomfort. No drama. Who wants for chaos and heartache? Who wants for drama? Karen Carpenter, unfortunately, and oh so sadly, propelled her pursuit of perfection to a level of chaos and heartache and drama, and it killed her. And if I had continued onward with my path of self destruction in my war with food, then who knows? I am very lucky. And grateful.

I have decided to call this chapter "Anorexia" because, in my brain, after crossing the border from anorexia to bulimia in 1999, it was my goal, for the next seventeen years, to achieve that state of "anorexia" again because it was the state in which I considered myself as perfect. For seventeen years, I worked arduously to rediscover that epic high which existed only momentarily at the age of seventeen. I never achieved my goal because, well, I rather found myself into a state of good health, thanks to my hard work, and thanks to the influence of then presidential candidate Donald Trump.

Anorexia was the theme of my eleven-year bulimic life. I was the bulimic with anorexic goals. And even after the bulimia ended, for another eating disordered years of six, "anorexia" continued to be my goal. And that is no way to live. But I did. Maybe you, too, own maintenance of constant unhealthy thin goals. Maybe you, too, battle with bulimia and other disordered behaviours like I did. Maybe you, too, have successfully restricted consistently and feel as empty. Maybe you, too, currently have some other eating "snafu" and just knowing that other people foster deep pain with regard to food will make you feel hopeful about your situation. This is why I am writing and publishing. People need to know that they're not alone. For a long time, I was alone. Until

President Trump. And if this book can reach one like-minded human who is dealing with an eating disorder, then I shall be so very happy.

My maternal grandfather, a settler from Italy, is a citizen of the United States of America. One of the hardest working humans that I shall ever have the privilege to know, he has laboured HARD for all of his life. Working the steel barges on the rivers of Pittsburgh as an expert welder by day and managing the house grounds of an affluent land owner by night, he did whatever he needed to do, to provide for his family. In fact, in 1959, he worked three jobs to afford the hospital's fee for birthing my mother. I am thusly so grateful for his hard work!

This man, my grandfather, once in 2008 gifted me with the opportunity to listen to his story of experience of World War II. It is a story of great pain. Of heartache. Of struggle. Of something that a human of this day and age could never imagine. Of a young child in Italy. Of his memory. He recounted the grim details of being evacuated from his village, of crossing an open field, of holding the hand of his older brother with one hand, a pail of salt with the other. During this village evacuation, he was target for the battle planes traveling above, the pail of salt blasted from my grandfather's little hand. He was just three years old.

He also remembers walking to and from the barn where his mother hid British soldiers underneath of a trap door. My grandfather's job was to pretend to feed the "animals," but he was truly providing nourishment to the hidden soldiers. After the war, these very appreciative, very affluent soldiers sent food and clothing to my grandfather's poor family. And, of most notoriety in my grandfather's story, is the village evacuation not, is the war planes shooting at him not, is his courageous helping of the British soldiers not. It is of the part of his food and therefore nourishment, or lack thereof. It is the part of how, when food supply extinguished, my grandfather, daily, walked to the housing of the occupying soldiers who offered their food scraps to my grandfather's poor family. But, one day, as my grandfather arrived to collect the scraps, one soldier unzipped his pants, pulled out his male organ, and urinated onto the food in a circus style spectacle, laughing at my grandfather, causing my child-aged grandfather to run to home, to cry to his mother. My grandfather told this information about the urinating soldier to me, just one year ago in 2018, and it rendered him to tears, just as the storytelling from 2008 did. It makes me saddened to know that a little boy, that my strong, wonderful grandfather, was treated like this and experienced such trauma and continues to feel triggered, nearly eighty years later. It makes me sick to my stomach to think of his lifelong secret, of his lifelong pain. But, it also makes me proud to know that despite his pain, he lived like a champion and continues to do so, now stationed at the age of eighty-one. After this awful encounter happened with the urinating soldier, my grandfather returned for food scraps not, rather fetching blood from the butcher who saved this liquid from the animals that he slaughtered, specifically for my grandfather's poor family. My grandfather's mother, my great grandmother, boiled this blood. When my grandfather's family had hearty food not, they ate boiled blood and dandelions.

Boiled blood and dandelions.

That was my grandfather's nourishment.

My grandfather, as a three year old, in World War II Italy, was forced to scavenge for food like a beggar.

When he first recounted this story of boiled blood and dandelions in 2008, I was, secretly, in my bulimic life, scavenging for food, too. Stuffing my face with pizza, donuts, macaroni and cheese, pies, cakes, pasta, cereal, cheese, muffins, and basically whatever seemed so naughty and delicious to my former starved self of nine years prior. Yes, it was nine years into my long war with food. Yet in the real war, in World War II, my grandfather, as a young boy, ate boiled blood and dandelions to sustain his life. It made me feel so very ashamed. It made me feel so very stupid. So very dirty. My grandfather would play an integral role in my eating disorder.

My eating disorder started on the February 14, 1999. I implemented the grandest of diets, in effort to look fabulous for the upcoming high school prom. At diet commencement, I weighed somewhere in the ballpark of 135 pounds on a five-foot, three-and-a-half-inch frame. And, like with everything that I do, I did it madly! It started as a "healthy" venture. Spending hours in the school library, printing nutritional details about every food that I considered as part of my new healthy diet, I educated myself on nutrients and proper fuelling. I grocery shopped after school, buying gorgeous vegetables which I cooked, as steamed, with no oil, in the family kitchen, completely rejecting the food which my mother so beautifully curated for the family. Most of my dinners were comprised of egg substitute plus delicious vegetables plus salsa, scrambled. Banana, mango, and skim cow's milk for dessert. I decided on my beautiful pink *Sleeping Beauty* style prom dress in March, and because I lost weight so rapidly due to my perfect calculations of calories in, minus calories out, the dress required two re-fittings, which of course costed extra money for my wonderfully giving parents, for which of course, I was criticised! The ever-so-expensive-child. They called me The Golden Child because they associated me with high dollars. Nowadays, in retrospect, in comparison with my little sisters, I was the least expensive financially (I never had a glamorous wedding or human children), but I was probably the most expensive in terms of "mental distress." Mind you, I think that mental distress is relative. One person's pain can be another person's pleasure. The dress fittings and alterations were pleasurable to me because it meant that I was succeeding at my goal of weight loss.

The prom came.

The prom went.

During which, all that I could think, during that long night and overnight of being trapped at the Embassy Suites in Moon Township, Pennsylvania playing silly casino games and chatting with humans that I loved not, was starting my afternoon and evening work shift at Wendy's Old-Fashioned Hamburgers where I could do the thing that I loved the most: WORK. It gave me such a glorious thrill and pleasure to perform perfectly in exchange for money. I accepted the orders, made the sandwiches (always perfectly applying the W shape with the ketchup as taught during my training), accepted the money, and distributed the product. I scrubbed the potatoes, cleaned the lettuce, prepared the salads, and kept my work station as clean and pristine. Under my care, everything was scrubbed and left as sparkling. Everything in my life, at that point, was about being clean. I skipped the day-after-prom picnic at McConnell's Mill because I cared not to socialise but rather wanted to work.

Classmates began using the word of "anorexic" to describe me.

In response, I felt accomplished. It was the end of my junior year of high school, and I had worked so very hard at Wendy's Old-Fashioned Hamburgers and on my physical body whilst everyone else played. They went to movies, smoked marijuana at bonfires, danced at clubs, went on dates, drank alcohol, etcetera. They did the things that "normal" teenagers do. I, on the other hand, was so addicted to earning money and to being thin, that I ignored what I interpreted to be chaos, rather living my life in the organised manner that I wanted. I thought that my peers were jealous, when citing me as anorexic.

And then I started getting reported to the high school guidance counsellor.

Calling me to her office, every few days, the soft-spoken counsellor asked of how I was "doing," and I interpreted this weak prodding as her way of saying that I was too thin, otherwise known to my brain as, "great accomplishment on your body!" I knew that she thought that she was stepping on hot stones, trying to be light, because "anorexia" was associated with "mental disorder," and one mustn't upset a girl with mental problems, right? This was how I interpreted the complete phoniness of our interactions. It was all a big waste of my time as I should have been reading about food on the internet, I thought. And when she began weighing me weekly, I felt like the best in show. The winner at being thinnest. There were a couple of other girls regularly lined up for the scale, but they did drugs. I, on the other hand, was a fitness queen! Or so I thought.

At this point in my epic "diet," I started to realise that a problem might exist. And we're talking a physical problem, not a mental or emotional problem. I was so confused because, as previously stated, "anorexia" was associated with mental and emotional issues whereas to me, everything problematic was rational and physical. Thusly, each night, unable to sleep, I stared into the family's computer screen, then hosting the AOL browser connected with dial-up internet. And I searched for more information on the word which fellow classmates had used to describe me. "Anorexic." I *Asked Jeeves*, "What is Anorexic?"

And, much to my shock, mostly everything checked off.

- Little white hairs decorated my body.
- I was extremely cold always.
- Loss of menstrual cycle.
- Irritability with other humans.
- Obsession with calorie intake.
- Obsession with calorie expenditure.
- Lower than prescribed weight for my height.
- Baggy jeans.
- Fear of food (for me, this meant not of big bad scary potatoes but more so, "I need to keep scaling back on calories so that the weight doesn't mysteriously creep-up again.").
- Etcetera.

There existed one particular website that earned my nightly encore visitation. AnorexicWeb.com. The site no longer bears resemblance to the original and is likely published by a different owner. But, back then, it was completely transfixing. Coloured in purple and black, I remember a welcome screen of a cobweb, suggesting that a visitor, perhaps an agent of anorexia, would enter into the spinning web of eating disorders forever, never to escape. It was a beautifully designed website, especially considering the young age of the internet, back in 1999. The website author was so very bright, publishing poetry regarding her situation, warning visitors that anorexia is something to avoid. But who knows, it could have been a fat man with a coding degree who wanted to mess with thin young girls. Whomever was the author of the website, I agreed completely. I wanted "to be" anorexic not. I simply wanted to be thin. I wanted to stay put at my weight which was, at that point, 117 pounds. What I disliked about the website was its message that once a person becomes disordered that they can never return to being "normal." In other words, they will be in the disordered mafia forever. They can never return to being a civilian. Despite this warning message, I knew that I could fix my problem, if I developed one. Nobody would tell me no and have the last word.

Spring of 1999 transitioned into summer, and my routine became more rigid. I stopped eating the egg substitute and vegetable concoction, replacing this dinner routine with a piece of grilled chicken, the size of the palm of my hand, plus a menagerie of steamed mushroom, plus salsa. Dessert remained as a banana, mango, and skim cow's milk. However, here is the caveat. By this point, weight plummeting to 110 pounds, my sisters began "telling" on me that I was undernourishing. People began commenting to my parents. And I began worrying that I would gain back the weight, or that my parents would force me to eat more, to gain weight. So, nightly, rather than feasting with the family, I ventured to the basement of our home where I pretended to eat, hiding half of my dinner creation in the sofa cushions wrapped into paper towel, returning late at night whilst everyone slumbered, collecting the hidden chicken, and flushing it into the toilet. I maintained a fake food diary so that my mother, upon daily review of it, thought that I was eating certain nourishing things. My real food diary was kept in my head.

I dropped out of beloved dance school and resigned from the volleyball team because I could no longer commit to hours of classes and practises, which would prevent me from exercising on my watch and accomplishing my needed calculated calorie burn to look a certain way. Extracurricular activities would also prevent me from earning high volumes of money. Similar to my input, without total control of my output, I would become fat and regular gain, and fat and regular were/are/shall always be unacceptable. And, just to be safe, I went to church every single day during that summer of 1999, lighting candles, praying to a god in whom I believed, to keep me as thin.

My weight dropped to its lowest of 89 pounds.

And then my first food binge happened on August 21, 1999.

I describe that first episode in full detail in chapter two of this book.

Immediately, after that binge, I proclaimed something divine.

"Okay, I am bulimic now. I must stop this immediately. I must write a book about how I arrived to this place. I must appear on Oprah. I must help others to become healthy. I must figure this out. I must win. I shall win!"

The next day, I binged and purged again.

In one month's time, I quickly gained weight, soaring my body from 89 pounds to 112 pounds.

Late September of 1999 arrived, and we celebrated the birthday of my grandfather, the same Italian grandfather described earlier in this chapter. No longer a little boy in the throes of World War II Italy, he was now a grown man, having supported a beautiful wife, four children, two sisters, and one father; now being grandparent to a count of ten. Surrounding him, singing happy birthday, all were joyous. It was just one month into my bulimic lifestyle, but having gained twenty-three pounds so rapidly earned the attention of those who loved me, even of those who loved me not.

At this party for my grandfather, I wore American Eagle jeans, size of zero and too tight. I refused to revisit my "fat clothes" with a size two tag so I punished my body by squeezing them into these most uncomfortable of pantalones complimented by a long-sleeved white Abercrombie & Fitch shirt featuring blue writing of the store name. As we sat about the birthday cake, I happily accepted my piece, very well knowing where it would go after I arrived to home. It would go from my stomach to the toilet. At this point, I was vomiting not, so it would leave my body by way of laxative abuse. See, this is why I gained so much weight in the early years of bulimia. For purging, I overdosed on laxatives after the binge, often consuming eight hours for the laxatives to perform. Calories were absorbed before the laxatives could work their magic. My binges were never planned. My binges began as restrictive "healthy" food days, only turning into full blown binges as the meal / eating period progressed. And even though my binges were planned not, my binges were organised and choreographed as they happened. The purging, in the early years, however, was chaotic. Never anticipating a binge, as they crept up on me, I was never prepared with my laxatives. So between the time of bingeing and laxative activation, my body absorbed too many calories, causing rapid weight gain. In later years, vomiting helped the efficiency of my bulimic work.

As I took the first delicious bite of my grandfather's birthday cake, he obviously assessed my body and very apparent rapid one-month gain of weight, and he said, from the head of the table, in his Italian accent, rubbing his chin, implying that my face had gotten chubby, "You look-a-healthy, Bella."

I wanted to disappear.

He meant this stated observation, as a compliment. He was happy to see that his granddaughter no longer looked like a skeleton. But, to me, it was a declaration of, announcement of, my failure.

Of my imperfection.

I immediately stopped eating his cake.

For the remaining months of my senior year of high school, I worked hard to stop my bulimia. Throwing myself back into exercise and "nutritional awareness," the food binges happened every few days versus daily. They were mild binges. I developed a habit of shopping at GNC, where, at the time, I could score things like "soy nut butter" and "pine nuts." Grocery stores in Moon Township, Pennsylvania offered not a "health food section" in 1999. I wanted to eat "healthfully," this time, and from what I had read, my restrictive diet of my six-month anorexic period was culprit to the eventual binge. I thusly needed to eat nourishing things. I needed protein. GNC is also where I discovered Hydroxycut and Ephedrine, two then-over-the-counter drugs to speed heart rate and therefore supposedly metabolism. Of course I became an addict.

I was cold, all of the time, and I slept away my senior year of high school in Dr. Phil's planetarium. He was a kind teacher whom I knew only in passing, but somehow, and I remember not of how, I converted all of my gym classes and lunches and non-necessary elective periods into "study halls," so, during my unregistered "study hall" free time, I slept in Dr. Phil's planetarium. It made me feel like I was living in another world. In outer space. On my "home planet" of Pluto! I wonder, how on Earth did I "graduate?" This daytime sleeping, accordingly, enabled me to work hard at nighttime at Wendy's Old-Fashioned Hamburgers and to exercise even harder before school or after my work shift. Because I had energy. Nowadays, such a napping planetarium arrangement could never be accomplished, as security and accountability at schools is so very tight. I fitted into that last leg of untracked humans on school campuses. I felt like a zombie during that year of school. I learnt nothing and passed through time like a ghost. The other thing that I would do: drop off my little sisters in the morning, leaving for a day of driving around the city of Pittsburgh, gazing at skyscrapers in downtown and admiring beautiful homes in Sewickley Heights, pining for the day of when I could afford it all, pining for the day of when I could afford to live in a skyscraper and to buy a house in the richest, most beautiful, old-money town in Pittsburgh, the one in which my great-grandmother had been a hard worker and queen. The only problem with this activity is that my newly established excessive absences had been detected, and my mother was therefore notified. My driving privileges were immediately revised at that point. I had never missed a day of school from Kindergarten until then at twelfth grade except for when I had the chicken pox in third grade, and that was a major blow because I was forecasted to be the grade champion for perfect recitation of my math times tables. But, due to missing class, due to being unavailable to compete, I lost the competition to a boy named Jonathan. I stayed MAD about that loss for so long! In fact, as I type this, I realise that twenty-eight years later, I am still bitter about losing! It taught me never to get sick again. It is proof that the weak always lose. Also, I missed a week of school in second grade for our divine family vacation to Florida.

I dated not. I partied not. I took drugs not (other than those which I thought influenced weight loss such as Hydroxycut, Ephedrine, and laxatives - and those which aided in my 1999 sleep when undernourished such as NyQuil). I simply existed like the robot that I loved to be. Work to me was fun, even at smelly Wendy's Old-Fashioned Hamburgers. I made the work experience into a beautiful art. At high school graduation, I weighed 112 pounds. Fit as a fiddle, or so I considered myself to be, I was super excited to start college and to find a sophisticated boyfriend to marry. And throughout the summer, before jetting off to college, I worked at a new, most wonderful job.

Resigning from my beloved post as drive-thru girl at Wendy's Old-Fashioned Hamburgers in May of 2000, I now worked as the front desk girl at the Best Western Airport Inn and Suites. Like my prior work arrangement, I loved this new job tremendously! And like the strong girl that I am, every time that I asked for a well earned raise, I received it. There was no need to march in a circle for it. Working for very good people, an Indian family with the name of Patel, as I always do when I meet humans of a different culture, I took upon the charge of learning the general salutations in their native language, in this case being Gujarat, earning respect of the elders. "Kamcho! Majama?" These people, these Indians, these hard-working LEGAL immigrants, made me feel like a part of their family. They made me feel loved and appreciated when I otherwise felt judged and rejected by everyone else in my life because of my eating disorder.

In late August of 2000, I went away to college.

And I gained The Freshman 69.

CHAPTER
VII

THE FRESHMAN 69

MOST COLLEGE KIDS gain the Freshman 15.

I gained The Freshman 69.

Of course I did.

That is my all or nothing personality.

The story of my life!

Back then, exerting the energies of my all or nothing reality in a harmful manner, I experienced so many highs and lows during that fall semester of college in the year of 2000, my eating disorder serving as percussion to it all. Everything that happened in my life at Westminster College in beautiful Amish country of New Wilmington, Pennsylvania happened with that dark cloud of the eating disorder presiding above. I shall herein recount a few of those "ALL OR NOTHING" items.

1.   My friendship with Julie.

Julie was my first friend away from home. She was my best friend for a long time. When I reminisce of our time together, I consider her as a forever piece of my heart. I hope that Julie will read this book, if only just this paragraph, because she was a REAL FRIEND of a lifetime, and I want for her to know that I am grateful for our memories. Sticking by my side during and after our first semester of freshman year, she was patient with me and kind to me, inviting me to sorority parties after I abandoned the traditional college lifestyle; inviting me to attend peaceful, heart-swelling Sunday dinners with her amazing, warm family in Hermitage, Pennsylvania; giving to me the privilege to be her maid of honour in 2006; and, sharing time together with our dogs for her birthday in 2009. But when 2011 arrived, having consistently cycled in and out of Julie's life for eleven years, always disappearing and hiding my body during fat bulimic periods, I royally screwed up, making myself unavailable during her first pregnancy, during a time that she needed my friendship and care. At the time, writing about my dislike of my then former bulimic fat at my blog, I gave Julie the impression that I disliked all bigger bodies, and she took this to include her pregnant body, thinking that this is why I stayed away from her. The real reason for my ghosting is that I was hiding my body because I had returned to bingeing on food and was embarrassed about how my body looked. I was embarrassed to admit to her that I had failed again, having gained weight. Despite living for one year as bulimic free, and despite writing about my "former" eating disorder at my new, fresh blog (www.theyogaballerina.com), I was back to ground zero. I refused to admit my failure to Julie. I had once again failed at finding correction to my eating disorder which had existed for all of our friendship. I am so sorry to Julie for being absent during her pregnancy. I am so sorry that she doubted my complete admiration of her beautiful body and ability to create and nourish a life, doubt which is completely justified by how I came across at my blog and by my unexplained absence from her life. I am so sorry for taking her on the eating disorder roller coaster with me. She deserved so much better. She deserved a friend who was all in. My heart was always ALL IN, yes. I truly loved her and still do, but my absence indicated otherwise. Julie hung with me, during my "all or nothing" periods, for greater than one decade, for longer than any friend of my life at that point thus far. And I am truly sorry that I allowed for our special friendship to fall apart. Julie is a heart of gold with the prettiest smile. A few years later, my friend Jillian lived the same role as Julie insomuch that when she needed me, after years of divine cocktails and movie nights and "extravaganzas," I was unavailable. And, like with Julie, Jillian's amazing family took me in, inviting me to parties and family functions. In 2008, Aimee came into the picture. But when she started her juicing business in 2012, I was an unsupportive bitch who fell off of the face of the Earth. How could I show enthusiasm at a juice bar as a fat girl? I bumped into her, several months and many pounds later in 2013. After spending so much time together, it was like bumping into a stranger. It was heartbreaking! And it seems, in retrospect, with Julie and Jillian that I was constantly seeking peaceful love from a "family" because my own family saw me as incorrect because of my eating disorder. I wanted to be seen as correct. And with Aimee, my great-grandmother had her last name, so we lived like "cousins" and that fact about being cousins made me feel loved and accepted by "family." To Julie, Jillian, and Aimee - thank you for the good times that we shared.

2. My biological family.

With my biological family, during this first semester of schooling, I was completely off. Constantly worrying about her little girl, because of the separation factor but also because of the eating disorder factor, my mother sent to me the loveliest of Hallmark greeting cards, telling me of how much she missed me, telling me of how my absence left a hole in her heart, yet I pushed her away because I was so embarrassed of my fat and of how I looked. I was so embarrassed of my failure to control food and to stay thin. My dear sister Stephanie who also sent cards to me, was pushed away, too. My darling paternal grandmother who visited me on weekends, buying for me delicious cranberry muffins at Eat 'n Park, unaware that they were like crack to me, propelling me into a day of food bingeing and purging after her departure, stopped receiving invitations for weekend visitations when I became huge. When I became huge, I disconnected from everyone. Always.

3. Film.

My love for filmography was then blossoming. Actually, it went straight from nothing to everything. All or nothing, indeed! That is me! I recall watching *Love & Basketball* every single day in the dormitory after being introduced by a fellow bulimic named Kate, my viewings accompanied at first by friends, but as the semester progressed, accompanied by piping hot oatmeal decorated with plump cranberries and raisins plus fat free yoghurt followed by pizza and cans of tuna fish and jarred peaches and *Peanut Butter Cap'n Crunch* etcetera in grand excess of volume. My binges always started off with "healthy" food, and then I ate ALL OF THE HEALTHY FOOD, and then I went to town on all of the naughty stuff. All in a few hours of time. My film viewing friends were completely replaced with food.

4. My studies.

There was no ALL about this factor. It was completely NOTHING. I studied not. I skipped so many classes. My ALL which should have been invested into studies based on the fact that my parents and I were paying for it, funnelled directly into two other specific departments: My eating disorder. And men.

5. Other than being at war with food 24x7, I was on the husband hunt 24x7.

My first kiss happened on a park bench by the lake at my school. I decided on Michael B for my kissing partner, and I thusly went to work on attracting him. I was more focused on earning his kiss than with earning good grades because with earning Michael B's attention, I was challenged. School offered not the same challenge as catching a high quality man did. Mind you, I had no physical urge to kiss another; in fact, in the 1980s, knowing that I would be strict in my interaction with the opposite sex, I made a hand-written contract with my Polish grandfather, confirming that if I were ever to kiss a boy, then I would owe to him dollars of five. And I refused to lose! As *Trump: The Game* proclaims, in life, the only option is to win! So I went straight through all of my pre-college schooling without kissing experiences, because, firstly, I had no urge to kiss, but, secondly, I refused to lose. But now, in college, I decided that I had won the bet as the opposite sex was no longer regarded as a population of "boys" as was the language used in my no kissing contract with my grandfather, as I now considered them to be "men" due to their age. Nowadays, they would be labeled as "guys" because a "man" is one who earns the title, example of a man being President Trump. Additionally, I wanted to be admired like a goddess by a man, and I wanted to seduce this specific Michael B, showing to him my gratitude for his admiration, with my lips. Everyone else was doing it, so naturally I must experience kissing, too, to be normal, I thought. After living for one-and-a-half years with an eating disorder, I would pour my all into finding a perfect boyfriend for the purpose of marriage. To be under the watch of a sophisticated man meant that I could be eating disordered not, I thought.

I remember nothing of the details of the pre-kiss conversation, but I do remember wearing my very sexy, extra-tight leopard-print slacks by Wet Seal. Dressed like a sexy little wild thing, intending to seduce my strong, tall, handsome company, I knew that my first kiss was on the verge of happening. And, as predicted, in the middle of conversation, his face raced toward mine, as though it belonged to a goblin! It was a pointless union of mouths. Pretending to enjoy the experience, I remember feeling as though I had truly won a challenge, that I had earned the right to be kissed and touched by the sexiest, tallest, smartest man in school, and that I had trumped the other pretty girls in this activity as related to Michael B.

After this awkward rendezvous with Michael B, I associated with a few other guys during that first semester, specifically with footballers. I have always preferred men who are much taller and larger than I am. And because I am naive, I know not if it was a trend ongoing since the Bill and Monica scandal of a few years earlier, or if this activity happens at college environments at anytime in history, but oral sex was all the rage. And I was blown away, pun intended, to learn of this activity in conversations with my girlfriends. Heck, I had just experienced my first kiss! It surprised my mind to learn that fellatio was a formal activity and that girls were literally putting you-know-whats into their mouths like it was their job. Again, "job" herein used as a pun. When a girlfriend explained this job to me, I was speechless. Akinyele's song, *Put It In Your Mouth*, which I had downloaded on Napster a few weeks prior, suddenly made sense.

We were all putting it in our mouths that semester.

My friends were stuffing theirs in acts of sex.

And I was stuffing mine with food.

I had started bingeing and purging again, thusly a growing kissing partner to Curtis. Curtis and I connected sometime after Michael B. I must have had a very amazing, sparkling personality for Curtis to spend so much time with me, as I never attended his football games, and I was quickly gaining the bulimic chub of a lifetime. On game days, rather than watching him play, I darted to the local Walmart using my roommate's car to buy yoghurts, oatmeal, and "healthy" things, only becoming so frustrated on the return drive to campus that I consumed everything during my drive except for the oatmeal because that required hot water but I prepared and ate that immediately upon landing in the dormitory, and then I used my meal ticket at the campus cafeteria, plus would venture to the little Amish grocery store for a box of *Peanut Butter Cap'n Crunch*, Hostess *Zingers* (the raspberry ones), pecan muffins, and laxatives. What truly makes me cringe is the memory of the obsession not and of the calories not and of the isolation not and of the weight gain not. It is the memory of the constant withdraw of money from my bank account, with the balance quickly zooming toward zero. Money that my parents deposited into a special account for emergencies was being stuffed into my mouth.

The year was 2000, and it was easy to hide purchases from your parents because everything happened in cash. It was also easy to hide your bulimic face and fluctuating body from the family when away at school. This was before video call and text pictures. This was before Facebook. Yes, we all had email, AOL, and AIM messenger (my beloved chat name, Fraggle15, rest in peace!), but such mediums reveal not of the body if one chooses to hide from the camera. I was very good at hiding my body. My mother had last seen me at about 117 pounds in the beginning of September (I estimate this date - it might have been at about 135 pounds in the beginning of October). Now, in early November, I weighed 155 pounds.

The Freshman 43.

My beautiful mother arrived to fetch chubby Nicole on election day morning, as I had intentionally ignored my absentee ballot because Bush and Gore appealed to me not, but she insisted that I vote in my first of-voting-age presidential election.

"You need new clothes. You've gained weight." my mother said as her greeting when we reunited in the parking lot of my dormitory on election day

Tuesday. Her statement carried with it the reality of disappointment, shock, and bewilderment. This was how I interpreted her inspection of me, at the scene.

No f*cking shit, I need new f*cking clothes. I'm a fat mother f*cker, and I f*cked up again. I'm f*cking angry and I'm f*cking starving myself starting f*cking right now.

I thought these things, with intense anger!

I was so MAD at myself for failing and for disappointing her that we spoke not on the entire drive to home. And, actually, I WAS wearing new clothes, khaki pants and an orange wool sweater by Abercrombie & Fitch, new clothes that I had recently purchased from a small mall in Ohio because I WANTED to lose ten pounds quickly and to fit into them. Fat clothes for my former 112-pound self. Skinny clothes for my then 155-pound self. Goal clothes for my growing, FAT, bulimic body.

Two months. 43 pounds.

That is a lot of weight to gain so quickly.

And although I was so angry at my mother's verbalisation of the elephant in the room, although I was so mad at myself for disappointing her, I would have rejected any coddling that she might have offered, thusly her straightforward, rational approach was the best way that she could have addressed the subject, for me, at that time, during my intense period of anger. And angry I was! When you are so filled with hatred for your failure at controlling your food and therefore weight, you can be nothing but angry. I saw the human body as the most intimate, closest, proximate, natural thing to control in life. I had control over everything else. Why not of my vessel?

That night, at home, in the suburbs of Pittsburgh, abandoning my declared starvation plan, I ate so much food. Kraft *Mac & Cheese*. Cake. Cookies. Jars of white buttercream icing. I basically ate the entire house. And when my family commented on my ox-like eating behaviour, I locked myself into the bathroom, pretending to vomit. At that point in my eating disorder history, behaving as just a laxative-abusing bulimic, I wanted for my little sisters to think that I was the real bulimic deal, the one that included vomiting. So I made vomit sounds, pretending to be purging through my mouth. I wanted for them to think that I was a strong bulimic. I wanted for them to think that retaining the garbage that I had ingested was out of the question. Returning to college on the next morning, I felt like the world was happening without me, that I was a separate unit from it all, that I was alone with no support or love. Everyone was glued to their televisions, awaiting a Florida recount. And I was glued to food. I would next see my family at Thanksgiving when I weighed 161 pounds. In January of 2001, I weighed 181 pounds on a five-foot, three-and-a-half-inch frame. My all time high.

I had achieved The Freshman 69.

At this point, just a few days before returning to school after winter break, I made the firm decision to postpone my return to Westminster College, rather attending the local Robert Morris College, commuting from home. In fact, I threw a temper tantrum, begging for my parents to permit this arrangement. My father said yes. My mother said no. I am so grateful to my father for winning that argument! I suppose that the mirrors at home were more efficient than the mirrors at school, and I could actually see the fat blob into which I had morphed resulting from bingeing and ineffective purging. Laxatives failed to address the food that had absorbed during digestion.

I was the fat bulimic.

Most people just saw a girl who ate too much food who visited the bathroom frequently.

They saw the girl who goes away to college and gets fat.

And it killed me that I could represent not my ideal. It killed me that I could flaunt not a thin *Vogue* body. It was all that I wanted. If only I could achieve that "anorexic" skinny state from my junior year of high school again, then the world would be perfect, I thought. I was grumpy to those around me. I wanted to stare them in the face and scream, "THIS IS NOT ME! THIS IS NOT ME AT MY FINEST! I AM TRYING SO HARD TO FIGURE THIS OUT! TO SOLVE MY PROBLEM! THIS IS WHY I AM NOT GORGEOUS LIKE MY LITTLE SISTERS! THIS IS WHY I CANNOT BE HAPPY! BECAUSE I AM BULIMIC! BECAUSE I AM FAT! I AM WORKING SO HARD TO FIX THIS AND TO BE HEALTHY AGAIN AND TO WRITE A BOOK ABOUT IT!"

I am certain that most humans who suffer from eating disorders do so in silence, and do so looking as "normal" or as "fat." The ones who resemble skeletons are the ones who earn the attention because they wear it like the cover of a book. My book was on the inside. The words. The story. The trauma. Inside of my brain, inside of my heart. Underneath of my skin. And it was killing my spirit slowly.

Freshman year of 2000 - 2001 continued.

After successfully begging my parents to permit school transfer so that I could commute from home during spring of 2001, it was my goal to lose the bulimic weight and to return to Westminster College in the fall, becoming the sorority girl of my dreams, dating the popular football player again, getting married, having children, and being the most perfect housewife on Earth WITHOUT an eating disorder.

But there was work to be done on my body to get there.

Speaking of work, the kind that one does in exchange for money, because I adored doing it, I used this opportunity of living at home to schedule shifts at the hotel where I began working one month prior to high school graduation until late August of 2000 when I left for college weighing 112 pounds. The hotel owner was a very nice Indian man named Alan Patel. A super, great guy. A legal immigrant. And during that summer before college, his legally immigrated family treated me like one of their Indian own, at a time of when my family and I were on the rocks because I felt judged for my fat, for my failure, for my bulimia, so I was combative at home, and therefore home life was a war zone. Coming to work was peaceful. Working made me happy.

Working allowed me to be an artist. To paint my canvas. I swear that I have been so fortunate with the most amazing of work experiences. But, to toot my own horn, one can lead a horse to water, but one cannot make the horse drink the water. I have always invested my ALL into each chosen work experience, making it my one big thing, as it should be. I have always overdosed on the work drug.

I had the work thing going for me.

I just needed to get the food thing controlled.

And then I could meet and marry the man of my dreams!

Now commuting from home to school and working at the hotel again, I hated the former and loved the latter. I despised attending class. Not only did I hate strutting in front of college males with my fat bulimic bottom, squeezed into a girdle so that it could fit into my very large-sized, fat-girl jeans, I also despised taking time away from working, the activity in which I actually earned money for my valuable time and effort. College was just a big waste of my time. I hated my new school of Robert Morris College. I was forced to study things that were giving to me zero return, things that I knew would never make a difference in my adult life. Communications? Hell, my writing style was better than my professors' writing styles. Group projects? Hell, I would immediately tell group members to take a few weeks of siesta. I would do their portions of the assignments because they needed to be done perfectly. I needed to control everything. And to make matters worse, I was paying for these nonsense classes,

BORROWING MONEY, for zero guarantee that they would ever do me any good! It made no sense.

And then I came face to face with my boss Alan Patel, having last seen him at my pre-college weight of 112 pounds. Now stationed at 181 pounds, just five months later, I looked like a different person. Rubbing his face like my Italian grandfather did one month after my entrance into the bulimic world, giving the impression of rubbing lumps of fat, Alan announced, in shock, this time with an Indian accent as compared to my grandfather's Italian accent, "You've gained weight."

F*CK.

The socially proper girl that I am, I simply accepted his commentary and replied, "Yes, I know. I am on a diet." But I really wanted to punch him in the mouth, asking if he ever heard of such a thing as bulimia and the kaleidoscope of calories in and out that painted the days and nights of my chaotic life with food.

Living at home with my parents and with two skinny younger sisters, I submerged myself into the basement bedroom that had been created for me, like an apartment, one to afford me privacy. And honestly, how amazing was it for my parents to make such a place of private comfort for me? But in addition to the constant judgement of my weight, I suspected, at the time, that despite their kindness, everyone thought that I was a loser for "dropping out" of the school away from home. Having a distance from them, albeit under one roof, was a good thing for all.

Working at the hotel and skipping college classes to binge on hot cheesy pizza on the floor of my 1989 Dodge Caravan SE in the construction lot of a future Walmart in Robinson Township, filled much of my time. And to burn those binge calories, I exercised in the middle of the night, wearing shorts because my legs no longer fitted into my exercise pants. I refused to buy bigger ones because I wanted incentive to be thin when the birds began chirping in April. I remember trudging in the blackness, snow falling onto my body, and RUNNING in cold temperatures, on icy ground, around and around and around the neighbourhood, legs freezing, brain ANGRY, working so very hard to shed my body of the Freshman 69. This happened at two o'clock in the morning. It was so dangerous! Now, in reflection, eighteen years later, I am amazed, in one part, of the activities into which I submerged myself, but I am also surprised not and therefore amused, as I am so very black and white.

In the spring of 2001, I met Daryl. I adored him. It was an amazing spring and summer of riding in his blue truck to country fields where we talked about life and kissed. I could have kissed Daryl forever. We met for coffees, we met for dates at my father's workplace as Daryl also worked from this site, we went to Daryl's home to lay in bed together, and we walked about downtown Pittsburgh holding hands and admiring architecture of exquisite churches. It was the perfect first romance for me. I found it exciting to date an older man. He was a tall, handsome, intelligent, sophisticated, entrepreneurial-minded man. He was the perfect man for nineteen-year old Nicole Marie Story.

Why did I end the relationship? I recall feeling suffocated insomuch that he wanted a forever girl. And I knew that I was that forever girl not. I wanted to experience a life of glamour, and he pined for glamour not, in my opinion. I saw him as a man who wanted a wife and child in the quiet country. I wanted to be a housewife with child, yes, but in the glamorous New York! But now, when considering it, I remember the exact moment of when it was over. We attended a Pittsburgh Pirates baseball game, where I would meet his older sister and family for the first time. He brought along for me a large polo shirt to wear over whatever I had chosen for the game. At the time, I had been obsessed with "Express" clothing, so that might help with conjuring an image of what I would naturally wear. A bit racy! He claimed this cover-up shirt was his idea because his sister was "conservative" and "Christian," thusly implying that my clothing choice would register as sister-rejected. I was so embarrassed and ashamed that he disapproved of my choice in fashion, and I honestly thought it was additionally because he wanted to cover my fat, not just my clothing. So I complied. I was physically hot and mentally mad from the big polo shirt and from his obvious judgement for the entirety of that baseball game, but, always socially graceful, I concealed my anger and disappointment. I would, in years later, experience this same scenario with Mr. Bikram on two occasions. We attended a wedding in 2008 for his cousin in Buffalo, and I had worked so hard to pick a perfect dress, spending $369 at BCBG Maxazria, $369 which I charged with no easy way to pay off, and he looked at me, from across the hotel room, after I had dressed, stating, "It's a family wedding." Shocked and horrified, I felt like I had failed. And it happened again at an awards dinner honouring his father's colleague and friend. The year escapes me, but I believe it was also 2008. My outfit, a White House Black Market business skirt and jacket, colour of black and white, bought specifically for this event, again, was an outfit outside of my comfortable price range. He looked at me and said,

"Buzz," implying that I looked like a bumble bee. I was mortified and sad that I had disappointed him. And yes, as I type this, I am amused to know that I once cared about what a man thought of my fashion choice! And that I stayed for the events after being criticised! Nicole Marie Story of today would never find herself in such circumstances.

I told Daryl one night that I could no longer date him, and we both cried. I cried because I knew that I would miss him. I know not of why he cried. I suppose it was because he loved me. He said something about a bird will find its way back, if it is meant to be. I have bumped into Daryl on several occasions during the past eighteen years. Randomly. On the street. It is always so wonderful to see him because I truly did adore and respect him, and during each encounter, I ask myself if I could be that bird. The answer is no. He was the perfect first boyfriend. And now he is happily married with a child in the country. I always want to hug him grandly at our random meetings because he meant so much to me, and I shall always remember his comment on the bird. It was very poetic and kind.

During the next few months, rolling into the autumn of 2001, according to my mother, I caused intense disruption in my family's life because I was combative and loud. I was, indeed, a hot ball of anger, constantly balancing my bingeing on food with exercising and laxative abusing. Hiding in the basement, I watched films to transport me to another place. To another time. Film viewing was my form of escapism from the eating disorder. From my fat. From my food. From my failure. I also enjoyed time with my friend from high school Valerie, developing a crush on her brother. One evening, when Valerie retired to her slumber early, leaving me and her brother in the basement of their home, we did things that young kids do. But, on the next day, when rumours spread that we had engaged in sexual intercourse which was, indeed, Fake News, my friendship with Valerie ended. Her friendship was important to me, as was her family, and our relationship was affected by the eating disorder in many ways. This is why I mention it herein. But to me, in 2019, they no longer exist.

When I remained disgusted with my body in the autumn of 2001, to my heart's chagrin, I chose to cancel my passionately desired return to Westminster College for my sophomore year, rather continuing forward with the local commute to Robert Morris College. But my parents had had enough of my seemingly disruptive company, thusly renting for me an apartment, generously footing the bill until I stopped attending university classes altogether. At that point, I was on my own.

There were a few dates with a few guys, here and there. But nothing special.

My focus was on starving myself, but, each day, when that plan failed, I entered into full throttle binge and purge mode. I remember leaving from my apartment on Moon Clinton Road in Moon Township at 1pm to drive to Krispy Kreme in Cranberry Township where, at the drive-thru, I bought a dozen of donuts, the ones stuffed with white cream and the ones of blueberry and glaze, all eaten to the tune of Fat Joe and Ashanti's *What's Luv* and Nelly's *Dilemma*. To this day, when I hear these songs on the radio, I think of Krispy Kreme donuts. I ate so hard on these donuts, driving another thirty miles to my place of work at the hotel where my shift began at 3pm, and, all night, I ate from the supply of hotel breakfast items: muffins, danishes, oatmeal, etcetera, ordering Italian eggplant parmesan and pizzas delivered when my brain went into super full throttle mode. All of this happened whilst maintaining a perfect composure. I never allowed for my problem to affect my work. And when the work night concluded, I abused laxatives, returning home to my lonely apartment where it all began again on the next day. Starvation plan. Exercising. And then I had lunch. And then I blew it, returning to Krispy Kreme and therefore into the bulimic mud cave.

The date turned to late 2002.

On the cusp of my twenty-first birthday, I met the monster. The ILLEGAL. Who got me pregnant. Who took advantage of my kindness, of my loneliness, of my vulnerability. Who helped to wreck my financial credit. Who helped to wreck my familial relationships. Who is a very bad, bad monster dressed in the skin of a fluffy sheep. Even after it ended, he had the audacity to call my mobile, from time to time, until 2017, pretending to be Microsoft offering to "help" with my computer. I will recognise that voice forever. That disgusting, nasally, ugly, oily voice. That cringe-provoking voice and creepy smile that haunts my mind. I changed my mobile number in 2017, so I have heard from him not, since that last "Microsoft" solicitation except I am very certain that he is one of the hate commenters at my blog. He follows me on Twitter and has hearted a few of my recent posts which surprises me that he can be so stupid given my public denouncement of illegal immigration and my public love and support of President Trump. And of course I am an Apple girl. The Microsoft insinuation makes me hate him, even more.

This is my formal report to President Trump. I am hereby reporting an ILLEGAL. Someone who is living in our great country. ILLEGALLY. It started with a work visa issued for the state of Tennessee. He moved to Pittsburgh,

Pennsylvania, illegally crossing the Tennessee state border. He is still here, in this country, seventeen years later. I am no longer angry and shall report this monster's name not, unless I am required to do so by law. But I simply want for President Trump to know that of all of the great things he is doing, cracking down on illegal immigration, on illegal entry, on expired visas, is the nearest and dearest to my heart because I was so very powerfully affected by the cancer that is the illegal. I am writing about this because although I might come across as a little twit making a big deal out of her first world eating disorder, I want for my readers to know that I did experience deep, real pain. Pain caused by manipulation by an illegal. Pain caused by someone who is reaping benefit from this nation because he feels entitled. Thank you, President Trump, for keeping your campaign promise to fight illegal immigration. We must finish building the wall now. We must deport illegals. We must deport the aliens who overstay on their visas. I think that separation of families at the border is necessary. I feel bad for the children, but their parents brought them here illegally, thusly there is no other option but to hold the children in detention. The United States of America is a sanctuary country not. We have our own problems to fix. We have our own prosperity to achieve. WE ARE NATIONALISTS. If you want to help other countries and you are a citizen of the USA, then do it on your terms, privately. This is also of how I think that Planned Parenthood should be funded. Through private work and donations. It is the job not of our government to take care of people who enter and exist illegally. It is the job not of our government to pay for abortions, of legals and illegals.

My abortion was very sad. I refused to mother a child fathered by an illegal monster. I refused to be pregnant without a comfortable life. I refused to say goodbye to my biological family. Existing in a family where interracial dating and premarital sex was unacceptable, I refused, at the age of twenty-one, to present my family with a monster's child. Additionally, my big thing, at the time, was my eating disorder and finding correction to it, and getting super skinny again. Nothing else compared to that, in my brain, including the action of terminating a pregnancy. I thought not twice about doing it. It was an item on my checklist of Friday, as though it were any old day. It was rational and unemotional. In this present day of 2019, I think that abortions are terrible and nobody should experience them - innocent child or mother. But, for me, at the time, in April of 2003 at the age of twenty-one, impregnated by an illegal monster two months prior, it was my decision, and I think that a woman should have the right to choose. I believe that the government should have zero involvement in the human body. But, additionally, in my current state of life, I consider myself to be pro-life because if I were to become pregnant, abortion would be unacceptable, unless the child were diagnosed with a condition that would make its life difficult, such as brain disease, and or unless it were a resultant of rape. This is why, for the first time in my life, I am proud to be a Republican after years of clinging to the Independent label. President Trump makes me proud to be a Republican. After his term, I shall likely change my party to Independent again, as I shall likely never be able to support another human who will run for the office of President of the United States of America.

Back then, at the age of twenty-one, I paid for my abortion completely on my own. And, to this day, nearly seventeen years later, when I see Planned Parenthood security, I stop to thank them for doing what they do - because it is dangerous. *If These Walls Could Talk* by HBO, despite starring radical crazy Cher, portrays this fact on danger so very powerfully.

A human being begins its first day on Earth when created in the womb. Thusly "birthday" has never meant much to me other than it is the point at which one begins counting its existence on Earth outside of the womb. I think that every day should be celebrated, not just a birthday. And, I really think that age counting should begin from the point of creation. So rather than stating that I am thirty-seven years, five months, and one day on Earth, I should state that I am thirty-eight years, two months, and one day on Earth. And when I became pregnant, resulting from one unprotected sexual experience, my very first experience of intercourse, on my twenty-first birthday on February 9, 2003, when I became so inebriated at the Indian restaurant at which the illegal monster made me celebrate and made me consume alcoholic drink after drink for which I paid with my credit card, that he forced me to touch him with my mouth in the bathroom downstairs, that when we emerged to a snowstorm, I could walk not, I could find my car not because it had been towed, and I needed to withdraw money against my credit card to pay the impound fees, and then I needed to direct the illegal monster to my apartment because he drove my car because I could drive not, due to inebriation, and then on that night, I became pregnant because he took advantage of me, when I was incoherent, I knew that I had no option but to seek an abortion.

Who was that girl?

Why did I become "friends" with this illegal monster? The answer is that my other Indian friends, the real friends, the legal ones, treated me like family when I felt so distant from my own because of the eating disorder. These

Indians were so kind and warm, and I thought that if I were coupled with an Indian male, that I could truly be accepted into the Indian culture and therefore family. I could drink divine chai tea all day with friends, I thought! Also, I had no idea that he was "illegal" throughout most of our relationship and knew not that "illegal" was such a thing. I was so naive! I just assumed that everyone followed the rules on existence. Why did I stay friends with this illegal monster after the sexual assault, pregnancy, and abortion? Why did I give my body to him, after the night of horror? The answer is, back then, he seemed like my only friend. And I rationalised that it was my choice to lose control of my alcohol consumption at my birthday "party" and that he simply wanted me completely and loved me completely thusly he took my body when it was relaxed. Nobody else saw me as beautiful, I thought. Nobody else wanted me, I thought. Nobody else would ever want me again, I thought. So I stayed.

Who was that girl?

I bought the abortion pills from Planned Parenthood on Liberty Avenue in Pittsburgh.

During the pelvic examination, the illegal monster stayed in the room and criticised that I had hairs attached to my private parts which the doctor would abhorrently see. He exclaimed, "Ewww that is so gross. Don't you shave?" I can still here his gross nasally voice saying those exact words. I remember nothing else about that appointment except that my credit card was gold and that I signed a receipt and was given the carbon copy in yellow. It was surreal to me, that such a simple transaction could terminate such a huge ordeal.

I drove my beautiful steel blue-coloured Mitsubishi Eclipse to Cincinnati, Ohio, gasoline for which I paid, where we rented a hotel room for which I paid where I ingested the pills and had my abortion for which I paid. For some reason, the illegal urged me to leave town with him for the procedure. Back then, my innocent mind thought he wanted to go on vacation! In retrospect, I realise that he did this to take me away from my family, in case there had been any complications. The illegal wanted to be released of liability. He wanted to hide. My family, I hope, would have held him as liable.

I remember driving to Pizza Hut whilst he stayed at the hotel to watch television, returning with cheese-stuffed crusted pizzas for which I paid. Because he wanted pizza. I was clearly his servant girl. I remember taking the pills. I remember getting angry with him for telephoning another girl named D. He instructed me to perform oral sex, which I did, as my abortion began happening. He threatened to end our relationship, to seek the company of other girls, if I refused his demand of oral sex. I feel so bad for that little girl who experienced this moment. I feel so very bad for her. That was nearly seventeen years ago, as I am writing this, yet it feels like a nightmare that was impossible of happening in real life.

Who was that girl?

As pains surged to my abdominal region, I rushed myself to the toilet where I began to bleed. The pains furthermore caused me to defecate. I remember feeling embarrassed for having to defecate in front of the illegal. I remember thinking that it was unladylike and would repulse him from wanting me, ever again. And when he acted as "grossed out," I instructed him to leave me alone. After it was finished, I returned to my bed and awoke desiring not to speak. I wanted silence. He called me cold-hearted and said that my attitude had ruined his big, planned surprise. He informed me later that he was planning to take me to a "beautiful" dinner at THE OLIVE GARDEN on the drive home to Pittsburgh. AND I FELT SO BAD. Like I had ruined his big, "divine" surprise. Like I had ruined our "divine" relationship. Like I had bruised his ego. Apologising, I cried. And begged for forgiveness. I begged him to reinstate his "gift" of The Olive Garden! And guess what, he did. And I paid for the meal.

OH MY GOD. Who was that girl?

In the almost one year that I spent being "friends" with the illegal monster, my family spoke to me on the rarity. They knew that the illegal was evil. And they wanted nothing to do with their damaged daughter as it would reflect poorly on them, if others discovered my reality. My family told me that I knew better. To my family, I was an embarrassment. And truly, as it pertains to my behaviours with the illegal, I was.

Four months after the abortion, in August of 2003, the illegal monster asked for me to drive him to Tennessee because, for his birthday, he wanted to see the girl that he loved, the one with an arranged marriage. He wanted to plead with D to end her marital arrangement, to plead with her to marry him. So I drove him to Tennessee. My car. My money. My time. Because I thought that I owed him something! OWED HIM WHAT?! I left them alone in a hotel room for one hour. In fact, he told her that a male friend had driven him to Tennessee. I was so brain-washed. My eyes bug from my head as I type this. And on the twelve-hour drive home to Pittsburgh, I got a speeding ticket. Basically setting my entire life deeper into the hole. Additionally, I want to mention another occasion, it might have been in late 2002 or early 2003 when he insisted that I drive him to a volleyball game in snowy conditions, on a wild day in which the

Pennsylvania Department of Transportation commanded to stay off of the roads, except for in emergencies. After delivering him to the "volleyball game" which I suspected, and still do, was actually a date with another girl, I had a terrible accident, totalling my car. He really was an asshole.

In September of 2003, when I awoke from the nightmare, I remember being at the Starbucks drive-thru, the illegal monster telephoning me, begging that I do something for him. I think it was something to do with co-signing a loan for a car, or for his education. I am unable to recall the specific details because at this point, I was done with him, but I remember my response. I said, firmly, "NO." And I continued, "I know that you're here illegally. I've talked with someone who knows the law." AND HE HUNG UP. It was the last time that I heard from him, for a long time. And then, sometime around 2011, when I started my blog work (www.theyogaballerina.com), the random calls started. And beginning on December 25, 2013, he direct messaged me on Twitter. After ignoring his repeated messages, I replied on June 16, 2014 because I wanted to keep him in my radar, just in case I could use this interaction to get him deported, but eventually, on September 15, 2014, I told him to leave me alone. I finally changed my mobile number in 2017, putting a stop to the telephone calls. And on President Trump's birthday in 2019, as previously stated, the illegal hearted a few of my posts on Twitter. He is an asshole. Yet I blame him not, for anything. I simply hate him for being a very bad person. Humans have no right to take advantage of the United States of America. And males have no right to take advantage of women. But blaming this monster for my former woes is counterproductive. I subscribe to the #MeToo movement not. I think that it is an overused label by angry liberal feminists as a way to condemn white rich Republican men and Bill Cosby. But assaults and rape do happen. I know this first hand. I simply recognise that it happened and hope that my writing about it can help girls to be stronger than I was, and to prevent their own unfortunate experiences. Additionally, for the record, I want to make known that although the illegal monster was, indeed, living here illegally as of our conversation at the Starbucks drive-thru in 2003, I know not if he has arranged for legal living conditions. Perhaps he found his way back to Tennessee and back to India where he devised a legal plan to return to the United States for lawful living. Perhaps he paid back JCPenney for the pants and shirts that I watched him steal. Whatever is the case, I care not. I simply know of how it was, as it pertains to me, at the time of our interaction. And because I know of the pain and damage that this illegal caused to me, I stand firmly with President Trump on his desire to build the wall and to kick illegals the hell out of this country.

During all of this time of my eating disordered life thus far, from February 14, 1999 to September of 2003, I lived consumed by food binges and purges. Gaining weight. Losing weight. Dropping out of university entirely. Having the abortion at age twenty-one. Abandoning over eighty grand in credit card debt, one year later in 2004 at age twenty-two, including a Subaru car loan that I believe the illegal monster opened under my line of credit. Having my own beautiful car repossessed during that same year, I worked "like a dog" to keep my bank account above zero when all of my money continued pouring into my food addiction. My war was a very stupid and expensive one.

But let us please rewind to the point at which I told the illegal monster to go to hell in 2003. In addition to my full-time job at the hotel, I now worked full-time as a service dispatcher for a security company. How did this second job come to be? One day, a large, cocky man named Brett, a hotel guest, asked if I would be interested in working for him. It was actually HIS gorgeous employee who sparked my interest. Her name was Jodi. Thin, beautiful, and watched closely by the men, I knew that if I could be in such a perfect girl's presence that I would be motivated to get thin and to stay thin. So I interviewed for and earned the job which I loved completely! In addition to becoming friends with the technicians who ran the core of the business (Hi, Jim! Hi, Walt!), I LEARNT the technical piece of the work from them. The technical piece is what swooned my brain. These technicians took the careful time to explain things to "uneducated" me, because, unlike my suited male counterparts, I treated these technicians like the humans that they are. I defended them in the office when they were otherwise treated like street rats. They became my allies. And because of these allies, I learnt of how alarm systems communicated to central stations. I learnt of how to protect businesses, people, and assets. I learnt the art of physical security.

When it came time for me to consider other options in the security company, I excelled because I knew the raw piece that makes a sales person a good sales person: I was the girl who knew what the heck we were selling! Surrounded by male bozos who knew not, I was set-up to get ahead except for one caveat: I believed in a contract. I believed that a handshake was a handshake. I believed in telling the truth. I believed that G was G. And, even more importantly, as handshakes no longer occur in this day and age, I believed that what was written must be done. The last real handshake on Earth probably happened when

Donald Trump negotiated air rights above Tiffany & Company with Walter Hoving. He writes about this glorious experience in *The Art of the Deal*.

I said goodbye to the security job in 2010 when I discovered that G meant not G in that world. When I realised that in order to earn a bonus next year, I needed to botch my numbers during the current year because I otherwise always performed perfectly, and in such scenarios of constant perfection, I would never again receive a bonus. The bonus system was rigged. And when I realised that "executives" were incentivised on three-year plans versus on thirty-year plans and that they would live on yachts in a few years because bonuses were their driver, not the well being of the company or its workers or its customers, I needed to go. When I realised that sales representatives were traded between security companies like prostitutes, I needed to go. Besides, this work bored me, and it was just another job holding me over until I could unleash my life's project of this book which you are now reading.

I worked very hard. My days from 2003 to 2005 existed like such: 7am - 5pm security company (salary - no overtime pay for my happily offered extra work), 6pm - 9pm university (I re-enlisted because the company offered full unlimited tuition reimbursement and I still, at that time, saw myself as a loser for having an incomplete formal educational record), 11pm - 6:45am hotel. I worked around the clock, and around the calendar! This was until I quit the hotel for good in late 2005, and I quit university in 2006 when, during my "senior year," the parent company divested its security division for which I worked and therefore canceled unlimited tuition reimbursement which left me in a very bad place because I had failed to pre-approve my prior semester of completed courses, as I had become accustomed to everything being approved and paid for afterward because I always earned As and my courses always complied with the "business nature" requirement thusly I was never rejected, but now I was stuck with a $15,000 bill from Duquesne University for the PRIOR semester of completed classes which I negotiated down to $10,000 concurrently forfeiting all unpaid credits. I paid this bill with money that my paternal grandfather had kindly loaned to me. And, despite having a canceled class registration card for the now current semester (I was permitted to schedule for the new semester despite having unpaid credits from the prior semester because, like President Trump, I am very good at getting what I want), I continued attending ONE class despite getting "kicked out" of college. *Introduction to Entrepreneurial Studies* by the great late Ron Morris. It was THIS CLASS that changed my life. I often bumped into this incredible man, years after the class, and he would always exclaim, "Ah! My one student who came to every class but never got a grade! I never understood of what happened there!" And, in reply, I always giggled. My giggles were all that he needed. I got the vibe that he knew that I was crazy wild for hard work like he was, and that I considered university schooling, in most cases, to be hogwash. If only he knew of the great impact that he brought to my life! I remember day one of his class like yesterday: he walked into that room, at 6pm on the dot on a Wednesday night, dressed in a three piece suit, long hair, and a rubber band secured about his wrist. And I absorbed his every word and every ray of energy like a sponge! *What? What do you mean you've worked for yourself and only for yourself for the past twenty years? What? You grew a huge company and lost it all due to a gambling problem, and this is why you wear a rubber band on your wrist because it stops you from succumbing to a gambling binge? What? You couldn't make pay roll and lived in your car? But you started again from scratch and made several successful businesses? And you recently found your beloved soulmate at this later stage in life? I want to do this, too!*

Ron Morris was an EXCEPTIONAL man.

Several years went by, and, sadly, in 2012, I discovered that Ron Morris had passed away, literally two weeks prior to my decision to then google him. Learning of his death prompted me to listen to every single one of his The American Entrepreneur podcasts, remembering that during my time in class with him, he was dreaming of this "podcast" idea before podcast was a household name. Incredible mind. Incredible man. Thank you, Ron Morris, for inspiring me to live. Thank you, Ron Morris, for shining your light onto this world. Also, thank you, for telling me that it made sense that I lived in Sewickley. Oh you had us both in stitches, on that fine night of class! Ha ha ha!

And, just a tad bit of clarification on my statement about earning only As at university. I also earned Ws. Withdrawals. When I realised that I hated a class, I stopped attending. And I accordingly earned an F. At semester conclusion, I refused to pay the tuition for these abandoned classes, rather pulling the "eating disorder / mental illness" card even though I did not (and do not) consider my disorder to be a mental illness. By pulling the mental illness card, however, I could convert the F to a W, leaving my GPA as un-compromised, leaving me without a bill for something that would never serve me in the long scheme of life. I was lying not, because in head doctor world, eating disorders are, indeed, classified as clinical mental illness. Agreeing with the label to claim it, was required not.

Throughout all of this, until 2010, I remained as a bulimic. I worked VERY hard. I played VERY hard. And I dated VERY hard. I "met" Mr. Bikram in 2004 but we never had a committed, functional, romantic relationship. Although many factors played into this reality, I ultimately accept responsibility for this fact of relationship failure. I had something significant that troubled me, even more so than the eating disorder, but something directly related to the eating disorder. I shall discuss this something in the next two chapters and in chapter fourteen. And, truly, of all of the men that have been in my life, Mr. Bikram is the great one thus far. He is the only one that mattered so much that I would have considered marriage. I loved him from our very first interaction simply because it seemed right. It still does seem right. I can go for years without seeing him after dashing off in one of my "pouting storms" as he likes to call it, or when I choose to disengage for the sake of "avoiding confrontation and argument" as I like to call it, and we reunite, as though only a day has passed. He makes me feel safe. And pretty. And smart. He has wanted my body at every size. And my dog loves him even though he is a jerk to her. I say this in all fondness because by jerk, I mean that he makes fun of her and calls her ugly. "She's so ugly that she's cute," he likes to say. He is a very good man. My future gentleman is the only man that I shall ever love more than I do Mr. Bikram.

CHAPTER
VIII

MR. BIKRAM

It is necessary and appropriate to dedicate one complete chapter to Mr. Bikram. He is my first love. He is my only love thus far in thirty-seven years of life. The only man that I shall ever love more than I do Mr. Bikram is my future gentleman who shall resemble a heroic figure of an Ayn Rand novel. Mr. Bikram shall always be in my life, and I shall always love him. But I shall never again give my heart to him. Although we had many happy times together, for me, it was mostly a war, running alongside my war with food.

Mr. Bikram was everything that a young Nicole Marie Story wanted: handsome, charming, affluent, funny, book smart, street smart, kind, Republican, older, Italian, and from a very good, respected family. As stated through earlier sections of this book, younger Nicole Marie Story thought that if I could earn the love of such a great, powerful man, then I could live in comfort as a housewife, abandoning the bulimic lifestyle because a perfect housewife could be bulimic not, I rationalised. To be under the radar of a powerful man would be my solution to failing thus far at life. This was my interpretation of my life thus far: that it had been a failure because I was bulimic, uneducated, and poor. Thusly, I charged myself with finding the perfect man. I knew that I could be a perfect wife, and I thought that being a perfect wife would be my answer to climbing out of my ugly hole. But the moment that I met Mr. Bikram, I knew that it would be impossible to sink my calculating clutches into him. He fitted the bill on everything that I wanted. But something else existed, something unplanned. That something was that I loved him. I loved him from that very first email. And because I was such a self-interpreted wretched person because of the bulimia and other self-perceived shortfalls, I thought that in order to earn his love, I needed to correct myself. Thrown from the window was my plan to first correct myself with a husband. Now I needed to correct myself for the desired husband. Everything was about fixing and correcting. I was obsessed with keeping him in my life for long enough to present myself, with a perfect body, on a silver platter for him to consume, to enjoy, and to love. I made a wreckage of this relationship from the moment that it started.

We met on match.com in December of 2004. This was before online dating was the normal. This was before swiping left and right to find one's match was a thing. This was when online dating was considered as inorganic. Online dating was for the weird. For the social rejections. Such was the case not with Mr. Bikram. He was la crème de la crème. And I enjoyed the online dating platform because in a world of where my weight constantly fluctuated in response to bulimic behaviours, I could hide behind a skinny profile picture of my August of 1999 or January of 2004 self, searching for my perfect man.

His first email to me read something about the moon and the stars. He later claimed that my dating screen name of PinkHearts1982 elicited such chosen prose. The email rendered me as putty in his typing fingertips. It was poetic. Kind. Mysterious. And sexy. This was six years before I read *Atlas Shrugged* for the first time, so although I would later compare him to the character of Fransico d'Anconia, at that point, he was my Tom Hanks of *You've Got Mail*. He even had a dog like did the character played by Tom Hanks. In fact, the first photograph that I ever viewed of Mr. Bikram was of he and a Labrador Retriever puppy, Mr. Bikram playfully gnawing on its ear. I was completely enamoured. I knew nothing of dogs, but something about his apparent love for this hairy creature made my heart smile. Refusing to meet with him in person, however, because I looked nothing like my skinny profile picture, I sat behind the computer screen with a big bottom and thick tire about my waist, using written prose to communicate. Despite my refusal to meet in the flesh, he continued emailing, as he seemed to genuinely like me for my raw and honest company. He seemed to like me for my words.

Corresponding daily in late 2004 through early 2005, we finally agreed to meet "offline." Despite my continuance of existing in a vessel of a fat bulimic blob, our meeting happened on May 18, 2005. And despite our daily correspondence, I knew nothing personal about Mr. Bikram aside from his formal profession of lawyer. I knew his last name not. I knew his exact disposition in the world not. And I cared to know not. It never occurred to me to ask for his personal information. I assumed that we would discuss such things on our first date. Trusting him from the get go, I knew that he was a lawyer by day who wrote captivating emails to PinkHearts1982 by night. That was enough. I enjoyed him. I trusted him. I was head over heels in love with him. After exchanging telephone numbers, migrating the conversation to text message format, I once asked him, around the 3am hour, "Do you ever sleep?" He replied with, "Want to come over and see?" It was an absolute turn on.

We arranged to meet for our first date. It would happen after my evening class at Duquesne University. Meeting time would be at 8:30pm at the school, and he would take me to dinner. Dressed in an obnoxious, shiny, pink poodle skirt, white blazer, and dark-pink, silk camisole by Banana Republic, complimented by chunky heels by Laundry and tan pantyhose with a built-in girdle, I was a fashion nightmare. My hair was really big, too, in a way that looked like it could house a bird's nest, as he often joked in the months to come. I thought that I looked pretty, bulimic fat aside. What was Mr. Bikram thinking? Why would he continue forward on this date after consuming the visual of this hot mess? Was he truly that intrigued with my personality to overlook my physical presentation? I was such a little girl. My age, twenty-three. He, thirty-six.

Lifting myself into his shiny Infinity SUV as though I had known him for years, I might as well had been securing myself into a space rocket blasting off to the moon because my head immediately filled with stars. He chivalrously closed the passenger door, returning to the driver's side from where he navigated to Opus, a restaurant located within The Renaissance Hotel of Pittsburgh. I can remember not of the car ride conversation and wonder if he does. It was my first ever downtown date, and I was glamorised. The skyscrapers. His fancy car. His suit. His tie. His spectacles. His sophisticated grammar. Offering his last name to the hostess, I heard his perfect name for the first time, and it seemed so very powerful. It took away my breath.

BIKRAM.

We enjoyed delicious, beautiful red wine from the most sturdy of wineglasses that I had ever touched in my twenty-three-year life thus far. I ordered "filet" because I thought that it meant "filet o' fish" (oh thank you McDonalds and my then unsophistication!). Having behaved as a pescatarian since 1999, imagine of how I handled that big, juicy, hunk of flesh on my plate! Well, because I REALLY wanted for this relationship to morph into something beautiful, and because I have always behaved as socially graceful, I ATE THE BLOODY FILET. It is humorous, in retrospect, to know that I compromised my value system and strict rules to impress a man. It also is humorous to know that I nourished so plentifully on a date. In front of a man! AND, AGAIN, THAT I ATE MEAT!

After dinner, he transported me to my parked car at Duquesne University, but before I departed from his vehicle, we "parked." Gifting me with a pair of green block shoes by Steve Madden, he made me feel like Carrie Bradshaw of

Sex and the City, so I behaved like would Carrie Bradshaw with Mr. Big. I slept with him not. But the current me would never behave as I did, on that first date. But, here is the weird unknown: if the current me were to have a first date WITH MR. BIKRAM, perhaps I would behave as I did. That is the thing: Mr. Bikram has always seemed to have this power of making me throw out my rules. And for anyone who knows me, it is understood and accepted that I am rigid and rule-governed. I suppose that Dagny Taggart of *Atlas Shrugged* felt this way as a seventeen-year old in the forest with Francisco d'Anconia. One thing is for certain is that nowadays, I would have smiled and asked, "Steve Madden? Oh, let me please teach to you about shoes!" Yes, I am a Tamara Mellon kind of girl, but, back then, the Steve Maddens were great and incredibly thoughtful. I know that Mr. Bikram is smirking at this comment, as he reads it, and of anything else that I have written in this book, the first thing that he will ask me, if and when we ever speak again is, "So, what was wrong with the shoes?"

On the next day, at work, I told a great story to my colleagues of this perfect first date. Excluding the information about "parking" and filet consumption, I discussed the skyscrapers and red wine, labelling this as the most wonderful date of my life thus far. Mr. Bikram's last name was immediately recognised by a coworker as belonging to a prominent family of Pittsburgh, and I immediately became obsessed with earning this man's love. It would be a challenge for me to correct my problems and to compel such a high quality man to accept a girl with a "history," with a "past." I always needed a challenge. And I truly wanted for this man to be my husband with all of my soul. Sadly, I would discover about myself twelve years later, that I thought of myself as undeserving of his love, because, for the past six years, from 1999 to 2005, because of the bulimia, I had been treated like a junkie by those closest to me and I therefore truly thought that I had a "history" and a "past" to correct because of how those closest to me made me feel. They made me feel like I was unworthy of trust. Of love. Of companionship with a good man like Mr. Bikram. Perhaps my family can offer a more compassionate account of this moment in time, but this is my interpretation of what I experienced. And my reaction to their reaction affected every relationship that I had, especially with Mr. Bikram as he would need the girl that he could trust with his everything. Because he had so much. Not just wealth. But a good family. A reputation. Friends. A real heart. And a bad girl with a "past" was unworthy of and unfitting of his world. There are many bad girls with ulterior motives, especially those who want a sugar daddy, and although I knew that I was a good lady, although I knew, completely, that I would give my all to him because I felt a true connection to him as though I had known him forever, I felt, at that moment, that I was undeserving of him. This intense guard was unrealised for another twelve years. My work at the blog, inspired by Gary Vaynerchuk, helped me to arrive at this realisation. My work at the blog made me determine that I am so very worthy of love and of trust, and I always have been worthy of such (www.theyogaballerina.com).

Our second date happened at Mr. Bikram's house. We watched *Batman and Robin* (1960s), drank red wine, and ventured upstairs to his bedroom. Mind you, he, on this night, would be my fourth time since the abortion. The second time happened with Joshua O. Joshua O and I met on the Pennsylvania Turnpike, in September of 2003, on the day after I told the illegal monster to go to hell. Cruising along in my 2003 Mitsubishi Eclipse, driving from Pennsylvania to Michigan because I wanted to buy a Tiffany & Co. bracelet from the same shop that my thin and beautiful coworker Jodie had purchased hers (or so I had thought that she had purchased hers in Michigan, therefore this purchase location may or may not be accurate), a present to myself to celebrate the end of my "friendship" with / freedom from the illegal, I caught the attention of Joshua O. One thing led to another during our game of highway flirtation, and he followed me to a rest station somewhere in Ohio, informing that he was traveling to Minneapolis but planned to celebrate that night with old college friends in Chicago, inviting for me to join his crew. So I did. Then aged twenty-one, with not a cent to my name despite years of hard work, scrapping my plans for Michigan, I followed Joshua O, a stranger on the turnpike, to his friends' condominium in Chicago. We had a fun night of partying followed by physical intimacy on the sofa. He and I remained as friends until he became married and his wife reportedly banned our friendship. He was my second time. After Joshua O, I played, just once, with the very tall, very blonde, very rugged, slightly older construction worker who stayed at the hotel at which I worked. It was very secretive. Very fast. Very naughty. I walked into his room, during my work shift. He sat on the sofa, waiting for me, his manhood extending like a skyscraper. I met his fiancé on the following weekend, and she was lovely. I knew not of his engagement until that moment and I therefore refused to meet with him again despite his urgings. Also, as a side note, this was the only time in my life that I actually looked at a male organ in the flesh. On my other meetings, I closed my eyes. His manhood was so perfect, and I never wanted to disappoint myself after that viewing. Next I met Lucas and Jason on match.com. Lucas visited at my

Sewickley apartment several times, and we kissed. Jason took me to a fun baseball game, and we became lifelong friends. In fact, still a college student at the time, Jason overextended himself to buy expensive tickets for the *Lexus Club* at PNC Park, tickets that I knew existed outside of his comfortable price range, but I had emailed to him a few months beforehand declaring that dating a poor college student was unacceptable for me. I was such a bitch back then. But I was so drawn to Jason and to his good looks and kindness, and somehow, by the grace of whatever, he gave to me a second chance, one that turned into a lifelong friendship. After that baseball game, I threw myself at him, and he rejected me, telling me that our first date was the incorrect time for sex. Back, then, in late summer of 2004, at the age of twenty-two, I was convinced that sex was required of me. I was so embarrassed by his rejection of me, but I was also so grateful. Despite he being a Democrat, ha ha, we shall be great friends forever. Well, he might actually be an Independent, but he definitely leans left! We have never talked about that first date, and, for that, I am grateful. He is a true gentleman. I had the great privilege of being his neighbour for a few years. And, I introduced him to his beautiful rescue greyhound girls Mega and Wunder. The team of Jason, Mega, and Wunder babysat my baby Gwendolyn one night in 2014 when I attended a baseball game with my dear friend Sheila. Hilariously, on that night, Gwendolyn discovered a package of hamburger buns that had been thrusted behind Jason's recliner chair! A package of buns that his sweet greyhound girls never detected. Of course Gwendolyn noticed. She is a food hound! She is my little Inspector Gwendolyn! She and I cherish Jason and his greyhound girls forever.

Meeting Mr. Bikram in 2005 came after Michael B, Curtis, Daryl, the illegal monster, Joshua O, the engaged construction worker, Lucas, and Jason. As I had only slept with three of the afore-listed, Mr. Bikram would be my fourth time but my first real lover. Being with Mr. Bikram made me feel so happy.

And then came the roller coaster.

Unable to articulate my feelings for Mr. Bikram, I was dually unable to accept that he seemingly rejected the notion of a public relationship with me (because I saw myself as unworthy for such a great man and that he would be embarrassed by me), so I let the relationship happen without structure. Without form. I lived in fear and in jealousy. I always feared that he was dating other girls. On a handful of weekdays, I drove to his house at 4am for running and sex, primping at his house and zooming to work by 7am. And this was a hike, as he lived across town. Who was that girl who DROVE TO A MAN?! We rarely spent days or evenings or weekends together, so after he once asked me to use spermicide after sexual intercourse, removing this tampon-like looking contraption from an open box, I became curious as to why he had a closet containing this product and went investigating. Finding a second profile of his at an adult dating site, and another at OkCupid, my careless heart closed. I became obsessed and even registered him at DontDateHimGirl.com, calling him dirty and used. And then, one day, in 2005, driving across the Sewickley bridge, talking to him on the telephone as rain poured, making the scene very 1940s film noir-like, I asked about what we were doing. He replied, "I just don't see myself marrying someone thirteen years my junior." It literally broke. my. heart.

So I went on a dating binge.

For the next eight years.

To get back at him. To make him jealous. Everything was done to hurt the man that hurt me. In retrospect, the "man that hurt me" was all in my head, as he was intending to hurt me not. I created this war, I created this "hurt," all because I was unable to open my heart in a healthy manner. I went on this dating binge, in full force. I remember all of the dates not, and I remember all of the names not, but I shall herein recount the ones that I do.

There was first SA1973. A sexy Italian Republican. A man with my value system. I was so obsessed with getting back at Mr. Bikram that I convinced myself that Mr. Bikram hired SA to take me on a fantastic date and to test me in terms of "behaviour." And, very badly I behaved. I wanted for this report to get back to Mr. Bikram. Of course it never did, because Mr. Bikram had zero knowledge of SA. I was creating the challenge and the "get back at him" game all in my head. SA and I have remained as amazing friends. He exists in my very selective circle of trust. He exists in my underground Trump railroad. He is supportive of my work and of my ideas and dreams. And I, of his. So, it turned out that my planned retaliation morphed into someone who means something to me. We slept together several times, and it was FUN. Wild and fabulous. True to Republican form, he is an animal in bed. Throw in the Italian stallion factor, and it was energetic and divine! When I got my Gwendolyn in 2007, he forced me to watch several episodes of *The Dog Whisperer with Cesar Millan* because he thought that I was being a terrible puppy mother, as I permitted my puppy to be the boss. Little did he know that my puppy would always be the boss. I hold SA as so near and dear to my heart.

After SA1973 came Paul the Italian attorney who mounted eight box-style televisions at his house so that he could watch all of the football games at once.

He was crazy. I slept with him not. After that was Disgusting Joe, who, at Willow restaurant in Pittsburgh on Camp Horne Road, ate his entire dinner, and then he began eating MY food without MY permission. I questioned on his continued state of hunger, suggesting that he order more food for himself. The reply? Please prepare to be repulsed. In fact, the memory of his reply repulses me, just as it did in real time! Grabbing my leg from underneath of the table, he whispered, "I want to eat more, yes. I want to eat you." I never again saw this guy, ignoring his emails and telephone calls. Additionally, he was a liar as he claimed to be an attorney on his match.com profile, but his true profession was paralegal. Back then, I certainly wanted a man with a fancy title, but the one thing that has remained constant is that I require a man to be honest. After that was Edward. I met Edward at Club Paris in Florida at my cousin's bachelorette party in 2005. Edward and I danced the long distance tango for a few months, flying back and forth between Pennsylvania and Florida, but I found him to be too wimpy. He called himself "Ed" which reminded me of the horse. He was obsessed with Frank Sinatra and always wore a *Smacks* cereal T-shirt. He was a nurse, and I wanted to date a doctor. Again, back then, it was all about status. I was such a bitch. I remember that we slept in the same bed, but I remember not the details of our being intimate. Then there was Mark U, a sexy, tall, Italian scientist with conservative principles. We met years before in 2004 at my divine cousin Tracy's wedding, maintaining a telephone flirtation until my divine cousin Terri's wedding in 2006, also in Florida. After Terri's wedding, Mark U and I rented a hotel room, spending the night together. He was great fun. Then there was Martin who lived on Mt. Washington. We enjoyed a lovely lunch together at Vincent's of Green Tree. Later that evening, he texted that I had made him so aroused that he needed to see me immediately. So I drove to him (who was that girl?!). As we became intimate, I suddenly wanted to leave because he had dirty laundry sitting in the corner of the bedroom, and it bothered me, so I immediately ended the rendezvous. And Jay who accused me of wanting "to f*ck the Mexican chef" because I offered words of gratitude for the chef's amazing meal. Jay was the jealous type. He sold Viagra and made tons of money and jogged wearing a black, plastic bag. I spent a few months driving to and from his house located in Columbus, Ohio. All of these men post Mr. Bikram, to this point, were much older and Italian. I was always seeking older, Italian men as an additional way to prove to Mr. Bikram, who is both, older and Italian, that I could be wanted by a man of this description despite his rejection of me, a rejection as perceived by me.

And then their was Adam in 2006. Adam was very sweet, and he would have made a superb boyfriend on our second go in 2011, had I been ready. He was a client in 2006 when I worked for the security company, and we conducted intimate meetings in his office. We continued as friends, on again, off again, for a long time; and when we both departed from the security world, he offered, in 2011, to whisk me off of my feet, making me his princess. I declined his offer, as I had much work to do on me. I think he is now happy, but I do worry about him! And then there was the Englishman. We met on match.com in early of 2007, met (in person) in New York in May of 2007, celebrated for several days in New York, flew to Miami, and cruised for seven days in the Caribbean. Yes, he actually lived in England. That relationship worked not because my breasts were floppy at the time due to bulimic weight fluctuation, and he wanted a tight girl. When he realised that my Match pictures were "photoshopped" because taping my breasts around my back made me look thinner in pictures, he was turned off. He drank like a fish. And he directed me, in that thick English accent, "Story, fetch me some melon!" There was no way on Earth that I could have been a servant girl, for the rest of my life. Yes, I wanted to be a housewife. But I wanted servants of my own. He was also too short for my liking. And then there was Terry. I had much fun with Terry. He treated me like a QUEEN. It was like a grown-up version of the relationship that I had with Daryl. I adored being with Terry, and my second favourite date of all time happened at the wedding which we attended together. He was so proud to have me as his date. I felt truly special. And then there was the man who bought me Gwendolyn. He is a very good man. I treasure him forever for gifting me with the greatest gift of my life. He is Gwendolyn's father. He is a friend who loved me and gave to me the world. I will be here for him, forever. Out of respect for his private life, I shall say nothing more than, thank you, from the bottom of my heart.

On December 12, 2007, I got my greatest love of all: my puppy. Gwendolyn. And, throughout it all, throughout all of this crazy dating, it was my main goal and mission to make Mr. Bikram love me. In fact, I got Gwendolyn because Mr. Bikram loved dogs! Thusly, I thought that if I had a dog, Mr. Bikram would love me.

But he never did.

In the manner that I wanted.

Next came Nacho, an executive at my company, who was very kind and generous but wanted sexual acts outside of my comfort zone. I sent him packing and to the airport, back to his home, on Easter Day. And Steve with a dog named Yogi. I ended this relationship because he failed to successfully back-up his boat into the water, needing my help. A man should drive like a man. And then a local meteorologist named Scott. He wanted to hold my hand and to take me to restaurants every single night. That was fine until he rejected puppy Gwendolyn's crawling on him whilst we tried to be intimate. And his hands were too small. When I watched him on the news, the hand size factor drove me insane! That was a mutual relationship ending. And Neil the teacher, a guy whom I met at my sister L's wedding in 2008. We had a very fun date at Kennywood (divine Pittsburgh amusement park), but, after the date, I returned to home, Mr. Bikram came to me, and we slept together. When Mr. Bikram left, I drank delicious red wine and ordered delicious Chinese food. Gwendolyn and I walked to the China Palace to fetch it. Steamed broccoli and shrimp with brown sauce on the side. I can still remember dipping the broccoli and shrimp into the heavenly brown sauce, using chopsticks. And I used too much salt. It was perfect. On the next weekend, I literally left my Gwendolyn at a dog hotel on the turnpike (one that Mr. Bikram recommended) when driving to visit Neil for a weekend in his nearby-to-Washington D.C. apartment. Gwendolyn contracted worms from this doggie hotel. Who on Earth was that girl who abandoned her baby for a guy?! And at some random place?! The next weekend, Neil visited me in Pittsburgh. When he petitioned the sleeping of Gwendolyn in my bed, I threw him out of the bedroom, giving to him the sofa. He reportedly stated to my sister L, on the next day, that I am crazy. Next came Andrew. I had one divine date with Andrew. Well, Gwendolyn and I had one divine date with Andrew. We met on match.com. He was warned against me by a former high school "friend" of mine, a mutual "friend" who had been his girlfriend during college. He saw through the nasty rumours and decided to have this date with me (and Gwendolyn) anyway. It was a date that reassured me that chivalry does, indeed, exist. Thank you, Andrew, for a wonderful date. You are a high quality man! Next came Michael the entrepreneurial fracker for whom I am grateful as he introduced me to *Atlas Shrugged* by Ayn Rand. We never slept together. He genuinely enjoyed my company, and I enjoyed his. We partnered well together in appreciating gin and wine, also sharing an affinity for fancy raw fish. One evening, after having a lovely walk date with Michael and our dogs, I recall walking to home alone with Gwendolyn, telephoning Mr. Bikram, telling him about this new relationship that I adored, and Mr. Bikram came right to me, and we had sex on the ground. After Michael came Potato Head who was incredibly kind and sweet. Very weird, yes, but genuinely a good human with a big heart.

He prepared a very thoughtful Christmas gift for me, and he is an excellent writer. I hope that he publishes his interesting stories some day and that he meets a girl who loves Christmas and family walks and weirdness as much as he does. And Pug Guy. Pug Guy was the last man that I have ever touched, aside from Mr. Bikram. Pug Guy is a damn fine man. Tall, handsome, and Republican. We met in 2010 at the bar at Jimmy Wan's in Cranberry Township, Pennsylvania. I was completely enamoured because he firstly had the sexiest of smiles and the most confident of natures, and he secondly had two adorable pugs and a pure capitalist attitude (pure meaning with heart). Because he had challenged me on something that I revealed at the bar, I spent the next few months trying to bump into him again. I like challenges. On the night of our second encounter, I was so affected by alcohol that I literally said to him, outside of my regular, conservative character, "Do you know what? You need to get f*cked." So we ventured to his house and engaged in sex. He is a very strong partner. I wrote about our interactions at my blog: www.theyogaballerina.com/pug-guy-comes-forward / www.theyogaballerina.com/review-date-with-pug-guy-at-vivo-kitchen. We dated a bit. But even if he wanted something more (of this I know not), I was never ready to forfeit my love for Mr. Bikram. To devote myself to the great Pug Guy who needed and deserved complete beauty and devotion meant that I must forfeit Mr. Bikram. I was unable to do this because Mr. Bikram was my love. And when, in 2012, I refused the advances of my touchy-feely, creepy, old-as-dirt landlord and was therefore given a sixty-day notice of termination of my apartment lease, the official reasoning being that he needed to raise the rent price and that I would be unable to afford it, Mr. Bikram helped me to fight the damages for which my landlord later billed (wanted to charge me for renovation of the apartment), and Pug Guy agreed to the arrangement of where I would care for his darling dogs and clean his home, in exchange for a room. I am so very grateful to both Mr. Bikram and to Pug Guy for helping me through those rough months. Living with Pug Guy was a perfect arrangement until I became obsessed again with the notion of being with Mr. Bikram. One thing led to another, and Pug Guy, rightfully so, ended our arrangement six months later, so I found an apartment in the city, which, despite overlooking an alley, I joked was my "penthouse." As a side note, President Trump referred to his first Manhattan apartment as the penthouse, too, despite its unglamorous view! He discusses this fact in *The Art of the Deal*.

Since leaving Pug Guy's home in July of 2013, I have slept only with Mr. Bikram. Yes, I have been with only one man for six years. And our being together during these last six years happened on the irregularity, going for long periods of time without seeing each other. I last slept with Mr. Bikram on June 17, 2018. And I have been with no other man since. My next man shall be my perfect gentleman.

Mr. Bikram is that kind of guy who you can trust with your entire world. He is that kind of guy who will keep your secrets. Who will guide you. Who will help you. And I am talking not only about the girl that he loves. Or the girl who is obsessed with him. Or the girl who knows that he helped her older sister, so she calls Mr. Bikram when she's in a scrape, because he is trustworthy and reliable and safe and consistent. I am talking about everyone in his life. He is so dedicated to being everyone's "get me out of a scrape" guy that I feel that he is unable to pursue his passions. He wants to travel. He wants to work in wine. He wants to write (yes, he is such a divine writer, so much that he can produce long segments of verse, making it sound as though I am the writer, and as one can gauge from this book, my writing style is anything but "normal."). Yet he continues with his boring, arduous law practice because he is good at it. He is good at running businesses. At telling people of how to run their businesses. At telling people of how to spend their money. And he is SO FUNNY. Once he told me that my dog Gwendolyn looks like a loaf of bread displayed vertically at Panera, with a tennis ball on top. Another time, he said that when Gwendolyn drinks water, it looks like she is bobbing for apples. And when he mocks me, he sounds like a girl duck from a 1960s cartoon. He is so funny. Bad aspects? His desk is CLUTTERED. His house is a CLUTTERED. In 2016, I told him that physical intimacy, for me, is impossible in such an environment; but the clutter aside, and the inability to say no when people beg for his help aside, and his inability to believe that someone can love him so fiercely, enough to stay loyal to him forever as I would have done in a ninth of a heartbeat, he is a perfect man. He is an amazing lover. An amazing friend. An amazing parent to a dog. Mr. Bikram's dog was Gwendolyn's first dog friend! I had this crazy, tiny, six-pound, seven-ounce very very very BAD beast of a puppy, and I let her loose around Mr. Bikram's HUGE "bully" breed of dog. Nowadays, almost twelve years later, I realise that in exposing Gwendolyn to this breed and to thusly a bigger dog from the get go, she saw herself as a big dog and would, throughout her life, be *The Pitbull Whisperer*. This is why we met our best friends Rebecca and Bella. This is why Gwendolyn met the love of her life Chico. Bella and

Chico, both pitbulls with "reputations" of being untrustworthy and unruly with other dogs, were putty in Gwendolyn's little paws! In addition to pitbulls, Gwendolyn is dominant with other larger breeds. Once, she made her boyfriend Mater the Portuguese waterdog drop a toy so that SHE could play with it. Once, she won a game of tug-of-war with Sophie the much younger and much bigger Labrador Retriever. Once, at her rooftop birthday party of 2013, Gwendolyn collected all of the party favours away from all of the other big dogs because she wanted them for herself! She treats puppies as though she is their mother. In fact, puppies recognise this mothering factor of Gwendolyn and lick her head constantly. It is hysterical to watch a huge German Shepherd licking her head. And if the puppy goes crazy, Gwendolyn corrects it. She has greyhound radar and refuses to budge when she sees one, until she can say hello because she remembers Sophia the greyhound who, in 2013, saved her life. She once served as a seeing eye dog for her beloved older "sister" Quinn the English Springer Spaniel. Now she is serving as a teacher / big sister to her beloved soul dog Lady, who, interestingly enough, is a descendant of our dear Quinn. Gwendolyn is incredible. She is a dog's dog. I shall always fondly remember of when Mr. Bikram's pitbull stole Gwendolyn's ballerina penguin toy, teasing her with it. Gwendolyn was so mad! I shall always joke that my puppy outsmarted Mr. Bikram's dog on that day, but it truly was the other way around. I think that Mr. Bikram's dog was very smart, just like Mr. Bikram.

Mr. Bikram is a wonderful man.

He is the one man who has meant something to me, thus far in my thirty-seven years of life on Earth.

Our last period of dating was perhaps the most intimate and special of all of the years of our friendship. Falling in love with NBC's *This Is Us* in 2016, we established a weekly ritual to watch the newest episode together. I still know not, of why, to this day, in March of 2017, I forcefully told him him to leave my apartment in the middle of the night. Did we have a disagreement? Was it because I wanted to eat dinner in private? Was it because my rules trumped his presence? Was it because I caught him investigating the contents of my iPhone? I know not. What I do know is that after I instructed for him to go, we conversed not for quite some time. I was very sad as I had come to enjoy those moments with him. And now they were gone.

During our break which followed this period of love, I achieved my epiphany which shall be discussed in the next chapter. As a preview, I shall offer that the shield that I built around my heart, oh so long ago, prevented anyone from truly loving me. Although Mr. Bikram never intentionally caused me to feel unloved, I already set myself up to feel as such. And when he refused to offer me a commitment, and when he refused to do subtle things like befriend me on Facebook, I honestly felt so rejected that I wanted to shrivel into a corner and never again offer my heart to anyone.

And, now, I am older than was Mr. Bikram, at our first meeting. My age, thirty-seven years. He is fifty. Almost one year ago, on August 15, 2018, he said something that made me so angry, and, in retrospect, I realise that my anger was really pain because it told me that he truly finds me as unworthy of his trust. I thusly have moved onward from Mr. Bikram because I am worthy. I am worthy of trust. I am worthy of love. Loving Mr. Bikram was a big chapter in my life. Although we shall remain as friends for all of time, the chapter of love is hereby closed.

CHAPTER
IX

WORTHY OF TRUST

"ANYTHING THAT PRESIDENT TRUMP DOES, I LOVE." This statement is true. Completely, unabashedly, perfectly true! It wholeheartedly reflects of how I feel about President Trump. And, although I lived as an undercover Trump supporter for nearly three years, silenced after many months of joyfully expressing my support of his campaign, silenced to protect my work and friendships, that when, in April of 2018, I decided to "come out of the closet," I held back not. Slamming the internet with my pro Trump reality, I again wrote about my love for our great president, just as I had done, before going into the closet, during the campaign of three years prior. And, my liberal friends, now shocked to learn of my freshly revealed truth, shocked to learn that my beliefs had never changed and that I was simply quiet throughout it all, presented me with daily argument about why they dislike President Trump, attempting to sell me on reasons for why I should disdain this greatest man on Earth. Because I argue not, and because I feel it as unnecessary to defend my reality, I firmly replied to their appeals, "Anything that President Trump does, I love." And, this response, seemingly, caused more "pain" for my liberal friends. Mind you, this book, *Donald Trump and My Eating Disorder*, is MY tell-all about WHAT I think. I refuse to hold back in the confines of this space. And I continue to no longer restrict my speech on social media and at my blog. But, in conversations with my friends? I do hold back. Because my friends are important to me. As previously stated, this is why I lived for nearly three years as an undercover Trump supporter. In addition to protecting my work, I did it because I cared so deeply for my liberal client and for my friends, and I wanted not to stimulate anyone more "pain" (as they describe it). Mind you, my rational brain thinks it is a double standard that I must be cautious of my words and that my liberal friends can say whatever they please. But sometimes friendships are more important than one's causes. And just to be clear, President Trump is my cause not. He is my reality.

One example of pain that I stimulated regards Rafael, a supremely handsome friend and divine father of a beautiful English Bulldog named

Lucille. A brilliant surgeon born in Puerto Rico, raised in New York, Rafael has volunteered, doing mission work outside of the United States. Witnessing hunger and lack of electricity, he thinks that immigration is a right because otherwise these poor humans will have no chance at a good life. I think that Rafael's work is admirable. But when I supported that President Trump called MS13 Gang members as "animals," my friend was highly offended because the radical leftists, and seemingly Rafael, interpreted President Trump's statement to regard all illegal immigrants as animals which was President Trump's message not. When Rafael appealed to me, regarding his cause, I blankly stated that I believe in President Trump. "Anything that President Trump does, I love" again, were my exact words. And my friend was genuinely hurt.

As she always does, my best human friend Rebecca, a radical Democrat, made me see the light. She taught me that to make such a blanket statement to someone who exists in pain, hurts them even more. So now I am aware. And I have changed my tune. Now I say absolutely nothing in reply to the appeals of my liberal friends.

A second example happened in October of 2018 when my beloved friend Kristin asked for me to change my Facebook profile picture to a black blob, to show my support for women, demonstrating to the world of what existence would be like without women. Rather than being kind, I laughed, rejecting her proposal. After weeks of giving each other the silent treatment, I realised that I had behaved just as I did with Rafael. Now we have made up. And, in future situations of where I disagree with her women's appeals and #MeToo petitions and putting together of GoFundMe campaigns to save old ladies' houses, I shall stay as silent. My reason for being silent is that I know what it is like to be hurt. To be in pain. To be denounced for my brain. I have felt the cold, critical reaction of others, of those closest to me, with regard to my existence. With regard to my former eating disorder. And, because of that cold reaction, I lived a challenging, lonely life, for a long time.

For nineteen years, I lived under the impression that I was a bad person. Because of the bulimia, I thought that I was unworthy of trust, of love, of intimacy. This is because those closest to me treated me like an incorrect human. Yes, they always loved me, and they saved me from rational things like when I blew all of my money on binge food (I always paid them back), like when I totalled my car and had one repossessed at age twenty two, so they loaned one to me / made a down payment on another car for me, but the eating disorder was, simply put, from that very first day, unacceptable. It was kept within the walls of our home. It was never to be discussed in public. It was an embarrassment. I was told that I should know better. From that very first day on August 21, 1999, I wanted to announce to the world that I was bulimic. I wanted to write a book about it, a book that could help other people. I always had bigger plans for the eating disorder, even in its infant stages! But, to my family, it was cause to withdrawal their trust of me.

It was cause to raid my apartment and investigate the garbage can to learn of my food victims. These unannounced raids were counterproductive. They embarrassed me, driving me farther away. During one of these raids, my parents found the receipt for my abortion. And during another raid, my mother thought that I had "overdosed" because nobody had heard from me, for several hours, and she thought that I was going to hurt myself. Did she think that I overdosed on food? Or did she think that because I had a food problem that I was also a drug head? My eating disorder was physical and strong versus emotional and weak. My mother understood this not. All that I remember from that night was she entering my apartment, and I was sleeping unclothed. I was so embarrassed that she could see my fat in its greatest reality. Because of all of this, I developed a blockage, one that lasted for nineteen years, one that convinced me that I was unworthy of trust. Of love. Of real, genuine happiness. With high quality humans. Mind you, this was my interpretation of their reaction to my behaviours. I am certain that they have a completely different perspective.

My family was in great pain, as our mutual hobby was the family. My sisters and I were a team. We were the Story Girls. Our parents, the drill sergeants. My volcanic eruption of the eating disorder was an unwelcomed reality. My interpretation of their way of responding to my eating disorder affected me so powerfully that it handicapped me from truly living, from being socially healthy, for nineteen years. I walked about this Earth with a guard, blocking humans from getting underneath of my skin, from getting to my heart. This epiphany of my social stunting and self deprecation arrived after living for nineteen years with a steel fortress around the beautiful thing in the centre of my chest cavity. I have never felt heart-swelling emotion as it pertains to a romantic love. I have never lived the King Edward and Wallis Simpson story.

My epiphany happened at the age of thirty-five in October of 2017 when consuming old blog posts dated 2011 to 2016. These blog posts provide a historical record of the healing that I underwent from the eating disorder (www.theyogaballerina.com). The manner in which I wrote about myself during those years indicated that I was A BIG BAD BULIMIC. That I was THE

COLLEGE DROP-OUT. That I was THE FINANCIAL MESS. That I was THE GIRL who needed TO EARN THE TRUST of my friends and of my family. That I needed to work OVERTIME on my human self to earn the trust from other humans in my life. That I was good enough not. That everyone saw me as questionable in character. And, one day, two years ago, it clicked. It clicked that I needed to do nothing extra special to earn trust because aside from lying about food from 1999 to 2016, I was the most honest, kind, hard-working, well-intentioned girl that could be! I am so glad that I documented my life at the blog to yield eventual achievement of this epiphany. I am so grateful to Gary Vaynerchuk for influencing me to start a blog, oh so long ago!

It consumed almost twenty years to figure out the monkey on my back. It took almost twenty years to stop thinking of myself as a child under the roof and food policing of my parents to realise that I was now an adult in her mid thirties, under the longtime care of myself and that I had formed a circle of friends and of trust. But why did I disallow my heart to truly open? The rational investigator in me went to work to discover the answer to this quandary.

Because of my work, I had keys to the most prominent homes in Pittsburgh. But a key to my parents' home? I had one not. My parents changed their locks and alarm code in 2001 after renting for me an apartment when it was determined that I was to be untrusted, because of my sneakiness with food. Additionally, I was to be untrusted because of my outbursts when the family criticised my high volume of food consumption and my dramatic weight fluctuations. Yes, I was an unpleasant human being - who can be pleasant when they are bulimic and fat? But sneaking around with food and my weakness as it pertained to bulimia meant that I was untrustworthy, in their eyes. This was their opinion, as I saw it. And, I agreed with them because it was the only thing that I knew, that being their approval or disapproval, approval being the one thing that I sought, each and every day of my life. I only wanted for their approval on my human self. I wanted for them to see and to celebrate my talents versus focusing on my newfound scarlet letter. But, because of the bulimia, because of my weight "problem," because of my associated anger, because of everything that I did that was ABC not, I was considered as an untrustworthy person with a questionable character. Turns out, I was a very trustworthy person. I was simply at war with food and judged for it harshly.

In 2013, my best human friend Rebecca allowed me to borrow her car when mine required emergency service. She offered her car to me. And I was shocked. I was shocked that an "adult," one of the approximate age of my parents, would permit then thirty-one-year old Nicole Marie Story to drive her car. Why shock? The answer is that just a few years earlier, my parents restricted me from driving any of their vehicles. My father will claim that the insurance company mandated this denial, but, at the end of the day, it was his decision, in my opinion. In fact, just a few months ago in 2019, my mother told me that I am unable to drive any of their cars during a planned visit to Pittsburgh. I never asked to borrow one of her cars. She offered this denial, unsolicited. And just to show the dichotomy of this relationship, even though I was banned from touching any of their vehicles, in 2013, my father was the one who fixed my broken car.

Two years ago, when I achieved my grand Worthy of Trust epiphany, I said to my mother that I am grateful for my experience in higher education because it permitted me to find my own rational conclusion that college was pointless for me. I recounted the time that my professor of *Business Law* assessed me with an A minus on a paper because, in his words, "Nobody is perfect." I disputed this "minus" until I received my rightly deserved A. I described a second example of when a professor of *Business Management* required that I list my incomplete education before my work experience, on a mock resume. At the time, I had WORKED MORE than I had received in education "credentials," and it made no sense to my brain of how an incomplete education could be more significant than my work in the dirt experience. This professor had never worked outside of academia. He lived in a land of make believe. I got my way with regard to creating the resume as I deemed fit. A third example happened in *Christian Understanding of the Human Person* where I wrote about my decision to have an abortion at the age of twenty-one after being assaulted by an illegal despite my then Catholic principles. The teacher offered to me the grade of D, demanding that I re-write the paper, explaining of why I committed a sin. I refused.

I have trouble with looter authority. This is why I was a bad student. This is why I shall never be a good student. I only want to listen to me. And I was almost always smarter than my teachers. Higher education teaches systematic ways of learning and of thinking. It is the school's way or the highway. I needed and shall always need creativity and uniqueness. Like President Trump who punched his music teacher in the second grade, I got into skirmishes of my own with teachers. In fact, I have a second grade story of my own to tell! The year was 1990. I brought a dixie cup to church for my First Holy Communion. The shared wine glass, to me, meant germs. In response to my action, the nun exclaimed, "How dare you suggest that Christ would make you sick in his house?"

Bottom line is that school and I meshed not. If I had human kids, they would be home schooled using YouTube, Fox News, President Trump's tweets, *The Art of the Deal*, George Orwell's works, Jim Henson movies, *Sex and the City* episodes, and Ayn Rand's *Atlas Shrugged*. And, I'd love for them to have an internship at The Trump Organization and with Elon Musk. When I explained all of this detailed reality to my mother in 2017, ending it with statement that a garbage degree would never have served me, she replied with, "Well, there is a stigma associated with a person who doesn't have a college degree."

My heart dropped. She was still disappointed in me. She was still embarrassed over her daughter's lack of completed "education."

And my mother's statement was very true, once upon a time. Without a college degree, it was hard to find work above a minimum wage-paying job. In 1990. But, in the day of Gary Vaynerchuk and entrepreneurialism where one can learn anything in the autodidactic fashion, and where one can create work from hobbies and passions, college matters not. It broke my heart to know that my mother still has this "my daughter didn't graduate from college" opinion of me. One year later, I broached this subject again, and she told me that she thinks this of herself, not of me. She thinks less of herself because of her lack of college degree. Well, let it be written and let it be known that college degrees are pure rubbish, in most circumstances. MY MOTHER was the greatest teacher of my life. I am certain that my sisters will agree with this statement with regard to their individual selves, and I hope that my mother's heart can smile, knowing that she did all of that, without a superficial degree. She is amazing. She is amazing even though she thinks that I am a loser without a college degree, ha ha!

Because I lived with an eating disorder and because I fostered zero interest with living according to the beat of the standard drum of college, office job, husband, human children, I was made to feel like an incorrect human, made to feel like a loser. My biological family's intention was never to incite these feelings, I believe. I believe that their intention was pure and that they meant zero harm to me with their distrust. But because of this distrust, I refused healthy romantic love and fruitful friendships in my life for nineteen years. I walked around, feeling broken, until I awoke from my trance and realised that I am amazing. And whole.

Why am I telling this to you? Because when people ask about how to deal with someone with an eating disorder, my most basic reply is to talk about it. To be strict. To be rational. To be loving. And to be non-judgemental. Example, don't call your child a loser. But make them understand that they will screw up their lives if they continue forward with their behaviour. Love your eating disordered person fiercely. Show them empathy. Judge them not. They shall obviously be grumpy, pissed, embarrassed, and defensive if they gain ninety pounds in one year. I suggest to treat them like a success even when they're failing in the eating department because even trying to breathe when you're living with an eating disorder is hard. And this is how we, the winning Republicans, must treat the losing Democrats who are close to our hearts. The other Democrats are fair game, but the ones whom we love, like Rafael and Kristin whom I mention in the opening of this chapter, should be treated with complete awareness and kindness.

Additionally, if your eating disordered person wants "help," find for them "help." If they want space, give to them space. Sure, there are cases where eating disorders are considered as mental illness and therefore fear of self-harm and suicide should never be ruled out, but one cannot live in a state of fear. As FDR said, "The only thing we have to fear, is fear itself."

Eating is the most basic function on this Earth yet it is so very chaotic for many of us. Thusly, for my second bit of advice, I suggest simplification. Remove the excess. Eliminate the jazz. Live like a Buddhist. Where there is less noise, there is more focus. More steadiness. More pace. More peace. Do Ashtanga yoga.

I want to create an analogy using the American Pitbull Terrier. There is a stigma associated with pitbulls. The stigma is that they cannot be trusted. There is a stigma associated with a person with an addiction. The stigma is that they cannot be trusted. Some pitbulls, because they are treated like this, develop a guard, unwilling to get cuddly or to reciprocate the love offered from a human. This is what happened to me. Because I was treated a certain way by my family because of my addition to food, I acted like a pitbull who was scared of love and of nourishment. Like a scared little pitbull, I developed a guard that was disguised as ferocity. AS A SOCIETY, WE MUST BREAK THE STIGMA. Regardless of what is a human's addiction, we must show to them love. Regardless of what kind of dog it is, we must show to them love!

On January 27, 2018, I wrote a letter to my parents, explaining about my grand epiphany on why I was reluctant to accept love into my life for so long, explaining about how I felt about my newfound discovery of their chronic distrust of me. I even suggested that we see a therapist together, not in a woe-is-me fashion, but rather insomuch that I think we need a mediator in order to discuss our issues rationally and calmly. My father's response was heartbreaking but clear. And I have moved onward and upward! I have opened my heart to accepting love into my life and to nourishing my friendships.

This includes nourishment with my sisters.

First is Stephanie. We have, after nearly two decades, achieved divine peace where we can be honest, open, and real with one other. We are so alike in our philosophy on existence, so much that we both quote from *Atlas Shrugged* and *Sex and the City* in our conversations, speaking as though Carrie Bradshaw and Dagny Taggart are real human beings. We say each other's internal thoughts aloud, when the other is thinking it. For instance, when using words that sound alike but have different spellings such as their, there, and they're, I know that she's thinking of the stated word's correct spelling in her head. For instance number two, just the other day, I used the word, "penalise," and I quickly followed it with, "I know you are thinking that penalise sounds like penis," and we both erupted into divine laughter because she was, indeed, thinking such. Our writing style is carbon copy. On the few times that she has commented anonymously at my blog, I've thought, "What?! Who is this comment author, and did we learn from the same teacher on how to write?!" I then proceeded to check the IP address of the comment author, which of course, led me to Stephanie! I am so proud of Stephanie. Gwendolyn is my heart. Stephanie is my star.

And with Stephanie, it became so very ugly, in those early years of the eating disorder. I remember, in 2001, when we departed from a family reunion, she wanted to fetch food from McDonald's. I pulled to the drive-thru window and ordered her food in my way. But she wanted for me to place the order using other verbiage. And a total battle erupted. I forget our exact argumentative words, but it was vicious. That was, in my opinion, the ugliest battle of our eating disordered sisterhood. Granted, she was emaciated, and I was the fat bulimic, so why should she trust the manner in which I ordered her food? My way would clearly turn her into a fatso! Additionally, because my parents interpreted me as a bad person at the time, she did, too.

Fast forward eighteen years to 2019. We now speak openly about our health. One morning, in May of 2018, during our morning sister call, she asked, "Nikki, do I really want McDonald's?" I replied, "No. Last week you felt like garbage. I think that you should declare this week as clean eating week. I did old school Tae-Bo bootcamp abs and twenty one miles per day on the Peloton, for the past two days, and I feel amazing! And I have returned to eating cleanly after a week of eating vegan cheeseburgers with ketchup in Chicago!" Stephanie replied, "You're right."

Three minutes later, she instructed, "Hold on, Nikki." Three seconds later and I heard, "Hello! Welcome to McDonald's." Ha! As she drove to the pickup window, I blurted, "Looks like I did a great job this morning as your life coach!" And we both motioned into divine laughter. If I had made such a comment five years ago, we would have spoken not for a year. Transparency about our eating idiosyncrasies is what helped us to achieve peace in our sisterhood.

Stephanie knows and understands me better than anyone else on Earth. She knows that walking through a grocery store is pornographic for me. Lured by peanut butter and white frosted cakes and white cream-filled donuts, I am! But she knows that I employ specific rules to permit peaceful existence and healthy experiences with regard to food, *unless I've had TOO much to drink and my brain tells me that it is okay to share a jar of Jif with Gwendolyn!.* And I understand Stephanie's rules. She is governed by calories and counts her Teddy Grahams.

For a long time, I was embarrassed about my failure to control food. And she distrusted me, because I spoke one thing, but my fat body said another. For a long time, she distrusted me as a human, and she tells me that it is because she understood not of how I could spiral so out-of-control. "With suspicion" was the general manner in which my family treated me.

When I started that first diet in 1999 that took me to 89 pounds, I was Stephanie's thin-spiration. She restricted so wonderfully that she, too, whittled to an unhealthy weight, but she was able to maintain her thinness. I, on the other hand, blew up like Shamu. Even though she understood not, she wanted to help me. In 2001, when I fired my last formal therapist, Stephanie offered to be my therapist. My sister was born with emotional intelligence. She assigned for me to draw pictures of how I saw myself (I drew a fat blob, of course), and she had me promise to report if and when I succumbed to bulimic activity. I never complied in reporting because each binge and purge, to me, was a failure, and I refused to disappoint my sister. Thusly, I would simply fix the problem and start tomorrow perfectly (or so I thought and hoped). The food issue + my relationship with the illegal monster + my "dropping out" of school + parents' opinion of me made Stephanie distrust me. But I was always a good person. I was always a hard-working, caring person. Stephanie and I now openly discuss those bad years. She is sad about the manner in which she responded to my pain. I, in turn, am sad about the selfish manner in which I responded to her own.

She left for the Disney College Internship in 2004. I was excited for and proud of my baby sister for accepting this big adventure. I called her, during her travels southbound to Florida. Traveling with my parents, she refused to accept my call. I can still hear her snippy, "No. I'm not talking to her." That exact moment in time demonstrates of how destructive an eating disorder is to relationships that matter.

Stephanie has always mattered.

Whilst she lived her beautiful Disney internship, we began chatting. Online. Slowly. It was very awkward at first. And then it became a part of our daily lives. During that period of time, we became friends again. Rebuilding a foundation and infrastructure would have been impossible to accomplish in person or verbally. It would have been too stressful. Too painful. The bond of our true sisterhood broke the barriers of the eating disorder that we both shared. We experience our periods of break-ups, because we are hard-headed drama queens! But we shall always be best friends and sisters.

Next is L.

As discussed in chapter five, in 1999, our relationship died. On December 29, 2017, I contacted her. On April 2, 2019, she responded. And it changed my life. We will be okay. For the first time in twenty years, I have two sisters again.

My family, as a whole, exists in a good place. I hold no grudges about what happened with regard to my interpretation of their reaction to my eating disorder, and I hope that they are happy now, too. I want to never discuss this boring subject again!

But there is something which remains. I do hold one grudge with regard to my family. And before this moment in time, I have never spoken of it publicly. It is very painful. It is the closest to "suffering" that I shall ever experience. I am hesitant to write about it, but I know that I must, to heal from the pain. Maybe I do need psychological therapy. Maybe I do need a straight jacket. Maybe I do need to cry and to scream like a radical Democrat. And now I reveal to you, this deep, dark secret. It is regarding my eyebrows. During my middle school years, my family so fiercely ridiculed my big thick brows, comparing me to Ken Rice, a news anchor on KDKA television. So, beginning in 1995, for twenty years, I tweezed, waxed, and underwent electrolysis. In 2015, for two complete years, I tried to regrow my big, thick, luscious eyebrows. I wanted the exotic Brazilian look, one that I harvested naturally as a child. And I failed. FAILED! It is the only venture in my life at which I passionately tried and failed. My eyebrows refused to grow back. Refused! My stupid eyebrows missed the memo from *Trump: The Game* which proclaims that winning is everything! My eyebrows are losers. And I blame my family completely.

CHAPTER

X

TRUMP DERANGEMENT SYNDROME

This book, Donald Trump and My Eating Disorder, is for the strong of mind, body, and soul. It is for those who think rationally. It is for those who subscribe to the value system of personal responsibility. It is for those who subscribe to the notion that hard work is what solves problems and creates opportunities. For whom is this book not? The answer is, this book is for the faint of heart not. For the weak not. For the emotional not. This is the kind of book that will provoke, in specific characters, the feelings of pain, panic, and fear. My perspective is madly aggressive. I am aggressive. In the words of Kanye West, like he, like President Trump, I have "dragon energy." Those who have dragon energy not? My book will likely leave them in a state of shock, in a state of being "triggered," maybe even in a state of tears. Who will cry? The answer is the ones who consider eating disorders to be something of "suffering." Something of "disease." Something of "woe." Something of "mental illness." Radical Democrats will cry.

Shakespeare won at the greatest contest of woe. "For never was a story of more woe. Than this of Juliet and her Romeo." Thusly, on the next moment that you are feeling weak and sad about your "state," please remember that it compares NOT to that of Romeo and Juliet; and who wants a second place trophy? If you do, then this book is certainly something that you should avoid. Romeo and Juliet won the best at the woe. So stop crying. Right now. And let us please, therefore, aim for something else, that being achievement of the greatest state of joy! Who wants to race me?

This was my way of seeing the eating disorder, for all seventeen years of it.

On that first food binge of 1999, I announced, in my brain, *"Okay, I am bulimic now. I must stop this immediately. I must write a book about how I got to this place. I must appear on Oprah. I must help others to become healthy. I must figure this out. I must win. I shall win!"*

It is twenty years later, and I am finally, after seventeen years of war followed by three years of peace, completing this non-fictional masterpiece!

Non-fiction. Why is it called such? Would a better label be Truth? Or Reality? Non-fiction simply seems to be so negative to me. It sounds like a term created by the "elites," the ones that President Trump mocks at his MAGA rallies. These "elites" value dollars and degrees over good, old-fashioned hard work. They value small talk about "classic" literature at cocktail parties. Can you imagine President Trump discussing John Keats at a cocktail party? LOL! Or, can you hear him talking about how magnificent is a boring piece of "art" hanging on the wall at a gallery? Can you hear him, softly describing to his followers about Robert Frost and that "two roads diverged in a yellow wood"? This is why he is President. He is real and relatable.

There is, however, one piece of song literature that President Trump might discuss at cocktail parties. It is called *The Snake*, an Al Wilson song. He has recited it at *Make America Great Again* rallies, using it as a cautionary tale about the danger of illegal immigration. It discusses, in poem format, a little old lady who takes in a snake, nursing it back to good health. And when the snake eventually turns on her, killing her, the snake explains that she always knew he was a snake.

I completely understand that everyone is different. And I know that I will offend so many humans with my writing as presented in this book. Such is my intention not. I want for every human to feel as lovely and peaceful and happy. But I know that my writing shall be interpreted as offensive. To those who hate me. To those who love me. To radical Democrats. To my friends who are Democrats. To fake Republicans. And, for that, despite being non-apologetic for the most part, I am, indeed, sorry because catalysing negativity is never my modus operandi.

Definitely, I shall offend Oprah. Writing about how Donald Trump was the ultimate influence to ending my eating disorder will raise eyebrows of the liberal masses! To the QUEEN of the liberal masses! To QUEEN OPRAH! But, I must state, for the record, Oprah's 1988 interview of Donald Trump registers as mesmerising. Search for it on YouTube immediately, please. And consume it, many times over! Oprah recognised presidential in Donald Trump twenty-seven years before his candidacy. I think that a young Donald Trump as featured in this video is dreamy. In fact, Donald Trump is dreamy then and now. And, despite Oprah's current public denouncement of President Trump, I also respect Oprah because she is a hard worker who speaks her truth. And, like me, she has seemingly battled weight and food for all of her life. Functionally. Thusly, despite our difference of opinion on President Trump, I think that Oprah will feel empathetic toward me. Because, I, too, have failed and failed and failed and failed with food. The war with food was the underlying factor of my thirty-seven year life thus far, up until three years ago. And I think that despite my adoration of President Trump, Oprah will open her heart to my story because it is so much like her OWN, pun intended. I viewed *The Oprah Winfrey Show* nearly every summer afternoon from 1992 until 1996 with my beautiful Italian grandmother Josephine who resembles the divinely glamorous Joan Collins, then and now, and our time together is a memory that I shall cherish forever. A memory complimented with potato chips and mozzarella cheese! Note, she lived nine doors away. I rode my bicycle to visit her. She was my caretaker not. Rather, she was my grandmother and friend. Hi, Grandma! Thank you for reading my book and for spending so much time with me, in the 1990s.

I am so very privileged that in today's day and age, I can express my voice without a major source, without an agent, without a publisher, without a stepping stone, without a bridge, without an Oprah! I can speak my religion without being governed. Freedom of speech never meant such truth until now. Yes, I shall adore to have the great Oprah read and discuss my book with her massive audience, but if she declines, that is okay. Same as with Ellen. Ellen is married to Portia who wrote the ONLY "eating disorder book" that I could continue reading beyond page fifteen. It is called *Unbearable Lightness: A Story of Loss and Gain*. For YEARS, I tried, over and again, to read Marya Hornbacher's *Wasted*, but it was just so sad to me! So helpless. Search "eating disorder books" on Amazon, and the titles will make you want to tear your brain out. They represent sadness, weakness, and negativity. So unlike MY disorder. I related to Portia's book insomuch that she binged like I did, purged like I did, and restricted like I did, valuing a thin body above all. And she healed herself with animals. Like I did. She's a beautiful human, inside and outside, and I shall be honoured if, despite my adoration of President Trump, that Ellen and Portia will read and share my book. My unique way of seeing the world might help a lot of people. Ellen's acting in *If These Walls Could Talk* stole my heart. She effectively communicated her message that it is okay to be different. That it is okay to be a lesbian! That it is okay to be same sex parents! It is a very powerful piece of filmography, especially for someone like me who was raised in a socially conservative family. And, her book, *Seriously, I'm Kidding*, had me engaged into stitches of laughter for its entirety! I shall love to know that my book, *Donald Trump and My Eating Disorder*, can compel Ellen and Portia to think, just as they made me think, with their incredible work. What a gorgeous couple. They are love!

Oprah and Ellen, despite being liberals, will likely feel unthreatened by my book. They are strong. If anything, because they are humans with hearts, they might connect with something that I have written regarding my war with food, or regarding my encountering opposition on my human self. And it shall be a privilege and honour for me, if tears flood to their eyes. Their tears shall be from a place of parallel feeling and experience. What is parallel not? It is the girl who lives in the therapist's office. It is the girl who is scared of her own shadow. Are you acquainted with the deer caught in headlights look? This is the impression that I get from the ones who are threatened by my very strong, bullheaded personality.

I tell them of my rigid opinion and or reality.

"No, I cannot meet for drinks tonight. I am working."

And it is like they have seen a ghost!

To most humans, Friday night is meant for going out and celebrating the end of a work week. To me, Friday night is the same as Monday, Tuesday, Wednesday, Thursday, Saturday, and Sunday. I am working. Or walking my dog. Or both!

This is my warning to anyone who is "struggling" because my book might be a "trigger" to them.

I am very rigid.

Such rigidness is unhealthy to many humans. Thusly, stop reading me, now, if you think that I shall trigger you into a state of unhealthfulness. BUT IF I SHALL INSPIRE YOU, and or if I shall entertain you, then please continue forward!

First let it be known: MENTAL HEALTH IS REAL.

My philosophy on mental illness, however, is a touchy subject, and I shall attempt to deliver it with gracefulness and kindness. Please remember that my beliefs are just that: MY BELIEFS. This is MY LANGUAGE. I encourage the adoption of my thoughts not. I challenge any opposing school of thought not. And my thoughts, as presented herein, exist for the subject of debate not, particularly in conversations, interviews, or the like, after this book is published. My thoughts exist. Peacefully and strongly. I simply state my truth. It is my right to express my truth. It is my right to express my reality. I refuse to defend or argue my reality.

This is my warning.

And this is my reality.

I DO NOT BELIEVE IN MENTAL ILLNESS AS A PATHOLOGICAL CONDITION.

I believe in deep sadness.

I believe in depression.

I believe in abnormality of the brain yielding terrible behavioural reaction such as schizophrenia. I believe in terrible events causing stress that is difficult to bear. Have you viewed the 1980 film entitled *The Elephant Man* starring Sir Anthony Hopkins? Have you viewed the 1981 film entitled *Ordinary People* starring Mary Tyler Moore? Have you viewed the 1942 film entitled *Random Harvest* starring Ronald Coleman and Greer Garson? Have you viewed the 1948 film entitled *The Snake Pit* starring Olivia deHavilland? All four films deal with "different from the normal" behaviours yet they are sold on the premise of "mental illness." In all of these scenarios, I disagree with this label of mental illness.

I believe that mental illness as a label is society's evil, socialistic, and IMPURELY capitalistic way of labelling a human's difficulty with regard to managing unfavourable situations. Such as vomiting food. Such as restriction from food. Such as bulimia. Such as anorexia. Such as any unhealthy behaviour.

I believe that eating disorders are psychological conditions not.

I believe that eating disorders are mental illness not.

That said, and as previously announced, I understand and respect that mental health is a real thing. Turning any negative aspect of mental health into a pathological condition, however, is crooked.

Mind you, never shall I judge a person who identifies with the label of mental illness. I respect every human and their unique ability to think, to relate, to identify, to understand, to live, and to love.

I simply identify with the label not, and I relate eating disorders to it not.

Even in the deepest, darkest days and nights of my bulimia, I constantly created a plan to correct it. I never once cried about it. I never once became so sad that I could, as a result of my condition, function not. I never considered my condition or actions to be related to mental wellness or to mental illness or to any degree thereof. I abhor the words of "struggle" and "cope." I feel bad for people who use these words.

In the early years, circa ages seventeen to twenty, it made no sense to me, that because I was eating food in unhealthy portions and expunging it from my body, that I "had" a mental illness. I felt completely fine and happy except for being disgusted with my food failures. My behaviours were simply in sync with my all on, all off personality. Thusly the eating disorder made sense. If I ate one bad thing, I needed to eat one hundred bad things. If I restricted, I could go for a long time without consuming high volumes of food, eating only healthy, divine things, in healthy portions. How did that count as mental illness, I wondered? How did my eating actions, resulting from what my brain instructed, be a sign of illness? Was it because my brain wanted all or nothing? But what was so wrong with that? To me, it seemed normal and rational. I either liked something or I liked it not. I was never half pregnant. And my brain choreographed every last detail of the binges and purges. I always maintained control of my binges and purges, as out of control as they seemed.

I was sent to a psychologist at the age of seventeen. My parents, as most humans do, classified my eating disorder as mental illness. They arranged for me to see a "well renowned" doctor in the field of eating disorders. A "doctor." Or, as I saw it, an old chubby Indian woman with a bindi who knew nothing about being a young, thin-obsessed, caucasian girl in the United States of America. She arranged for me and my parents to have group therapy sessions. Sitting around a table, we passed around a puppet, only permitted to speak when holding the puppet. When the puppet came to me, I held it into the air, snottily, dramatically sealing my lips. I spoke not a word.

I wonder of how much money my parents paid to that quack. I would like to pay them back! Again, my parents did exactly what a text book advises to be correct. And I am grateful for their love and care.

A couple of years later, as a snobby, self-righteous nineteen year old, I sought my own "divinely sounding" "doctor," this time a psychotherapist named Doctor Zebra (name changed). She still occupies that same office space in Pittsburgh. I know this, because sometimes, for many years, I walked by with my dog Gwendolyn, and seeing her name on the roll call of building occupants, I smiled, remembering it all. But, back then, I smiled not. I compare my expectation of Doctor Zebra to the episode of *Sex and the City* where Carrie Bradshaw meets Bon Jovi. I wanted for my experience to be sexy, to be fashionable, and to finally get me to stop bingeing and purging so that I could be thin again. And then I could meet a sexy, powerful man waiting to see the therapist after my appointment, and we would marry and live happily ever after! It is nowadays hilarious to me that I considered dating a hypothetical "man" who cried to a therapist.

For my first appointment, stationed at 181 pounds and ferociously engaging in bulimic activity, I wore black pants and a blue peasant top by Express, with a metal belt circling my waist, paired with clunky black heels. I thought that I looked good, fat considered, and I wanted for Doctor Zebra to talk to me in an adult-like, rational, glamorous fashion.

So I told her about myself. I told her about my bulimic behaviours. And her reply?

"We need to get you to a nutritionist to lose some of this weight."

F*CK.

She totally misunderstood me. I was the bulimic with anorexic goals. It was my every desire to lose weight. And she was basically calling me a fatso. I needed a controlled system developed by myself, not by a nutritionist. I needed to do it my way. I had been anorexically thin, just two years ago, and I could accomplish it, all by myself, again. Oh, yes, and she wanted for me to draw pictures.

I knew, right then, that Doctor Zebra knew nothing more than the text book definition of eating disorder. She knew that bulimia meant "ox hunger." I shall afford her with that compliment. But she realised not the pain that I experienced by her suggesting that I lose weight. To have my failure called out, that of being unsuccessful with weight and food, was the worst thing that my ears could hear. Listening to her words made me want to punch her in the face.

I was so mad at my chronic failure to maintain a state of thin for more than one year.

I was so mad at my failure to control food.

I was so mad that I no longer looked like a fitness queen.

I was ready to be finished with my eating disorder so that I could write a book about it!

In exchange for poor service, I gave zero dollars to Doctor Zebra. I refused to pay her bill because she lied to me in that insurance would cover her "services." It turned out that insurance covered nothing, thereby leaving nineteen-year old penniless me with an enormous bill. She stalked me for a few years in pursuance of her fee (fee for what?), eventually surrendering. I wonder if she retains record of notes from our sessions? It will be interesting to see if she publishes them in an "academic" paper, in response to this book. Maybe she can strike it rich, riding on my book's coattails. She will need my consent, however, to quote from this memoir and to release my file to the public.

In writing this book, in fact, I became curious as to her "work" so executed a Google search, quickly finding her website. It's humorous because it's the exact kind of "therapy" that makes my head spin into circles. Art therapy for eating disorders? Really? Well, maybe, in a broad scope, she's onto something. My art is yoga. My art is writing. All of that has, indeed, helped me to work through the healing needed from those eating disordered years. I hope, that at the end of the day, Doctor Zebra is only trying to be a good person and really wants to help people who are challenged. But something about her approach made me feel like all she wanted was my money, like she was a crony capitalist pretending to be a social worker. Like a bad guy from an Ayn Rand novel. Like a James Taggart. Something about her sat unkindly with my brain, and seeing her picture on that website also elicits those feelings. I speculate, with all confidence, that she is a radical Democrat.

Is the brain separate from the body? No. Then why, when considering undesirable behaviours, do we assign an intangible disease to the brain? Here is an interesting way to look at it: Why can the brain get "depression" but the vagina cannot? Why, for the brain, is it turned into something intangible? The answer is that head therapists and pharmaceutical companies can make money from it.

Well, allow me to backtrack, please. I revise my comment about vaginal depression, as any *Sex and the City* fan knows that Charlotte's vagina was diagnosed with depression in season two of episode four. LOL! I first discuss this episode in chapter one when highlighting the infamous scenes of *Sex and the City* featuring President Trump.

For the physical disease of the brain, in my opinion, a person can self-medicate with proper nutrition plus Ashtanga yoga, balancing it themselves. A change in behaviour might result. And for the record, please allow me to state that I think that healthcare is a right, but insomuch that "healthcare" means access to clean air and healthy food and movement. NOT CONVENTIONAL HEALTHCARE. An example to back my statement on healthcare is that when my dog Gwendolyn, at the age of nine, for a second year in a row, produced tumours that behaved as mast cell, instead of conducting surgeries and chemotherapy and drugs, I chose a holistic approach, implementing Chinese herbs for good immunity and Essiac tea and an overdosage of raw goat milk and copious hours of daily exercise. All tumours disappeared. And, as this is published, we are celebrating one year, six months, and seven days of a tumour free state. I think that much of the human and canine condition is related to inflammation. If we eat things that cause inflammation of the outside body (bloat and fat), then how do we think our brains are responding? The brain is likely inflamed, too. To me, this means that the brain is sick. To me, this means not mental illness. Eliminating and or reducing processed foods and gluten is my suggestion. TRUST ME, I LOVE my naughty tofu burritos by Soul Vegan dipped into ketchup on Saturdays and Sundays, and I never miss this tofu burrito beat. But with a more rigid focus on good food, the exterior of the body look great, and the brain will feel great! I think that food and movement is at the root of health. This is why ending my war with food was so very important.

Anorexics claim to be afraid of food. THEY FEAR FOOD. Gosh, imagining fear of food is outside of my realm of comprehension. "Ooooh help me! Help me! The big bad scary potatoes are frightening me!" It sounds so ridiculous. The only thing on Earth that I fear is a height. I hate being up high, when motionless, and when moving slowly! Such as driving in the high mountains. Such as riding a ski lift. Such as riding the ferris wheel. Even looking at the ferris wheel frightens me! But, I honestly can imagine not of how a person can fear food like I do heights. Fearing food sounds so childish and irrational to me (this coming from someone who lived with an eating disorder for seventeen years). Yes, I hate fat. HATE FAT. Hate fat. ON ME. But I fear it not. So yes, maybe medication will cause someone to stop fearing food? Let's say it's true. A change in behaviour might result. Great. The anorexic no longer fears the calorie, so she'll eat. This is analogous to treating the vagina with cream for itchiness. If your vagina is itchy, the doctor will prescribe something. And you stop the scratching. But why is under-eating considered as a mental illness whereas over-scratching of the vagina is not? Does the brain not control both undesirable behaviours?

It's all about fear mongering and of what society can label into a "mental illness" comfortably. The popular activities that get classified into mental illness include sleeping, sexing, eating, drinking, and gambling. Oh! The basic elements of life, drinking and gambling aside. Oh! And two big ones additionally: perfectionism and narcissism. How dare a person love themselves madly?! How dare a person strive to live perfectly?! Also, did you know that once upon a time, until the 1980s, homosexuality was considered as a mental disorder? The *Diagnostic and Statistical Manual of Mental Disorders* is such a f*cking joke!

At my blog, I have been accused of being "autistic" because I rarely sit still and have a one track mind. Someone recently told me of a child who was tested for autism due to his antisocial behaviour and weirdness, and this interested me to learn more about this "mental illness." Firstly, I confirmed that it is, indeed, listed with many "subtypes" in great detail in the *Diagnostic and Statistical Manual of Mental Disorders*. This blows my mind. *Psychology Today* writes that autistic people are obsessed with schedules and rigidness, that they're socially awkward, that they lack the ability to understand perspective of others, and that they engage in behaviours like finger twisting. So basically an introverted perfectionist who practices yoga? So basically me? How is this a brain disease?

Society mongers with fear because they make money from it. The socialist state makes money from it. Well, things are changing under President Trump's ruling. Yes, the divine First Lady's cause is opioid addiction, but it is being treated rationally. We must keep illegals out of the country because they are bringing in the drugs. Eliminate the root cause, and eliminate the addiction. If there are no drugs to take, then there is no drug addiction.

Many question about how the capitalist nature of my brain can repel this ponzi scheme of crony capitalism. The answer is that I am a pure capitalist. I believe in doing things in the correct and honest way, for the betterment of society and for human existence, not for the betterment of the fat socialist doctor's pocketbook.

Anorexia is traditionally defined as "without appetite."

Bulimia is traditionally defined as "ox hunger."

And modern head doctors have turned these basic words into definitions of emotional dysfunction. Any dictionary will now tell the researcher that anorexia is "an emotional disorder characterised by an obsessive desire to lose weight by refusing to eat." Any dictionary will now tell the researcher that bulimia is "an emotional disorder characterised by a distorted body image and obsessive desire to lose weight in which bouts of extreme exercising are followed by fasting or self-induced vomiting or purging."

How absolutely positively ludicrous to define eating disorders as emotional.

Heck, let us please take any bad behaviour, slap "emotional" onto its description, and sign it up for a formal mental disorder to again, line the socialist state's pocketbook.

There is a great episode of 1980s *Dynasty* of where Adam Carrington suggests to Colby Anders that she is suffering from "sexual anorexia" and must therefore be wanting him badly, at that time. If one were to make such a comment in this day and age, they would be thrashed! I found the comment to be amazing. In fact, it turned me on, and if my future gentleman were to whisper that into my ear, I shall be very drawn to him. Radical Democrats probably consider lack of sexual activity or appetite to be unhealthy and therefore a mental illness. Of course this directly opposes the celibacy limb of Ashtanga yoga. Does this means that yogis who practice celibacy are mentally disordered? Bottom line is that anorexia is a choice, unless of course, it is a physical, medical condition.

The ox hunger origin of bulimia is spot on. Similar to anorexia as an eating disorder, bulimia is a choice. And for me, ox hunger extends beyond eating. It applies to EVERYTHING that I do. I want everything divine in huge amounts. So is my entire life a disease? If it is a disease to want everything in grand amounts, then please, define me as mentally ill. Please! Sign me up.

If socialists insist on keeping eating disorders in their *Diagnostic and Statistical Manual of Mental Disorders*, then I motion to add one more "condition." Of what condition do I write?

TRUMP DERANGEMENT SYNDROME.

Trump Derangement Syndrome is the truest of disease. Wikipedia defines it as, "a neologism describing a reaction to United States President Donald Trump by liberals, progressives, and anti-trump conservatives, who are said to respond to Trump's statements and political actions irrationally and with little regard to Trump's actual position or action taken. The term has been used to discredit criticism of Trump's actions."

I truly hope that my book can help to cure humans of their disorder, of their Trump Derangement Syndrome. The Fake News, radical Democrats, the Bush family, and "the forgotten president" Jimmy Carter exist amongst the humans that require deep psychological treatment for their mental disorder of Trump Derangement Syndrome.

The other day, I spied a little boy, likely aged three or four, walking with the assistance of a medical walker. Smiling and giggling, the boy probably knew not of his handicap. It delivered tears to my eyes because this joyful little boy had bent legs and a face that indicated some sort of brain disease. And he was joyful. He was living with a smiling heart. Three hours later, I spied the SAME little boy. Smiling and giggling. Trudging forward with his medical walker. And it made me feel so very stupid for moaning and groaning about the injured shin of my left leg. About the bone spur on my left foot. About the plantar fasciitis of my left foot. About my double sided bunionettes! About my missing toe nails! About the blisters on my toe pads! I shall never again complain about my "problems." This joyful little boy really affected me. His reality made the old eating disorder and battle with yoga and complaining about screwed up feet seem as so very shallow. Additionally, this wonderful little joyful boy reminded me of the amazing children whom I saluted daily at The Children's Institute of Pittsburgh. Unloaded from their school buses, mostly all in wheelchairs, these children all had brain diseases. They all did. I have no doubt on this statement. It is appalling to me that people live in their woe and think that they are something special because they have an addiction to food or other bad behaviour and define it as mental illness or depression. Look at these beautiful children who require grand assistance to function, children who actually do have a brain disease, and you shall feel ashamed for clinging to the label of "mental illness" for your selfish eating disorder or other problem with living.

For more on how I think on this subject, please read *The Myth of Mental Illness* by Doctor Thomas Szasz.

The former eating disordered girl in me, if given my soapbox, wants to firmly grab onto the shoulders of one who is living with an eating disorder and exclaim, "Nothing is wrong with your brain! Something needs to be changed with your behaviours so that you can eat and be joyful. Nothing is wrong with your brain! You simply need to create peaceful conditions so that you can think clearly. It was really hard to end my seventeen-year war with food. But I succeeded. And President Trump helped me greatly. I won the war. You can win it, too."

I hereby refer my readers to a wonderful song by the talented music artist who goes by the name of Ice Cube. The song is called, *You Can Do It*.

Yes. You Can.

CHAPTER
XI

FAKE YOGA

I STARTED PRACTICING YOGA BECAUSE OF MY DOG.

I mean, really, now that you have read this far into my book, you likely assumed that it had to be one of two reasons: My dog Gwendolyn or President Trump. Ha! In this case, Gwendolyn deserves the credit. And, of course, there is a dramatic tale to tell!

It was a cold, dark evening in January of 2009 when I arrived to Gwendolyn's daycare of Misty Pines Dog Park Company of Wexford, Pennsylvania. On the cusp of the closing time of daycare, I understood not of what could be so important that the workers would shoo me from the daycare after paying Gwendolyn's fee. They normally encouraged friendly chit chat, sharing stories of Gwendolyn's big day, even though it was customary for me to telephone and to check in several times per day, like a crazy mom! But on this night of subject, the beautiful red-headed girl on duty named Sherry stated, with peppiness, "We are going to yoga!" Smiling, I secretly rolled my eyes.

Who would waste their time with getting zen when they can be working-out and burning calories? I thought.

Two days later, it was deja vu. Gwendolyn and I were shooed away because the worker girls needed to be at yoga.

On the following week, they invited ME to yoga.

The ever-yearning to be "normal" and therefore included, I thought, *Okay, a few months ago, we saw 'Marley & Me' in the theatre, and now they extend a second invitation for social activity? Maybe they really like me? Maybe I should go, just this once? Maybe I can have real friends? Yeah! Fellow dog mommies! But yoga? Really? And what if they think that I'm fat?*

Racing to home to drop-off my baby Gwendolyn at our Sewickley apartment, I nowadays ask myself, "Who was that girl?" I left her all day at daycare during my pointless hours of working at corporate America, and, now I was dropping her off at the apartment so that I could leave her to race back to Wexford where I entered the studio of Amazing Yoga. Seriously! Who was that girl?

Renting a yoga mat, as I owned one not, I noticed just one thing: FEET. Everywhere. AND I HATE FEET. Also, the room was so hot that my skin felt tarred and feathered. I thusly had zero expectation other than I would hate the next hour. *This will be my first and last time at yoga*, I thought.

BUT IT WAS AMAZING.

What?! I love this! sang my brain.

I literally wanted for the practise to keep going. The graceful poses connected by vinyasa immediately electrified my everything. It was the closest physical HIGH that I had experienced in the past ten years that permitted expression of my long ago, most beloved, dance training, the one that I had abandoned for my eating disorder. Yes, it had been exactly one decade since quitting dance school to enable better control over exercise and therefore purging of calories and constant sculpting of the perfect body. Ten years is a long time to be without the thing that makes you tic and toc. And, at that time of ten years ago in 1999, I had flirted with a yoga-themed VHS tape by Karen Voight, a VHS that I had purchased at Kmart, the same Kmart from where I later purchased pizza and laxatives during my first binge and purge as depicted in chapter two of this book. I remember fondly of how the movement as depicted in that yoga VHS tape caused me to feel. It was intoxicating. This 1999 flirtation with yoga reminded me of my long ago 1991 flirtation with *Trump: The Game*. And, here, at Amazing Yoga, in 2009, this was that same feeling. It was a feeling greater than what I had achieved with dance. It was a feeling greater than what I had achieved with a perfect body. Yoga matched the exact high that nine-year old Nicole Marie Story felt when investigating *Trump: The Game*. I wanted to scream about my newfound love to the world!

So I did.

Because Nicole Marie Story loves attention.

Next evening, following a morning of running on the treadmill, lifting weights, "working" in corporate America, then returning home to my sweet dog Gwendolyn where we darted off onto our adventure walk including a stop for coffee at the Crazy Mocha Coffee Company, I noticed my friend Barb working at one of the coffee shop computers.

"Hi, Barb!"

"Hi, Nicole!"

"Did you workout today?"

"Yes. I went to yoga."

"Oh my god! I went to yoga last night!"

"Where did you go?"

"Amazing Yoga."

"Oh, Nicole. You need to come to Teacher X's class." (name changed).

"No, Barb. I love Amazing Yoga!"

"Nicole, I see how you exercise at the Y. You will love Teacher X's class. It is the best. It is so hard!"

"Okay. Fine. I shall attend."

I attended Teacher X's class on the next evening. And I never stopped. Until I was kicked out. Every Tuesday and Thursday from 6:30pm to 8pm. Every Saturday and every other Sunday from 9:30am to 11am. And then I began using my vacation days in half-day increments to practise with the affluent housewives on Monday from 9:30am to 11am and Friday from 9:30am to 11am. I crushed very hard on the sexy powerful Republican man at yoga. In fact, I came to practise wearing yoga pants and high heels, toting a copy of *Atlas Shrugged*, as I knew it got his attention. His attention made me high.

Suddenly I found myself being accepted and loved by a group of beautiful housewives with perky breasts and thin bodies. I unquestionably became teacher's pet. Teacher X invited me, and only me, to weekend workshops, including an Ashtanga workshop with the great Tim Miller! I had NO IDEA as to Mr. Miller's reputation and history in the yoga world. I simply thought that I was attending a workshop with someone who got really deep, spiritually and physically! I had no idea of what Ashtanga yoga meant, but I knew that what I practised daily with Teacher X was some fashionable derivative of it. Mr. Miller "played" something called, *The Hanuman Chalisa*, and it rendered me to tears! I am the girl who cries on the rarity. Yet this song, presented in Sankskrit, prompted me to tears. I had no idea as to what I was experiencing, yet it made me cry. After the workshop, Teacher X said to me, "I wasn't impressed." Something about that comment sat unrightly with me. It felt like the soothsayer in *Julius Cesar* had warned, "Beware the Ides of March."

In late 2010, I decided to pursue a yoga teacher certification and dazzling yoga career. Teacher X warned me that "There's no money in this. Don't do it." But I loved it. I loved yoga! And I was headstrong that I could make money from it, that I could make money from whatever most interested me. Thusly, because Teacher X offered not a teacher training program and I thought that one was required to teach yoga, I enrolled at The Yoga School Z for teacher training (name of school changed). At that point, I added two more daily classes with Teacher X thusly attending every class that she offered. People began coming into Teacher X's studio, introducing themselves to me, thinking that I was the teacher because my body looked so lean, long, and strong. Additionally, I attended eight-hour Saturday and Sunday "torture sessions" at The Yoga School Z for "yoga teacher training." But teacher training it was not, I soon came to learn.

IT WAS FAKE YOGA.

On that first day of "yoga teacher training" with The Yoga School Z, I entered into the classroom, fit as a yoga fiddle (or so I thought), ready to learn anatomy, philosophy, history, and to pump out chaturanga after chaturanga with my fellow students and fellow teachers in training. What did I find? A room full of chubby housewives, old stinky hippies, and recent skinny college graduates who claimed former eating disorder status and that yoga had saved them. LOL. It was a freak show with a few thousand dollars as admission fee. None of these fellow students had been exposed to downward dog (aside from maybe one or two of the "ex bulimic" college graduates). And it was obvious that nobody had studied yoga for any great length of time, like had I. Well, that was my perception of my "studies" to that point. And that was my perception of my fellow "teachers in training." But despite my reservations, I attended these boring sessions, every weekend, for about one month's time. I would rise before the sun, in the wintry months of 2011, to walk my Gwendolyn for two hours in the enchanted forest of Sewickley Heights, to tire her so that she could sleep whilst her mommy attended eight hours of "teacher training."

One thing led to another, and although this does, indeed, sound very angry on my part, I despatched the following letter to the "President and Spiritual Director" (LOL) of The Yoga School Z on the March 16, 2011, herein deleting small parts and changing names. But just like the Fake News scan legally sell newspapers, **FAKE YOGA** can legally sell yoga teacher certifications, and The Yoga School Z cooperated with my refund request, so I shall cause zero harm to their business. It is important to share this information, however, to demonstrate the harm which they could have caused to me, if I were a weak person. It is important to use this data to prove my point that **FAKE YOGA** exists and that most western yoga is Fake Yoga. By sharing this letter with you, the picture of what I endured is properly painted. It sounds like something that President Trump would direct his attorneys to write, in my opinion, to the Fake News Media! I hereby present to you, a 2011 letter sent to The Yoga School Z, otherwise know as Fake Yoga.

"16th of March of 2011

Dear President and Spiritual Director,

This email serves to communicate my immediate demand for resolution to a scam concerning the The Yoga School Z. I expect written emailed response concerning the school's disposition of my full refund request of ($xxxx.00) by 16:00 hours on Thursday, 17 of March. If the school options to decline my request for full refund, then I shall contact my colleagues at the *Pittsburgh Tribune-Review*, *Whirl Magazine*, and *WPXI* television regarding this situation. Additionally, I shall contact *Yoga Journal*, *The New York Times*, and the *Yoga Alliance* to report on this scam. This potential exposure to the press shall happen tomorrow. Most importantly, I shall sue The Yoga School Z for discrimination, lost wages, intentional infliction of mental distress, and associated damages.

Miss Fake Yoga (name changed), a 'teacher' at your organisation, contacted me during this afternoon at 13:45 hours. She informed me of her opinion that my vinyasa flow style does not compliment The Yoga School Z theory and therefore she counseled me to seek other options for achieving my yoga teacher certification. I informed Miss Fake Yoga that my intentions exist to complete the program as I'm fully open to learning of practices other than my passion. Furthermore, I had invested six months of time and money into the training. She understood my expectations when she accepted me into the program as my application clearly stipulated my passion and daily practice of vinyasa yoga. Furthermore, when I expressed my concern regarding the difference between hatha and vinyasa styles during our initial telephone interview, Miss Fake Yoga stated, 'Oh, vinyasa is hatha yoga.' She was simply trying to secure another $xxxx.00 of tuition.

At that point, Miss Fake Yoga attacked me with statements such as the following:

'You will not allow me to correct you in class. I remember a specific incident during downward facing dog. You had tears in your eyes.' - In response to Miss Fake Yoga's accusation, I reminded her that during correction of subject, she questioned, 'How does that feel now?' My response was, 'It does not feel powerful.' To my reminder of this dialogue, she responded, 'Well that confuses other students in the class. You're disagreeable.' Am I to lie of my opinion when questioned?

Miss Fake Yoga informed me of being late for every class. This is not true. I have arrived earlier than most of the other students, even when arriving a few minutes late due to parking issues or jolting from another yoga class.

Furthermore, I have attended all classes. How are excessive absences of other students being handled?

I informed Miss Fake Yoga that it's my intention to finish the program considering the time and money that I have invested. She responded that she will not pass me. I informed her that I will immediately contact The Yoga School Z headquarters to report on her attack. Her response existed, 'They will not pass you either. I've already informed the board. Sure, I'll accept your money, but I won't pass you.' Miss Fake Yoga waited until more than half of the tuition was paid to inform of this? By definition, this is a scam.

When Miss Fake Yoga questioned of my dissatisfactions, I stated the following, 'I was uncomfortable with moving a bone in my knee as instructed, and teacher M responded that I'm not happy with myself.' I could not move the bone because I was not happy with myself? M stated that I needed to search my soul to correct the issue. When I informed Miss Fake Yoga of this, her response was, 'That is what The Yoga School Z tradition is all about. It's about growing.' I am certain that the media shall appreciate that The Yoga School Z attempts to make young girls feel bad about themselves in attempt to earn revenue.

She then accused me of pressuring other students to attempt my vinyasa flow style. I don't speak much to the other students. I am a quiet, shy person. The other students approached me on Sunday to question if I could provide them with instruction on inversions. We agreed that I would send Miss Fake Yoga an email to request usage of the Pittsburgh space for providing my fellow trainees with a complimentary vinyasa flow class. It is now my belief that Miss Fake Yoga arranged for these girls to pique my interest with teaching a class and to therefore request usage of the space. Miss Fake Yoga is using my love of yoga against me. Miss Fake Yoga stated, 'You can't teach a class. You're not certified. You don't even know how to properly do the poses. And you can't talk about opening your own studio when at teacher training.' I can't? I can't talk about opening a studio when I'm questioned about my current teaching practices?

Miss Fake Yoga stated that she doesn't observe my progress in terms of meditation and relaxation. She doesn't believe that I enjoy it. Does my enjoyment level, high or low, relate to achieving certification? I have, indeed, successfully instructed relaxation and meditation in the class which I believe is the expectation.

From the very first class, Miss Fake Yoga has glared at me with cold eyes and harsh commentary. Despite my discomfort, I have been nothing but cheerful and positive. My ankle was severely sprained this weekend, and she roughly questioned, "What's wrong with you?" It took one of the students to fetch a container of ice to help me. Miss Fake Yoga's mother treats me in the same manner, as though I don't manner. Do not allow Miss Fake Yoga to contact me, ever again. She is rude and threatening.

Bottom line is this:

1. Issue full refund within five business days.
2. Communicate disposition regarding the full refund via email by 16:00 hours tomorrow.
3. If items one and two are not fulfilled, then I will go to the public as stated through paragraph one.

Regards,

Nicole Marie Story"

My yoga heart was broken. Broken! But broken hearts heal. And I continued practicing with vigour and love every single day with Teacher X until the day, seven months later, in October of 2011 that I published my first YouTube yoga video. I called it "Kitchen Yoga." It was like Instagram yoga work, before Instagram. A few hours after publishing the video, I received an email from Teacher X, informing of my expulsion from her yoga school. Yet again, it was **FAKE YOGA.**

6 October 2011, 08:54:222 AM EDT

"Dear Nicole,

It is with great regret that I am informing you that I will no longer be able to teach yoga to you. I have worked very hard over the last decade to develop a style of yoga that is unique to me and extremely personal. I do not give my consent or the rights to publish it in any manner. I will be sending you a check for the balance of your pass.

I wish you the only best,

Teacher X"

And that was the straw that broke the yoga camel's back.

I basically died inside.

I tried really hard to keep up the practice.

And despite being one year, three months clean from bulimia, I opened the door to resumed disordered eating. Not bulimic this time, just a binge eater. A too much eater. And I got fat. I lost my yoga. And my body fell apart.

I was back to ground zero.

In fact, I was below ground zero in a place called Hell.

Fast forward to March of 2012, and I was transformed back into a chubby cow, an angry girl, a lost soul. I did it to myself. It was me trying to find balance when I needed a system of black and white rigid principles. I was listening to the world instead of to my heart. I had so much work to do. At this point, I could understand not of why I was getting so fat. The answer was that I drank like a fish, I ate like a man and or an athlete (which I was not, at the time), and I stopped practicing yoga. Well, although I practised yoga here and there, it seemed like stopping completely compared to my former everyday twice per day routine. I popped into random yoga classes throughout the city, where nobody knew me as the former skinny yoga girl. Dealing with the grimaces, or should I say, dealing with the grimaces that I imagined, was outside of my scope of capability. Nobody else really cared about my fat. Sure the fat would be a shocker to anyone who knew the former skinny yoga girl, but at the end of the day, it only mattered to me.

With regard to the various classes that I attended, I enjoyed Three Rivers Yoga in Coraopolis, but it was too far from my home in mileage, and the hours were incompatible with my work schedule. Also, it was a little too "yeah man hippie" for me. I shall proclaim, however, that the instructor is the real deal. Yoga Bob, flaunting a big teddy bear heart, knows his yoga. As a side note, I am friends with a divine undercover Trump supporter who practices at this studio and described of how, on the days after the election, the energy of the students was so very low. Everyone existed as "horrified" and in puddles of tears. LOL. Next I experimented with Salt Power Yoga in Cranberry Township. I enjoyed it. I enjoyed the people. But it challenged me not. To my brain, it was "regular boutique yoga," not "high fashion obsessive compulsive boutique yoga." I also attended a few Bikram classes with Mr. Bikram. And, on Bikram class number two, the young, snotty, just-out-of-yoga-teacher-training, just-out-of-college-twit told me that I had no choice but to use a towel atop my mat. She literally scolded me in the middle of class because I refused to use a towel. I appreciated her attitude not and thusly quietly rolled my mat, exiting from class, departing in my haughty nose-in-air fashion, listening to her whiny voice trailing behind, begging for me to return. I think, at this point, although he agreed with my decision to politely leave because the "teacher" indeed behaved like a snotty jerk, Mr. Bikram deemed me as the angriest yoga girl alive.

AND YES! I was so very angry. I had all of this artificial yoga. I had **FAKE YOGA**. I wanted the real thing! I wanted that thing which made my heart go pitter patter. I wanted my new zsa zsa zsu. THE YOGA that I practiced from February of 2009 to October of 2011 was my old zsa zsa zsu. And then it went into a coma. My yoga experiences to follow were like trying to date again, with my true love being in the hospital. You can't give your heart to something simply because it has the label of a man. You can only love that which you love. And yes, my zsa zsa zsu would need to evolve from what I had known, but I knew that it would have the same base. I would shake my yoga from its coma, and I would figure it out, no matter how long it would take.

The period between getting kicked out of two yoga schools and succeeding at finding my yoga, those exact dates being October 6, 2011 until April 27, 2015, was torture. Having a three-year history of practicing happy yoga for nearly every day, only to have it completely ripped from you, then improvising with downward dogs without electricity and love, was like eating spaghetti without marinara sauce, was like eating a peanut butter and jelly sandwich without the jelly, was like eating a tofu burrito without ketchup!

It was like being suffocated.

It was like walking on a ninety degree day in the middle of the summer.

It was like losing your soul.

My body continued growing bigger and farther away from that heightened state that I knew when I practiced boutique yoga. It was devastating to know that I was capable of something beautiful, once upon a time, only to now be incapable. My eating was chaos. I weighed between 145 and 160 pounds on any given day during this period. I hated the skin in which I lived. I hated the skin in which I walked. I hated the skin in which I breathed.

I met Mr. Bicycle and his amazing family in January of 2013. A fellow admirer of Ayn Rand, Mr. Bicycle became my mentor. Inspiring me to be my best person, he read every blog post. And he genuinely cared. Someone of high quality recognised the high quality in me. And I knew that if I committed to something at my blog, I would succeed. I knew that Mr. Bicycle was rooting for me.

So on January 1, 2014, I started my new big project, Finding My Yoga, in which I dedicated all of my free time to finding that which I had lost. I went to work in a hard way. Attending studio classes. Exploring different methods of online yoga classes. Doing practices of what I remembered from my old boutique days. And I blogged daily about my trials and tribulations. Pairing with yoga, of course, were stories of my dog and of my eating, and many pictures of my abdominals. In 2014, my experiment spanned the entire year without success.

In year two of Finding My Yoga, almost four years of living in Yoga Purgatory, almost four years since getting kicked out of two **FAKE YOGA** schools, I had my telescope facing forward, at all times, determined to find my Yoga Planet. And, on April 26, 2015, my rocket began descent. Suddenly, the formula for landing on my Yoga Planet became clearer to my brain. Suddenly, I wanted an exact prescription of yoga, but it was different from the yoga that I had known. After so many years of trying every fancy practice under the sun, I wanted something without the pizzazz, at least without pizzazz on the cover. I wanted something quiet. Strong. Passionate. Black. White. I wanted the peeled back onion. The raw. I wanted the pictures that I had seen in my book entitled, *Light on Yoga* by "some man" named Iyengar.

Why did I have this book? It is because my former "teacher" told me that it was her yoga bible. It had thusly sat on my shelf for four years, and I had skimmed the words and pictures but never actually delved into it because it was plain. But all of a sudden, it piqued my interest. It seemed to match that which I suddenly craved. Visiting YouTube, searching "Iyengar Yoga," I queried the most incredible, most intriguing, most beautiful video of B.K.S. Iyengar from (I believe) the 1970s. So there I had it! I would now be an Iyengar Yoga practitioner! The declaration blog post, dated April 26, 2015 still exists at my blog: www.theyogaballerina.com/my-sunday-yoga-pressie-to-you. I immediately wanted to share this practice with the world. My heart felt so happy. In retrospect, I see that I am a good person because I wanted to share my findings immediately as compared to my former "teacher" who wanted to keep her practice as a big fat secret. The video continues to inspire me, today in 2019, four years after my first viewing it, just as it did on that very first day in 2015. When I am feeling like a lazy yoga sloth, I watch this video to be inspired! But what happened on the next day, on the April 27, 2015, happened by complete accident. An accident of divine fate!

On the next day, on April 27, 2015, exactly one years, four months, and twenty seven days into my project of Finding My Yoga, exactly six years and three months since beginning a dedicated yoga practise, by pure accident, I did it. I found my yoga. When setting up for asana (physical practice) on this very special day, rather than finding the Iyengar video of the prior day, I stumbled upon a video of Sri K. Pattabhi Jois instructing an intermediate series practice. And I fell hard. I fell hard in love. After nearly four years of living in a yoga coma, after one year, four months, and twenty-seven days of actively working hard to find my yoga again, I found it. I found my zsa zsa zsu.

I FOUND ASHTANGA YOGA.

CHAPTER
XII

SURVIVAL

On December 20, 2018, I was attacked, beaten, and mugged.

Walking in a very affluent area of Chicago at 8:20pm on a weekday, in one of the highest taxed neighbourhoods in the United States of America, I suddenly found myself on the ground, with a very large, strong male on my back. Punching me. Kicking me. Dragging me. Telling me to shut up. TO SHUT UP! I was screaming for help. "Help me! Help me! I'm being attacked!," the video surveillance reveals of my breathy screams as I fought the monster, scrambling to escape. I believe that he was trying to lift my body to move me into the alley to rape me or to throw me into a car to kidnap me and to sell me on the internet. From inside of their homes, neighbours heard my screams and came running to my rescue. Noticing the alerted neighbours, the monster ripped the bag from my body and ran away, joining two other monsters who had watched the attack. It was only at this moment that I turned around to face the monsters who were dressed in black masks. All three disappeared into the dark alley, the sound of running feet and rain, closing the scene of terror.

All that I could think of during this attack was to survive. *"I must get home to my Gwendolyn… I must get home to my Gwendolyn… I must get home to my Gwendolyn."* Scrambling forward on hands and knees, I tried so hard to get away as he grabbed my hips, dragging me backward, trying to lift me. As I fought harder, he grabbed my neck, shoving my face to the ground. But I kept my brain on the mission. To survive. Falling onto the ground, that night in Chicago, crawling forward, fighting for my life, I punched backward with my elbows and kicked backward with my legs. My body was of blood and bruise. But I healed. I am built to survive.

The monsters got away.

A bystander, running to me after the monsters bolted, handed to me his dog, "Here, take my dog," he said, proceeding to chase the monsters into the alley. He returned, accompanied by a policeman, and my bag, which had been discarded by the scoundrels, with my wallet missing but keys and knife safely inside. Thank goodness that my keys remained as unharmed so that I could return home to my Gwendolyn. Thank goodness that they had used not my knife, or other physical weapon, against me. Thank goodness that I was unharmed. Thank goodness for those kind people who fearlessly came running to my rescue. Thank goodness for karma. Or an angel. Or whatever you might believe, was watching over me.

I thought that my survival mode had ended when the eating disorder did.

I thought that I could let up my guard and walk around in a state of bubbly joy.

But I was wrong.

As backbone to it all, the message of *Trump: The Game*, the one that I had admired as a child in 1991, strummed through my brain. My only option was to win. This mantra is what guided me to succeed with the eating disorder, with the attacker in Chicago, with every challenge that I have ever faced.

My training in Ashtanga yoga, Tae Bo by Billy Blanks, and work on the Peloton bike made me physically strong to handle the enormous attacker who was twice my size. This exercising helped me afterward, too. I got right back out into the world. People were surprised when I showed no emotion. That is how I am.

I want to thank my sister Stephanie. She was the first whom I informed about the attack. On my birthday, a few months later, she posted the following to Facebook:

> *"Today is my oldest sister, Nicole Marie Story's, birthday! I am so thankful for this beautiful human (and Gwendolyn!). I did not share this previously, but on the eve of my birthday in December, I received the worst news I could have. She was attacked, mugged, and beaten in Lincoln Park, a very affluent area of Chicago. She is a fighter and survivor. I could have lost her that day. I am so lucky to have her in my life. I hope you have the best day today, Nikki! We love you!"*

Everyone showed so much love. Stephanie, my best human friend Rebecca, my parents, my Aunt Linda, my grandparents, my friends, my Uber drivers! And, most importantly, my little dog Gwendolyn.

If it had been not for those gracious humans running to my aid, then I might be a sex trafficker at this moment (but I assure you that I would have fought the trafficking system with goal to write a book about it). I might never have published this book (or it would have been significantly delayed). And, most importantly, my little dog Gwendolyn would never have known, what happened to her mommy (but I would have fought like hell to have made this untrue).

A few hours before the attack, I had napped. During this nap, I dreamt that a male approached me, from behind, on a bridge in Pittsburgh, with intention to rape me. In reality, seconds before I fell to the ground with the male on my back, I heard pounding, running footsteps. I think that my dream prepared me. I think that I shall hear those footsteps forever, in my head.

On the night of the attack, before leaving my apartment, I filled, for Gwendolyn, two glass water bowls, something that I had never done before. My ritual was to fill one glass water bowl. Again, the dream really did tell me to prepare. As I sit here, writing this chapter, Gwendolyn is snoring at my side. We are a family. Our hearts make the other's smile. And everyday, when I leave the apartment, I am equipped with three knives and pepper spray. Soon I shall apply for my license to carry. I believe in *The Second Amendment to the United States Constitution*, protecting an individual's right to keep and to bear arms. I am grateful for it. I am grateful for President Trump's support of the National Rifle Association. I am grateful for the Chicago Police Department who investigated this crime until they were pulled away to waste resources on that terrible actor who faked a hate crime in "MAGA Country." Additionally, I believe in lipstick kisses. Each time that I leave Gwendolyn, if only for a few minutes, I make certain to kiss her so many times, leaving remnants of lipstick kisses on her head, just in case.

I never saw myself as a victim, ever.

I have never believed in suffering.

I despise the words of "suffer" and "cope."

I am a fighter, a survivor, a winner!

In my college admissions essay to Duquesne University, I was asked about how the mind, body, and spirit are related. At the time, I wrote some BS piece that earned my entrance to the institution. But now I can truly answer that question.

Only a strong person, only a fit person of mind, body, and spirit, can beat an eating disorder, can beat the Fake News Media, can beat off attackers and physical assailants, can lead the United States of America when opposed by radical Democrats, can write and publish a book about their own survival in effort to help others with living. President Trump and I both fall under this category of fit persons who are built to survive, conquer, and inspire!

Just like Carrie Bradshaw who, in episode two, season four of *Sex and the City* got up when she fell on the runway, completing her glamorous catwalk appearance alongside Heidi Klum, I got up each time that I fell. Because I am a survivor. I am built to survive and to thrive. I deserve to live an amazing, glamorous life. I just need to fight for it! And I shall, every damn day.

CHAPTER
XIII

GWENDOLYN

If I had been told, twelve years ago, that a puppy would become my little heart with floppy ears and a curly tail with a very opinionated brain and demanding "woo" and sophisticated prance, then I would have laughed at the notion. But it is true. My puppy, now aged eleven years, eight months, and twenty nine days has helped me to mould the world that I dreamt, has helped me to become the person that I want to be. And in proper writer fashion, I present this chapter, in the form of a letter, to my dear little puppy Gwendolyn.

July 9, 2019

Dear Gwendolyn,

This is my favourite chapter.

You are my favourite chapter.

I want to pour my heart and soul into this letter because you mean more to me, than anything else in space. As a little girl, your mommy enjoyed writing letters to her next door neighbour, Mrs. Palumbo. An older, Italian woman, Mrs. Palumbo was my first friend when I lived in that old house, the one that I loved so dearly, the one in which I admired *Trump: The Game*. Mrs. Palumbo smelled of basil and of spaghetti sauce. Her husband, Mr. Palumbo, had a tomato garden. Blinded of colour, he often asked for my help, in choosing the red tomatoes that needed picking. That would be the extent of my life's work in gardening, ha! I had a fruitful love for that old house and for Mrs. Palumbo that after we moved in 1991, I sent Christmas cards to her every single year, each Christmas card containing a letter, one that updated her on the state of my life. It was my annual autobiography, and she was my dear audience. She was aged into her eighties when I invited her to my high school graduation party. It had been nine years since our last physical encounter, but she happily attended because I had written to her for all of those years. At this point, I existed as one year of being eating disordered, and all that I could think of was, *Will she think that I am fat? Will she think that I am fat? Will she think that I am fat?!*

It was a terrible time in my life. After that high school graduation party in the year of 2000, I never saw Mrs. Palumbo again. I never tried to see her again because my eating disorder trumped everything else. But even after she moved to a convent to be cared for by the nuns, I sent Christmas cards until her death. Those letters to Mrs. Palumbo were important to me.

And now I write a letter to you, my darling Gwendolyn.

The eating disorder and my finding resolution to it trumped everything in my life, for a really long time. Yes, I have a blog about it. Yes, I have this book about it. Yes, I might have my very real, very raw memories of it. But, at the end of the day, it is you who witnessed it. In real time. Behind closed doors. In the flesh. You experienced my eating disorder firsthand. You were the one thing in my life who I could ignore not, who I could put on hold not, to whom I could say not, "Let's put our friendship on pause for a little bit - I need to get skinny again before we can socialise." I know it sounds stupid to so many people, but you changed everything. And because of my eating disorder and the path that my life chose, I have you as my baby.

The questions lingers, when deciding on the content for this chapter, "How does one pay tribute to their heart?"

Because you are my heart.

How does one publish a formal statement with an ISBN about the living, loving, breathing four-legged, curly-tailed canine sophisticate who, for the past eleven years, six months, and twenty-eight days, has been the entire world?

Because you are my beautiful world.

I am grateful to have been afforded the privilege to love you, my little Gwendolyn, since our meeting on December 12, 2007. That is 4,228 days of love!

Longer than I spent as a bulimic.

Bulimia registered at 10 years, 10 months, and 14 days. That is 3,971 days. That is 257 days less than I have loved you, my little Gwendolyn.

I have loved you for longer than I lived as a bulimic.

Up until this point in my life, nothing that I have done, has happened for longer than the bulimia. Up until this point in my life, bulimia was the record holder on the "thing that I have done for the longest." Now, you, and my love for you, stand as the record holder, my Gwendolyn. It can be stated that I have loved you for longer than I have done anything else consistently in my life.

And, I hope, wish, pray even, that we will be our Mommy and Gwendolyn team for longer than my eating disorder in its entirety. The entirety of my eating disorder registered at 17 years, six months, and eight days. Or, 6,399 days of hell.

Even if you give me only one more day, one more hour, one more minute, I shall thank you, every single moment, for the rest of my life, with all of the strength of my heart, for allowing me to love you, for loving me in return, and for accepting me, with all of my flaws, as your mommy.

You know that I rarely cry, my dear girl. But tears have begun to stream along my face as I write this, as you sit inside of the diamond shape that my legs are forming in baddha konasana of the Ashtanga yoga system. You are snoring, so loudly, like a man! And I am writing away, as I want to have this book completed so that we can celebrate care-freely, with a bestseller. We shall celebrate the bringing awareness to the war-like nature of eating disorders, and to the amazingness of our great President Trump.

I knew nothing about dogs. Before you were a twinkle in my eye, I had memories of Midnight who was my parents' dog during my mother's pregnancy. In fact, she thinks that because Midnight watched over her, when the doctor required strict pregnancy rest, that I have some amazing cosmic connection with you. In 2007, before you, I considered dogs to be hairy monsters. And slobbery! So why did I get you?

One day, in December of 2006, whilst socialising with my dear friend Julie, I met a puggle. And I immediately knew that I was seeing something unique. I spent the early half of 2007 dating and galavanting about the globe with rich men until one day, in December of 2007, I decided that I wanted a dog. Mr. Bikram loved dogs, and I thought that if I had a dog, he would love me. So I found you! I searched the internet for "puggle" and found a beautiful website belonging to Bernadette Santana of then Amish Puggles, now Roly Poly Puppies. She's still in business, and my heart sings with recommendation for her puppies! Scrolling through the list of puppies, I stopped on the only puppy featuring a black snout and black ears. I wanted this puppy. She was defined as a "pocket puggle" in this case meaning puggle x pug, whereby the puggle mother was created by pug x beagle. And the father was a pug. Thusly, this puppy would be smaller than a standard puggle, taking on the traits of the pug more dominantly than the traits of the beagle. She costed $850, exactly $100 more than the regular puggle. And she was beautiful. BEAUTIFUL. I immediately loved Baby Gwendolyn. During our telephone interview, I said to

Bernadette, "I want the one with the black snout and ears, the one named Emma!" She replied, sternly, that the dog must pick its owner. And it happened. You picked me.

Walking into Bernadette's beautiful Victorian home in upstate New York, I experienced the most amazing moment of my life. Surrounded by your fellow litter mates, these cute little things cooed and cooed, completely taking away my breath! And then you came to me and stayed at my side. You were the only of your litter with a black snout and black ears. I was so nervous to dress you in the Nicole Miller sweater that I had brought along, so Bernadette dressed you for me. We captured our first picture together, I changed your name from Emma to Gwendolyn, and then we ventured off to our home. We were accompanied by the wonderful man who bought you for me. Only my sister Stephanie and my best human friend Rebecca know of his identity. We drove away in first class in his very fancy luxury automobile. Your first ride happened with heated leather seats until we arrived in Erie, Pennsylvania when I returned to my vehicle which was a beaten up Toyota Camry. We said goodbye to your father and ventured home to Pittsburgh.

Our adventure involved stopping at Target for a smaller collar, as the red leather Coach collar that I had prepared was too large for your tiny neck. We stopped at Panera Bread, but I kept you crated so that I could enjoy my Veggie sandwich and mushroom soup from the driver's seat, and you barked at me during the entire meal. We stopped for gasoline in Wexford where I walked you on the snow-covered grass. When you urinated, I thought that it was the greatest accomplishment of my life! I still remember that moment, and my celebration of it, like it was yesterday. During that entire six-hour journey to home, you slept on my lap like a little 1980s glow worm. When we arrived to home, I locked you in the crate as I had been directed by "dog experts" to do so, but you barked at me, so I collected you into my arms and we slept on the blue sofa, a hand-me-down piece of furniture from my parents, purchased at Kaufmann's. It was the first night that I slept soundly in my life.

Awakening the next morning, I carried you to the bathroom where I closed the door and began primping for the day. As I soaped my hair in the shower, I peaked outside of the curtain to find you posing elegantly. I admired your beautiful pose until I realised that you were urinating on the floor! I had so much to learn! I would need to first take care of YOU before ME! For the next few months, each morning, I carried you to the large kitchen where you used a "piddle pad" for your relief needs. In my infant stages of being your mommy, I was too prissy to think about venturing outside into the snow at such early hours. Oh, my dear Gwendolyn, how you have changed my life, honey!

Nearly twelve years later and you continue to love me, even when I require that you "enjoy" a five-mile walk in a snowstorm. But I am confident that all of your walking has kept you as the spry puppy that you seem to be, today on the cusp of your twelfth birthday. Oh I love you so much!

As I have stated in earlier sections of this book, you are *The First Corinthians*.

"Love is patient, love is kind. It does not envy, it does not boast, it is not proud. It does not dishonour others, it is not self-seeking, it is not easily angered, it keeps no record of wrongs. Love does not delight in evil but rejoices with truth. It always protects, always trusts, always hopes, always perseveres."

And now I cry again.

But please allow this love letter to fool you not! You have been quite a pill, too! You are a blanket sucking, panty munching, television animal barking, food delivery barking, toy stealing, dehydrated fish stick demanding, blanket humping royal pain in my rump! And I would have it as no other way.

People on the street tell me that you prance. That you strut. That you are confident. That you are sophisticated! And you are nearly twelve years but your teeth are pearly white! As I often joke, your story is called "The Curious Case of Gwendolyn Button." You seem to be ageing in reverse. Yes, we had a few cancer scares, but with the guidance of the great Dr. Maro and team of Ellwood Animal Hospital and Cranberry Holistic Pet, I feel very confident in our Chinese herb solution (NewVita - pills for immune health and energy) plus an overdosage of raw goat milk, plus Essiac tea, and I feel so confident that everything is working nicely inside of you. If I ever did one thing right in my life, it is mothering you, my darling. But the question remains: how did you come to be so beautiful? When I ask you, in my baby voice, "Gwendolyn, how did they make you? What did they do to make such a pretty little goo? Such a unique little goo? The most beautiful little goo in all of the wooold? You da cootest mushkie in da bookie! You ma schmookie!" As you can see, as my dialogues to you progress, I sound more and more like the Swedish Chef of *The Muppets*. Well, the cocking of your head is answer enough for me. Thank you for cocking your head for me, for all of these years. Thank you for smiling at me with your kiss-me-face. That face which resembles a hamburger housed between two pieces of a sandwich bun. That face which resembles a bow-tie if you throw in the black ears! The fact that my voice elicits such a passionate response in your pretty little face, in your very big heart, makes my heart smile to Pluto and back.

Thank you for going to town on my takeout boxes at dinnertime. I always awaken to boxes scattered across the floor and to you sleeping soundly curled to my side. It is obvious that I fall asleep immediately after our midnight dinner, and you take care of cleaning the boxes and putting yourself to bed!

Thank you for expecting a good morning, good afternoon, good evening, and good night cookie at the elevator, preceded by three gnome kisses. And thank you for wagging your tail in the elevator, as I tap dance for you.

Thank you for watching 1940s film noir with me. And every episode of *Dallas*, *Dynasty*, *Sex and the City*, and *The Nikki Haskell Show*, too. Thank you, my little girl, for walking with me, for all of these years. Thank you for bringing love into my life from other humans when I felt that I was undeserving of it.

Thank you, for loving your Auntie Stephie. And for making her cry, when she existed as your babysitter, in those early days, because you bit her ankles and barked at her. We shall always fondly remember the naughty little puppy that you were. You were our tiny beast! Thank you for loving your Auntie Becky, Auntie Kristen, Auntie Jillian, Auntie L, Auntie Janice (Precious Pets of Sewickley), and Uncle Brandon. Thank you for loving your grandparents and Aunt Linda.

Thank you, for loving your Lady, Quinn, Bella, Phoebe, Sophie, Lana, Lolita, Sophia, Shae, Frida, Chloe, Chico, Miles, Khan, Ajax & Bella, Murphy, Pepi, Stella, Benji, Lucy, Buckley, Buddha, Shadow, Pugsley, Mater, Alexander, Lambo, Blanca, Katrina, Buddy, Ally, Coach, Carter, Maple, Harvey, Mega, Wunder, Andy, Oliver, Foxy, Jazzy, Scooby, Vincent, Artie, FLGM, Mona, Maeva, Linus, Buster, Spike, and Hayden.

Thank you for loving your mommy.

When people ask me of whether or not I regret anything in my life, I say no. The eating disorder was a challenging time, but without having ventured down that path, I never would have met you. I never would have been gifted with this once in a lifetime experience to love you. For the rest of of my life, I shall love you and honour you.

To my beautiful baby, to my sweet puppy, I love you with all of my heart and shall hold you inside of my smiles and dreams until my last day.

Love,

Your Mommy

CHAPTER
XIV

LOVE

This is the final chapter of *Donald Trump and My Eating Disorder*. It is about love!

Most of this book seems like a dream.
Who was that girl?
Who was that girl who lived with chaos?
Who was that girl who lived with destruction?
Who was that girl who lived without love?

In the overture of this book, I write a passage taken directly from a dream that I had recently. When I awoke from the dream, I existed in a state of confusion. The dream seemed to describe a recent interaction with Mr. Bikram, but some of the details were different. Yes, I had recently said goodbye to Mr. Bikram as the dream recounted, and yes, a tear rolled along my face as he walked away, because I somehow knew it might be the last time that I would offer my heart to him. Also I thought that perhaps he would never again see my dog Gwendolyn. The way that he said goodbye to her, in real life, made my heart cry because I could see in Mr. Bikram's face that he, too, thought it might be the last time.

But the passage that I wrote, in my dream, indicated that it was cold outside when, indeed, it was hot. I have yet to figure out why this weather condition changed, in the dream. And also of difference from the real life scenario, is the dream indicated that I would no longer seek to win the love of Mr. Bikram, but I would rather seek to win the love of myself. This confused me because I do love myself. I am proud of who I am. I always have been such, even in the throes of my eating disorder. Why then, did I dream such a bold statement?

I thought for many months on this quandary. And then it occurred to me: In order to love myself completely, I need to grant myself permission to be loved. My heart has been closed for so long. I have disallowed myself the pleasure of being loved. I have been unable to share my heart with another human in the exciting, romantic, rational, kind, honest intelligent way that I truly want and deserve. And in denying myself of this freedom, I was therefore loving myself incompletely. I was punishing myself all because of those years of war with food, all because of my eating disorder. This was the message of my dream. The dream was giving me permission to be completely happy.

And now, as I bring closure to this book, as I bring closure to *Donald Trump and My Eating Disorder,* I know what is next.

The first answer is to campaign passionately for the reelection of President Donald J. Trump.

The second answer is exciting love.

I shall love myself so passionately that I will be able to love another human, in the right way, for the first time in my life. And yes, I have his exact description created, of course! He will be tall like a skyscraper, athletic and energetic, too. His eyes will sparkle with life, creating stars when they meet my own. Sleep will be a need versus desire. He will be selfish and giving, through and through. Brilliant like a CEO with his business, he will respect and admire my work, too. And at the end of the night, he shall own my body completely. I am ready to meet the gentleman whose value system matches my own.

Just as my chapter about Gwendolyn was difficult to write, this final chapter is difficult to write, too, because it is the lasting impression that my readers will have of me. What impression do I want my readers to have? The answer is that I am Nicole Marie Story.

I am ready for this book to be completed. I am ready for my next book to begin. On the moment that I press, "publish" of this autobiography, I begin the next exciting adventure with my little dog Gwendolyn at my side. The date is July 9, 2019.

Thank you for for reading a book about an ordinary girl with an extraordinary story.

The end.

ACKNOWLEDGEMENTS

Thank you to Lady, Raí, and Piggie for listening to me read this book, over and over, during the editing period throughout 2018 and 2019.

Thank you to Gary Vaynerchuk for inspiring me to start a blog in 2011 which formed a living breathing document of my process, helping me to achieve the greatest epiphany of my life thus far, and for helping me to see the vision for completion of this book which consumed twenty years to write!

Thank you to Mike, Eadie, Sheila, Steve, Candace, Juliana, Mary, Lee, Janice, and Rebecca for believing in me.

Thank you to Brandon for loving my monkey and for watching *Brief Encounter* with us, one hundred thousand times.

Thank you to Kristin, Jillian, and Erica for being my girls!

Thank you to my parents, grandparents, and Aunt Linda for loving me.

Thank you to my sisters for forgiving me.

Thank you to Mr. Bikram for being my free lawyer when my big mouth got me into trouble on many occasions.

Thank you to Gwendolyn, for it all.

Nicole Marie Story

Blog www.theyogaballerina.com
Twitter @yogaballerina
Instagram @theyogaballerina
facebook.com/theyogaballerina
YouTube: The Yoga Ballerina
iTunes Podcast: The Yoga Ballerina Show

www.ingramcontent.com/pod-product-compliance
Lightning Source LLC
Chambersburg PA
CBHW070747310526
45791CB00029B/1748

* 9 7 8 1 0 7 4 4 2 3 7 7 3 *